The Dramatic Landscape of
STEINBECK'S SHORT STORIES

Photograph by Paul Farber. Courtesy of Elaine Steinbeck.

The Dramatic Landscape of
STEINBECK'S SHORT STORIES

by John H. Timmerman

UNIVERSITY OF OKLAHOMA PRESS

NORMAN AND LONDON

By John H. Timmerman

John Steinbeck's Fiction: The Aesthetics of the Road Taken
(Norman, 1986)
The Dramatic Landscape of Steinbeck's Short Stories
(Norman, 1990)

Library of Congress Cataloging-in-Publication Data

Timmerman, John H.
    The dramatic landscape of Steinbeck's short stories / by
John H. Timmerman.
        p.   cm.
    Includes bibliographical references (p. 317)
    ISBN 0-8061-2258-7 (alk. paper)
    1. Steinbeck, John, 1902-1968—Criticism and interpreta-
tion.   2. Steinbeck, John, 1902-1968—Criticism, Textual.
3. Short story.   I. Title.
PS3537.T3234Z927   1990
813'.52—dc20   89-25019

The paper in this book meets the guidelines for permanence
and durability of the Committee on Production Guidelines for
Book Longevity of the Council on Library Resources, Inc. ∞

This study is gratefully dedicated to my colleagues in the Department of English at Calvin College, whose unfailing support and good humor have always been a harbor.

Contents

Acknowledgments

IN ADDITION TO my indebtedness to the rich tradition of Steinbeck criticism and to fellow scholars in the field who have encouraged this study, there are specific parties to whom particular thanks are due.

I would like to thank Calvin College for providing me with a generous Calvin Research Fellowship, secretarial help, and travel expenses. I thank the National Endowment for the Humanities for a travel grant to visit the necessary manuscript collections. Those collections deserve both praise and thanks, particularly the John Steinbeck Collection of Stanford University; the Steinbeck Memorial Library of Salinas; The Steinbeck Research Center of San Jose State University; the Harry Ransom Research Center of the University of Texas at Austin; the Steinbeck Collection of Ball State University; and the Houghton Library of Harvard University.

Nor would this study have been possible without the encouragement of Tetsumaro Hayashi—*il miglior fabbro*, and my editor, Thomas R. Radko. I also thank John Ditsky, whose advice and insights I have deeply appreciated.

I especially thank Mrs. Elaine Steinbeck for providing the photograph of her husband used in the frontispiece of this study.

But above all, to my colleagues in the Department of English at Calvin College, to whom this study is dedicated, goes my unreserved gratitude.

Introduction

IN A 1958 LETTER to Eugène Vinaver, John Steinbeck wrote,

A long time ago I learned a trick—or perhaps it might be called a method for writing. I stopped addressing my work to a faceless reader and addressed one person as though I had only that one to talk to. I gave him a face and a personality. [*SLL*, p. 590]

In the early years of his career, it must have seemed to Steinbeck that he was the only audience for his short stories, the only "one to talk to." While he was learning the tricks—"or perhaps it might be called a method for writing"—during those years, he frequently addressed notes to himself in his ledger notebooks, explaining what he wanted to do and why he wanted to do it.

Although *Tortilla Flat* appeared in 1935 to a sudden burst of publicity, and five years later *The Grapes of Wrath* propelled Steinbeck to world fame, his long and arduous apprenticeship has remained something of a mystery. The evolution of his art occurred over a decade, from the stories written as a student at Stanford University through 1934, when he drafted the stories of *The Long Valley* collection.

This decade posed a critical juncture in Steinbeck's life. He was keenly aware of his desire to be a writer but was in the process of discovering the artistic means to achieve that goal. The stories crafted during this period provide us access to the developing mind of the artist. They reveal his experimentation with, and eventual mastery of, narrative points of view, character, plot, setting, and patterns of imagery. It is a dramatic revelation, and one that also discloses a great deal about the novelistic triumphs of later years.

Although most of Steinbeck's short story writing occurred during that early decade, he practiced the form throughout his career. In his later years, Steinbeck published relatively few short stories designed independently as such, but the short story form may be found as an influence upon other works. The intercalary chapters of *The Grapes of Wrath* and *Sweet Thursday* may be seen as miniature short stories. The journalism he engaged in throughout his life is colored by the influence of the short story form.

The aim of this study is to examine the entire body of Steinbeck's short stories in their chronological development, using methods of both textual and literary criticism. By such an examination, one can discern a great deal about Steinbeck's growth as a literary artist, his ideas about art, and his literary achievement. Steinbeck operated dangerously as an artist, working from idea and actual events to literary art. Yet, the substantial risks he took as an artist and the resiliency of his craft—tested, developed, and proven through his short stories—became the characteristics of his achievement.

Several ambiguities have plagued efforts to examine these short stories. Several of them have had disputed authorship, now for the most part resolved by earlier studies. The composition of a number of them is extremely difficult to date accurately. The relationships between certain short stories and both the major novels and major events in Steinbeck's life have often been puzzling to scholars. Several resource tools have appeared in recent years that have helped sort out these puzzles and ambiguities. The publication of four volumes of Steinbeck's letters—*Journal of a Novel: The "East of Eden" Letters* (1969); *Steinbeck: A Life in Letters* (1975); *Letters to Elizabeth* (1978); and *Steinbeck and Covici: The Story of a Friendship* (1979)—and the greater availability of unpublished letters held by private collections are valuable for tracing an accurate chronology. Items of historical and bibliographical importance appear throughout these letters. Any collection of letters, however, is finally an unreliable guide to an author's work and life, lacking the objective ordering of biography. The appearance of the authorized biography by Jackson J. Benson has set in order many of the lacunae in the author's life. And the availability of Steinbeck's original manuscripts has helped determine the chronology of composition, the process of revision, and the author's intentions through notes accompanying the stories. Even with these superb tools, however, a considerable amount of literary detective work is necessary to arrive at an accurate chronology.

Since this study will rely heavily upon the original manuscripts, some description of them is in order (see appendix). It should be noted that while the ledgers containing the original drafts provide many valuable clues about the order of composition and Steinbeck's intentions in the stories, he sometimes wrote in several notebooks simultaneously. Furthermore, not all the ledgers contain reliable pagination. Nonetheless, they are the most valuable single resource for a critical and textual study of Steinbeck's short stories.

In a letter to Louis Paul in 1962, Steinbeck wrote, "Let's face it. In 60 years I've left a lot of tracks" (*SLL,* p. 751). If one were to apply his comment metaphorically to the short stories, the early years were sometimes like a wandering maze, riddled by dead ends and doglegs as his peripatetic mind investigated new possibilities. Eventually, however, the path became more certain, the artwork more sinewy and muscular, the destination more clearly in view. Examined from beginning to end, it is a most remarkable and rewarding journey.

Abbreviations

THROUGHOUT THIS STUDY, quotations from Steinbeck's notebooks and letters will be identified by parenthetical abbreviations as follows:

IDBN	*In Dubious Battle* notebook
LVN	*The Long Valley* notebook
POH-1	First *Pastures of Heaven* notebook
POH-2	Second *Pastures of Heaven* notebook
SLL	*Steinbeck: A Life in Letters*
TFN	*Tortilla Flat* notebook

Detailed descriptions of the notebooks are provided in an appendix.

The Dramatic Landscape of
STEINBECK'S SHORT STORIES

1

Flaming Youth: The 1920s

THE DECADE OF the 1920s was, as Warner Fabian declared it, the era of "flaming youth." Although the smoke of myth hangs over the age, students in the twenties provided plenty of fire. Administrators preached prohibition before going home for a drink. After the administrators left, students sauntered over to waiting automobiles where bootleggers sold their stock from the copious trunks of Stutz Torpedos. An official of the YWCA warned, "Pet and die young!" The young plotted seductions as if their lives depended on them. It is a wonder they had the energy after whirling to the Charleston.

But an odd and vulnerable innocence lay just under the extravagance. One of the most popular college magazines of the age, boasting 80,000 readers, was *College Humor*, to which the *Stanford Chaparral* contributed this knee-slapper:

Moronia thinks the postage stamp is a dance.
Well, letter.

There was a lively press of literary magazines as well, from *True Confessions* to the *Atlantic Monthly* to the emerging *New Yorker*, which even then believed that the world stopped at the Passaic River. *Scribner's* magazine was banned in Boston for serializing *A Farewell to Arms*.

It was a good time to be a student, the twenties. The dreams unfurled like banners across a bright sky and nothing seemed impossible, even for a student who fancied himself a writer of fiction.

The direction of John Steinbeck's short story writing in the 1920s was a bit like that of someone learning to swim by being thrown in the lake. The instincts for survival are there, but a great deal of energy is expended on random strokes until those that bear the weight and direct the body are learned.

Steinbeck had a fierce instinct for storytelling and writing. The techniques of the craft, which may be general qualities but which every writer must appropriate as his own, were learned in often fumbling ways, occasionally with strokes of rare genius. The 1920s was a decade for learning, a time in which dogged determination was often the only thing that won out over apparently insuperable obstacles—among them, the lack of an audience. The artistry matured with confidence and grace in the 1930s, but it was forged in a crucible of insecurity and awkwardness.

It is really very difficult to determine just how many stories Steinbeck wrote between the fall of 1919, when he first enrolled at Stanford, and 1934, when he completed the *Long Valley* stories. In a letter to Katherine Beswick, written in 1927 or 1928, Steinbeck indicates that several of his stories had been sold, but we have no record of such: "You ask about old stories of mine. Everything was turned over to the agents Brandt and Brandt on Park Avenue with orders to do anything they wanted with them as long as they didn't use my name. They sold about two thirds of them and I received checks for the agents so I haven't the least idea where they appeared, nor do I want to know. That was stipulated. I am ashamed of them Katherine."[1] Was the claim simply part of a young, struggling writer's pose? It is difficult to tell. The relationship with Beswick was an unusual one, and Steinbeck often projected an image of himself to her that reality didn't support. While expressing his dislike for literary agents, Steinbeck wrote, "Why, one man wanted to charge me ten dollars for reading two very short sketches and telling me they were no good. I refused to pay him, and was later justified in my kick by receiving one hundred eighty dollars for the two."

Preston Beyer, a devoted collector of Steinbeck materials, suggests that Steinbeck wrote many pseudonymous stories in the twenties. In "The Current Status of John Steinbeck Book Collections," Beyer quotes from a letter by Steinbeck to him on the subject of a pseudonymous story:

You see, I don't really know whether that story exists. I don't remember what it was about nor to whom it was sold nor under what pseudonym. There were quite a number of little stories, which during my shy and experimental youth, were sent out and some printed. Except as oddities, I think that their disappearance is a good thing. To the best of my knowledge, they were lousy.[2]

While very little of the writing of the twenties made print, such items indicate that there was, nonetheless, a fair amount of writing.

Steinbeck also wrote of having destroyed a number of stories from the late twenties. In a December 1931 letter to Amasa Miller, Steinbeck wrote, "Before the Cup [*Cup of Gold*, 1929] the stories are so feeble and childish that I destroyed them all as a matter of course."[3] Not infrequently Steinbeck burned work of his that he thought was no good, and he knew well when his own work was going badly. More than one failed short story in the ledger notebooks ends with a note such as this one after "The Cow": "Wrong again all wrong. What the hell's the matter with me" (*LVN*).

On the other hand, Steinbeck never seemed at a loss for subject matter for short stories. His letters throughout the twenties and thirties brim with ideas. In an April 7, 1924, letter to Carl Wilhelmson, he described several short stories he had written, including one description of faces around a campfire that would eventually find its way into chapter four of *In Dubious Battle* and chapter six of *The Grapes of Wrath*:

I wrote of miners' faces around a fire. Their bodies did not show in the light so that the yellow faces seemed dangling masks against the night. And I wrote of little voices in the glens which were the spirits of passions and desires and dreams of dead men's minds.

And Mrs. Russell [an instructor] said they were not real, that such things could not be, and she was not going to stand me bullying her into such claptrap nonsense. Those were not her words but her meaning, and then she smiled out of the corner of her mouth as nurses do when an idiot child makes blunders. And I could not stand that, Carl, so I swore at her because I had been out all night in the making of my pictures. And now she is very cold, and she means to flunk me in my course, thinking she can hurt me thus. I wish that she could know that I do not in the least care. [*SLL*, p. 7]

Later that spring, Steinbeck wrote,

There have been six short stories this quarter. I wonder if you remember the one about the machinist who made engines and felt a little omnipotent until his own machine pulled his arm from him. Then he cursed God and suffered retribution at the hands of God or thought he did. That has finally been done to my half satisfaction. Of the others, one was perfectly rotten, two were fair, three were quite good. About the only thing that can be said for them is that they do not resemble anything which has ever been written. [*SLL*, pp. 7–8]

While seldom satisfied with the quality of his own work during this callow period, Steinbeck was at least working hard at it. The indomitable urge to write was strong in him, and it found an outlet, if not a clear focus, at Stanford University.

THE STANFORD EDUCATION

The years at Stanford University, while negligible in purely academic terms, were critical years for Steinbeck's growth as an artist.[4] There he found sympathetic listeners who would actually read his stories. Although described as "a near-recluse who knew a lot of people,"[5] some of the people whom he knew exercised a tremendous influence upon Steinbeck's awareness of himself as a writer and sometimes upon his writing. In particular, these people included members of the Stanford English Club, including Carl Wilhelmson, John Breck (Elizabeth Smith), Grove Day, and Katherine Beswick, and fellow contributors to the fledgling *Stanford Spectator* such as Webster Street and Frank Fenton. Steinbeck enrolled at Stanford with the intention of learning to write, nothing else. In his introduction to *Letters to Elizabeth*, Carlton Sheffield observes, "He refused steadfastly to take courses required for graduation and when told that they were necessary for a degree, he calmly answered that he wasn't interested in graduation or degrees—the only thing he wanted was to learn to write and to take those courses that would teach him to do it."[6] One such course in story writing was taught by Edith Mirrielees.

In the early 1960s Steinbeck was asked to write the preface to Mirrielees's book, *Story Writing*. The preface was reprinted in 1963 as a short essay, "On Learning Writing," in *Writer's Yearbook*. Here Steinbeck recalls what he learned about writing at Stanford:

Although it must be a thousand years ago that I sat in a class in story writing at Stanford, I remember the experience very clearly. I was bright-eyed and bushy-brained and prepared to absorb the secret formula for writing good short stories, even great short stories. This illusion was canceled very quickly. The only way to write a good short story, we were told, is to write a good short story. Only after it is written can it be taken apart to see how it was done. It is a most difficult form, we were told, and the proof lies in how very few great short stories there are in the world.[7]

As Steinbeck recalled it, the basic lesson he learned was at once liberating and, to use Steinbeck's own term, heartbreaking:

A story to be effective had to convey something from writer to reader, and the power of its offering was the measure of its excellence. Outside of that, there were no rules. A story could be about anything and could use any means and any technique at all—so long as it was effective. As a subhead to this rule, it seemed to be necessary for the writer to know what he wanted to say, in short, what he was talking about.[8]

This fundamental rule was liberating in that it gave free scope to the writer's imagination, but heartbreaking simply because it opened so many avenues to the aspiring writer. Subsequently, Steinbeck's search for an artistic voice would wander erratically. If the only measure of success was effectiveness, it still left him to discover those stories that would be effective for him.

Beyond this simple but overwhelming challenge, it is certain that Edith Mirrielees imparted valuable guidelines, probably very much in keeping with her book, *Story Writing*, which provides worthwhile comments ranging from shaping character to keeping proper time sequences. More importantly, however, her comments nurtured the writer's sense of creative impulse by insisting that the urge to write is itself valuable and necessary. Passages in *Story Writing* would still fuel the spark of imagination in an aspiring writer:

The best way, even if not necessarily the only way, to write a first draft is to want to write it, to get continually more excited by the thought of it, and finally to sit down and write.

It is not the lack of experience which handicaps any writer. What it is, is the purblindness that prevents his seeing, or his seeing into, the experiences he has had.

For most stories and most writers, deliberate ornamentation needs much scrutiny before it is allowed a place in finished work. Phrases pushing up like mushrooms above the level of the narrative have a habit of turning out to be toadstools.[9]

Mirrielees refused to be a rule-setter, even while passing out some monumentally good rules. She was a nurturer, one who understood the psychology of writing. One of her comments in *Story Writing* is echoed frequently in Steinbeck's letters: "Writing can never be other than a lonely business."[10] Steinbeck's letters, particularly from the early 1930s, are shot through with expressions of the loneliness of the act of writing, the immense daring of picking up the pen and battling the empty page with nothing more than imagination, intellect, and a reservoir of stories to back him up. As late as a 1957 letter to Dennis Murphy, Steinbeck spoke of the "holy loneliness" of writing.[11] An aspiring writer, liberated to write about anything he wishes so long as it is "effective," convicted already of the loneliness of his craft, nonetheless writes for someone. It is essential for him to have his works considered by others. In this respect, the Stanford years were also important years for Steinbeck, for there he found an audience, even when he had to impose his work upon whatever audience he could find. The primary of all human virtues for Steinbeck was friendship. He treasured his friendships, and rupture of those relationships caused him profound grief.[12] In the 1920s his circle of closest friends drew Steinbeck out as an artist. He had an audience among them for his work, and well into the thirties he made a practice of sending draft manuscripts to trusted friends for comments.

Discussing one's work with friends, however, is quite different from seeing one's work in print. This is the anointing for the new writer, the confirmation of one's aim. To fully appreciate the excitement for the young writer of publishing in the *Stanford Spectator*, one must also understand the impact of the magazine on the Stanford community. A relatively young publication, only entering its second year when Steinbeck published, it reflected the student spirit of the 1920s. Marked by a kind of sophisticated snobbishness, an arch, laconic tone, and a heavy trend toward satire, the magazine was a remarkably polished production. While relying upon student publications, it was nonetheless a commercial venture, retailing for twenty-five cents and enjoying a readership beyond the Stanford campus. As such, the *Spectator* accepted community advertising, which in itself gives a fascinating portrait of Steinbeck's age and this singular academic community.

Stanford students, dwelling in a hub with the playgrounds of San Francisco, Half Moon Bay, Santa Cruz, and San Jose on the periphery, were apparently very much on the go.

Transportation advertisements dominated the pages of the *Spectator*. The Pacific Auto Stages, Inc., known for its "Orange Painted Pierce Arrows," boasted that "CARS LEAVE EVERY 30 MINUTES IN BOTH DIRECTIONS." The ad fails to indicate precisely which directions, but Stanford students would know.

In a series of adjectives that might have made Steinbeck wince and Edith Mirrielees positively quake, the University Creamery advertised hot waffles: "What is better than a hot, crisp, greaseless, buttered waffle on these cold, damp days? Have you tried our secret process electric waffles?" The Creamery also allowed that they had used 4,000 pounds of malted milk in their "CHOC MALTS" during the past year.

Just as fascinating as a portrait of the student age are the literary offerings of the *Spectator*, February, 1924, which included in its pages "Fingers of Cloud: A Satire on College Protervity," by John E. Steinbeck. He was in good company. Frank Fenton was literary editor. Carl Wilhelmson, who wrote music and book reviews, served on the editorial board. Webster Street was book review editor. These intensely intelligent, talented, slightly cocky people were also some of Steinbeck's closest friends at Stanford. Often their intelligence and cockiness erupted in satire.

The literary offerings were probably overshadowed, then, by the lead article, "What's Wrong with the Stanford Klan," by A. Sleuth, a devastating piece of student satire. Webster Street, reviewing *Streets of Night* by John Dos Passos, offers the opinion that "In twenty years from now, John Dos Pasos [sic] may be a fairly good writer—but it is doubtful." His music review of a Jascha Heifetz concert proved more accurate: "That Jascha Heifetz will be regarded by the future generations as the outstanding violinist of this age is becoming a certainty."

The tenor of the *Stanford Spectator* is the same as that of most student publications: bold, brash, arrogant. To a certain extent, all three adjectives also apply to Steinbeck's contribution. That is at once the promise of and the problem with "Fingers of Cloud." One observes the genius—the memorable depictions of the migrant camp that testify to his ability to recreate vivid scenes from experience, the fascinating character portrait of Gertie, and the sense of a story wanting to break through. The problems lie in the author's almost gladiatorial wrestling with a plot that wants to break free in several directions at once. Is it a story about Gertie? Or about migrants? Or simply a wild fantasy? Or a Stanford-inspired satire propelled by high-octane symbolism?

We meet the main character, the teenage orphan Gertie, in a portrait as immediately intriguing as any that Steinbeck wrote:

On her flat, pink face there was a benign smile that seemed glued on; her hair, as white as a washed sheep's wool and nearly as curly, bobbed knowingly on the top of her head, and her pink eyes blandly regarded everything on the street, accepted houses and fences and grass plots, enjoyed them and cast them aside for new houses and picket fences and grass plots.

Gertie is sweeping a porch and, heartily tired of her labor, simply runs away.

Gertie has one call on her heart: the mountains. She plunges through a stream and romps through a meadow toward the dusky hills. Here the first artistic uncertainties appear, in a tension between fantasy and realism. Whimsically enough, the yellow mayflowers of the meadow say, "Boo! You're running away, my girl." To which Gertie replies, "I am not running away. I guess I'm eighteen and know my own mind. Besides, I'm an orphant, and an orphant can't run away because she ain't got absolutely nothing to run away from."

Still in the vein of fantasy, Gertie climbs to the top of the mountain, longing to touch a cloud. This mysterious pull of the mountains upon the human spirit would surface in later works of Steinbeck's, most noticeably "The Great Mountains" of *The Red Pony*. In this instance, Gertie is mesmerized by the pull of the high places. She lies down on the mountaintop, amid the high clouds. "A big grey one brushed her eyelids with its hanging shreds until they closed; a smaller one rushed up and pressed gently, and she slept." If the story had stopped at this point, one would call it an unfinished attempt at fantasy. The main character responds to some mystical urging, very much like Joseph Wayne's in *To a God Unknown*, and amid the high mountains experiences a supernatural event. One also senses in Gertie a character and theme that would emerge more powerfully several years later in the portrait of Elisa Allen of "The Chrysanthemums." Gertie possesses the same powerful longing for freedom, and the compulsion to pursue her dreams.

Quite suddenly, however, the story shifts to a Filipino migrant camp, and Steinbeck thrusts us into the domain of symbolism. The Red Man, a bootleg whiskey peddlar, enters: "Heavy steps sounded on the porch, the door was flung open and a large red man came into the room turning down his coat collar. His hair and eyebrows were red, and red freckles covered a red face. He looked very big and blustery beside the quiet brown man." A clue to the symbolism lies in the subtitle of the story: "A Satire on College Protervity." *Protervity* appears to be a portmanteau word formed from propensity and perversity; thus the college students' propensity toward perversity. Bootleg whiskey was not uncommon on the staid Stanford campus of that era, and the Red Man bears the Stanford color.[13]

The confrontation between the swaggering Red Man and the deferentially polite Filipinos sets up a delightful little interlude. While the Red Man haggles with the migrants, Manuel slips outside to filch the supply from his car. After the Red Man drives off, the Filipinos settle down to some hard, pleasureable drinking. A little story within a story, this duping of the braggart by the migrants, it at once echoes Steinbeck's own service with migrants of the Spreckels ranch and points forward to the delightfully resourceful paisanos of *Tortilla Flat*. But Steinbeck has nearly lost track of his main story and Gertie.

Perhaps when she was on top of the mountain among the

lowering clouds, Gertie failed to realize that such clouds usually signal rain. In any event, as the Filipinos steadily empty the bottles, they hear a cry. Pedro, the boss, opens the door on Gertie, who is struggling toward him through the rain. Mud-splattered and soaked with rain, Gertie washes and retires to Pedro's bedroom to sleep. She smiles fetchingly at the Filipino on the way to the bedroom. With a line that might have been taken directly from *Tortilla Flat*, Steinbeck describes Pedro's reaction: "Pedro went out feeling attractive and warm and dizzy. 'I am going to marry the woman,'" he announces. But with that announcement, the story shifts once more, from fantasy, to satire, now to a kind of stark realism of life in the migrant shack.

Teased by his companions for his lust for the albino woman, Pedro goes back into the bedroom to conquer the lady. The next morning they are married. Gertie, the half-witted orphan accustomed to little more than pushing a broom, is suddenly queen of the migrant shack. She has married the leader; the followers fall over each other waiting upon her. Yet, she feels a curious instinct, calling her back to the mountains. This reality fails to satisfy her dreams.

As the summer heat grows more intense day by day, her longing for the cool spaces of the mountain increases. The summer heat also hardens the realism of the present circumstance:

"The summer heat irritated Pedro, and well it might, for the dust stood in the roadways in powdery quilts. The yellow ground and the dun grass threw all the heat of the sun back into the air. On an evening when his back was sweaty, he beat Gertie with a curtain rod. She whimpered and discovered that he was very black, but she stored the knowledge for later use."

Once again, symbolism changes the tenor of the story. Here and in subsequent passages, Pedro's blackness is sharply identified in opposition to Gertie's albino pallor. This too may arise from the rather waspish setting of Stanford in the twenties, and also from Steinbeck's own experiences among migrants in the fields surrounding Salinas.

The intrusion of the symbolism, however, signals Steinbeck's artistic uncertainty in this early story. He has a moving, unusual story developing, but feels compelled to deck it out in artistic apparatus that will make the story seem complex and sophisticated. The increasingly irritable Pedro vents his frustration on Gertie. He forces her to sleep on the floor. Gertie retaliates, threatening to leave him because he is black. She is, in fact, very much like Pedro, a misfit in society, an outcast with no place to go. But she has been made queen for a day and wants to rule forever.

One day she tries to escape from the blazing heat, which by now symbolizes the strain between her and Pedro as much as the cause for that strain, by soaking in the fire barrel. While raising the lid, she discovers the horse heads that Pedro has placed there. Gertie insists that Pedro remove the heads, and when he refuses she climbs back into her mountains, hoping to recover the dreamlike experience that can change her life once more.

The flaws in the story are obvious, if understandable. In the Stanford environment, Steinbeck was uncertain about his simple story of a retarded orphan and a migrant camp of Filipino workers. Unwilling to let the story stand on its own, he tried to affect artistic sophistication by means of symbolism and an arch tone. At many points, the figurative language also gets out of control, as in the description of the rainstorm:

The sky was splitting. A cruel, crooked line of light brought Gertie to a sitting position. Then there was a crash as of two giant freight cars hurtling together and the pop-pop of fragments falling on the roof of a tin warehouse. Suddenly the black air broke to pieces, the hills sounded and resounded, the moving air moaned, drew back and charged, buffeting and tearing at the ground.

But the prose also often bears that sure, clean touch of description that marks the later works with power.

While bearing obvious flaws, "Fingers of Cloud" nonetheless is a very significant story for Steinbeck as a writer.

Besides the fact that it was his first important publication, he was discovering techniques and themes for future use. The very fact that he draws upon the scenes that he knew well from the migrant camps marked a direction for him. Steinbeck was most at ease as an artist when writing about events that he had experienced or that grew out of his personal interest. Some years later, Steinbeck was to recall the migrants in terms that echo this story: "We brought in Filipinos to cut and chop the lettuce and there were interesting results. No Filipino women were allowed in and the dark, quick little men constantly got into trouble with what were called 'white women.'"[14]

Moreover, in Gertie he located a character type that he would explore more fully in the future. Gertie is possessed by huge dreams and urges but finally has no place to go with them. In her, one sees a foreshadowing of Elisa Allen, who sees a bright shining in the distance that she will never fully realize.

The story unlocked a certain artistic sensibility in Steinbeck, a sense of setting and theme. In his second Stanford publication, however, he was to reject this entirely in an effort to write straight satire, this time with Stanford itself as the subject.[15]

The June 1924 issue of the *Spectator* featured more work by members of the English Club. Katherine Beswick published a sonnet. Carl Wilhelmson published a story titled "Sir Galahad of Pisagua," and Webster Street a story titled "Mute." And John Steinbeck, having dropped his middle initial, published his satire "Adventures in Arcademy: A Journey into the Ridiculous."

A little satire in the hands of student writers is a dangerous thing; a lot of it is devastating. The writers of the *Spectator* used a lot of it, often wielded like a mace against gnat-sized issues and petty discomforts. While in the Western literary tradition satire enjoys a noble history, students tend to care little for tradition or history. Give them satire as a weapon, and they often don't know much about nobility either. It is the axe that grinds their opponents down.

The episodic journey to "Our Academy" travels on a blistering surge of satirical energy, often losing its way in lightning at the expense of clarity. Curiously enough, for so vicious and headstrong a piece, it is told in first person, one of only a handful of Steinbeck's stories told from this point of view. His disenchantment with Stanford was at a peak, and it certainly piqued the venom of this piece.

The story is framed, beginning and ending, with a young man whistling along the road to Stanford. What happens in between changes the tune slightly. The persona is naïve at the outset, traipsing a white road of innocence: "Blithely the white shell road slipped by under my feet, and now and then, in an unthinking way, I whistled whimsical tunes which had no endings and very, very immature beginnings." Along that road he meets the "mysterious stranger," stock figure of many satires. But this is a very odd stranger indeed: "He was dressed in those clothes which an old man would wear were he young or a wise man were he a fool. That is to say, his coat hung loosely from his neck and his trousers were entirely made of bits of pliable glass in many colors which fitted his crossed legs in no uncertain manner. When he moved the glass tinkled quite nicely." The many colors of glass in the stranger's costume seem to signify that he sees nothing whole and certain. His costume is disjointed and ill suited, as learning will be for the young man at Stanford. The stranger points toward the university, indicating where the young man can obtain trousers just like them.

As he heads in that direction, the young man notices that the shell road has grown pink. The direction of the satire is also clear at this point. The repository of arcane knowledge, of mystical and intriguing pursuits guided by eminent authorities, lies at Stanford. But his arrival at the hallowed gate signals something quite different.

The way grows increasingly nonsensical, a kind of *Through the Looking Glass* world in which the glass is pink-hued. The young man meets people howling madly. When some try to guide him, others protest that it is "time wasted from howling." The portrait suggests, in the academic setting, scholars desperately protecting their turf by insane howling, rather than providing clear directions to seeking minds. The road stops before a wall "built of small tombstones piled up flatwise." The lively academic environment proves to be a charnel house of restrictive rules: he has to purchase a ticket to enter.

Thus far, the piece seems a rather common work of student satire, particularly from one who fought the bridle of academic demands with a notorious propensity for avoiding the classroom altogether. The context changes dramatically, however, with entrance to the campus. We have slipped into Wonderland, a surreal world of cartoon characters, each of whom suggests a certain pedagogical dogma: "In one line there was a rabbit of good figure which sniffed of the beginnings of things, and in another an undergrown buffalo snorted of Botticelli and certain frowned-on theories." While faculty members move ethereally on the airs of their doctrines, quite detached from reality, the students are very much creatures of the earth. In obvious symbolism, a group of boys jumps for fruits on the trees just out of reach—students groping for success, or grades, or a degree. Meanwhile a group of girls plays merrily in a mud puddle. The dean of women, presented here as a gray goose (all the administrators are birds), looks upon her charges wallowing in the mud and tells them, "I don't approve of this, but as long as you do not fall in the pool you will not be wet." Whereupon one of the girls runs up to her and exclaims, "See, I am not wet." The college girls, who frolic in a moral mud, put on a shameless face and announce their virtue to the dean, even as the mud drips from them. It's all a game.

Suddenly attention rivets on the narrator. Pouter Pigeon, a leading administrator, accuses him of heresy. His vile fault is not being thoroughly red. He has not been entirely assimilated into the Stanford milieu. He reflects: "They denounced me because I was only partly red (for I had forgotten to remove my cap when I had come into the field and my head was untinted)." So he is cast out. That Stanford can stand no dissension and will reframe reality to fit its image of itself seems to be Steinbeck's message. Muddy Stanford girls will appear clean because they say they are, and the Gray Goose approves. Gasoline and alcohol will not mix, even while students industriously support their local bootlegger, because a voice has told them they will not mix. The faculty, like bloated animals, will ruminate on their pedagogical cuds and snort Botticelli because it is the thing they do. Voices will continue to howl, fearing the silence that will remind them of the inanity of their own howling. The attack blisters everything it touches. The narrator, recognizing that he has no place in this sound and fury, turns back to the road. Steinbeck subtly changes the wording of the ending so that it doesn't simply frame the beginning, but reverses it into a devastating comment on Stanford itself: "The walls closed behind me, and I was sitting on a smooth bench at a turning in the shell road, and along the path came one who whistled a whimsical tune which had no ending, and an exceptionally immature beginning." The narrator sees the shadow of himself, and the reader is left wondering what advice will be offered. In a July 1924 letter to Carl Wilhelmson, Steinbeck wrote,

I think rebellion man's highest state. All that we regard most highly in art, literature, goverment, philosophy, or even those changes which are the result of anatomic evolution had their beginnings in rebellion in an individual. Here you will say that rebellion for its own sake is not good, but even that I deny, for many things are and have been found in rebellion for its own sake.[16]

Although the comment may be dismissed as the intemperate statement of a headstrong young man, as some might view the short stories of this period, it was very much Steinbeck's spirit during the Stanford years.

"Adventures in Arcademy" served a cathartic function for Steinbeck rather than an artistic one. In another sense, however, the short piece was an important crossroads, for Steinbeck had a natural inclination for such satire. It appears not infrequently in his early work, spicing passages of

Cup of Gold, serving as the subject of the few poems he wrote, and appearing occasionally in later works as well, from *Cannery Row* to *The Short Reign of Pippin IV.* In a sense, his Stanford publications gave him an either/or. Would he pursue the stories of migrants and common people, as in "Fingers of Cloud"—the stories that he knew best and that originated from personal experience? Or would he unleash his flaming intelligence in vitriolic rebellion against his times? The solution—some years off—came in his sensitive portraits of common characters in conflict with their times, and often themselves. But there was a great deal of writing and personal frustration ahead before he found that dramatic synthesis.

After the spring quarter of 1924 at Stanford, Steinbeck took a summer job, joined by Carlton Sheffield, at the Spreckels factory at Monteca. It was a hot, sweaty summer as he labored over the sugar-refining cookers. Fired for fighting with a worker, a sequence of very odd jobs followed: from selling a new radio called the Echophone (about which Steinbeck knew nothing and from which he made $2.50, half the commission on precisely one sale) to mailing Christmas seals. He returned to Spreckels in the late fall and returned to Stanford, for the last time, in January 1925. Now scarcely a part of the academic community, Steinbeck roomed in a toolshed attached to a stable (one thinks of Crook's room in *Of Mice and Men*). Jackson Benson describes the quarters:

It was damp, since it stood near the bank of Francisquito Creek, and only half of it, a little more than six by six feet, had been cleared for living space. There was no stove, gas, water, or electricity; urgent bathroom problems had to be taken to the main house; and it was infested with pill bugs and spiders. He put his battered Corona typewriter on a wooden box and bought an old army cot, which he put near the wood stacked at one end of the shed. He made do with water from a garden spigot and a little outdoor fire pit. He called the place "The Sphincter" and paid five dollars a month rent.[17]

The tool room became a haven for the discontented, the evenings passed in long wine parties and no study. Stanford had virtually ceased to exist for Steinbeck. His writing consisted chiefly of "A Lady in Infra-Red," which would grow over four years into *Cup of Gold*, and several short stories: "I have written the Jael-Sisera story, and there are several others. Some of them are fairly good, though I can get very few outside myself to believe that."[18]

The unpublished Jael-Sisera story survives in manuscript form as "The Nail," held by the Houghton Library of Harvard University. Using a biblical tone that he attempted also in *To a God Unknown* and perfected in passages of *The Grapes of Wrath*, Steinbeck recounts the story of Judges, chapter four, with several variations. Most notably, he casts the pagan Canaanite culture as remarkably rich and liberated compared to that of the rigid Israelites. Some of Steinbeck's truculence toward Stanford's rigid decorum touches this story also.

Sisera was the military commander of Jabin, king of Canaan during the time of Deborah, ruling judge of Israel. Under Deborah's direction, Sisera's army was routed and the commander fled to the tent of Jael, wife of Heber. Heber and Jael's tent lay in a region where they were dependent upon the protection of the Israelites, rather than Heber's native Kenites. In the biblical account, Jael's motivation for slaying Sisera with the tent peg was, therefore, an act of self-defense in the Israelite cause. Steinbeck supplies a different motivation for Jael, however. Sisera reveals to her that he has killed a Jewish leader whom Jael recognizes from his description as her own son. Moreover, Steinbeck has Sisera coming to her wounded in the leg, an item not found in the biblical account, to elicit sympathy for Sisera.

The significance of the story resides primarily, however, in revealing Steinbeck's fascination with the biblical story. The Bible would become one of the foremost influences upon his later fiction, often providing a rich symbolic texture. While not drawn to the Bible for personal spiritual reasons, Steinbeck found in it a powerful series of stories, an experience of religion, and a symbolism that had infiltrated the consciousness of Western culture. These were to become important artistic resources for him in coming years.

NEW YORK AND NEW WRITING

Several other unpublished stories exist from this period of the late 1920s, and they raise a problem of sorts in Steinbeck criticism. When a reader studies the works of an author for some time, reading and rereading the major works, led by insatiable curiosity into the lesser works, several dangers arise. They often arise because the reader's own emotions—this love for the work which drew the cords of interest in the first place—sometimes blind the critical eye to the quality of the works themselves. While we place the highest value upon the literary work that gives us reading pleasure, the dangers that can arise are common ones: to gauge the artistic worth of the works by the pleasure derived in reading them; to dismiss those that fail to give reading pleasure as of lesser artistic worth; to long for more works, of whatever quality, to extend the pleasure.

Perhaps because of these dangers, an odd enthusiasm has marked the modern age for the unpublished stories of a writer. In some instances—J. R. R. Tolkien and C. S. Lewis in Great Britain; Ernest Hemingway, William Faulkner, and F. Scott Fitzgerald in the United States—a small industry emerges for publishing posthumously the previously unpublished works. The residue of a writer's career suddenly receives the limelight. It doesn't always glisten.

Steinbeck left one complete, intact, book-length manuscript, "Murder at Full Moon by Peter Pym," and a number of short stories unpublished. It is somewhat a credit to Steinbeck's legacy that, with the exception of the unfinished *Acts of King Arthur*, for which Steinbeck expressed clear intentions of publication, the temptation to bring the unpublished works to the general public has been resisted.

In *Beyond "The Red Pony,"* the first critical work to sys-

tematically explore Steinbeck's career exclusively in short
stories, R. S. Hughes speculates that "since these Steinbeck manuscripts are available for inspection, it may be jus-
tifiably asked why they have remained so long in obscurity.
Six largely unknown stories by a major American author
would ordinarily become the focal point of critical activity."[19] Hughes suggests two reasons why this is so. First, for
many years the manuscripts were privately held and not
generally known. Second, the authorship of four of the
stories was in dispute for several years, although they are
now generally acknowledged to be Steinbeck's.[20] Hughes
overlooks a third possibility: the decidedly uneven quality
of the unpublished stories. The fact of the matter is that
some unpublished works are better left that way. "Fingers
of Cloud" and "Adventures in Arcademy" are clearly inferior works in comparison with the later Steinbeck canon,
and were it not for those later works, no one today would
pay any attention to them. Nonetheless, their publication,
albeit as student publications, is a matter of historical record. The works were submitted to an audience and, with a
clear understanding of that audience and the time, they may
also be submitted to critical scrutiny, particularly to assess
the mind of the author in apprenticeship for the later works.
    Steinbeck did not always have enormous scruples about
what he did publish later. He could easily burn a manuscript that he thought inferior, but he was also inordinately
fond of some works that were largely, and deservedly, ignored in his time. As late as 1949 he still thought *Cup of
Gold* had smashing possibilities as a film, even though in
1939 he called it "an immature experiment written for the
purpose of getting all the wise cracks (known by sopho-
mores as epigrams) and all the autobiographical material
(which hounds us until we get it said) out of my system"
(*SLL*, p. 17). In an unpublished letter to Wanda Van Brunt,
dated March 9, 1949, Steinbeck wrote, "Do one thing for
me! Get Cup of Gold and tell me whether you don't think
with rewriting and some arranging it wouldn't make a hell

of a picture. I know it would but you read it and think about it too."[21]

Upon leaving Stanford in June 1925, Steinbeck put his aim of being a writer into practice. Perhaps that aim in itself turned him toward New York, for this is where the big talent seemed to go, where a small army of agents swarmed, and where the heart of the publishing industry beat most powerfully. In November he boarded a steamer and made the long voyage through the Panama Canal to New York. Few places could have been more uncongenial to a young man from the temperate climate of the Salinas Valley. Instead of the sprawl of hills, he found the endless maze of buildings. Instead of the warm sun, a steely cold. Instead of familiar faces, the averted glance of strangers. A decade later he wrote, "I guess I hate New York, because I had a thin, lonely, hungry time of it there. And I remember too well the cockroaches under my wash basin and the impossibility of getting a job. I was scared thoroughly. And I can't forget the scare" (*SLL*, p. 9).

Steinbeck gives his own best portrait of this period in an article written for the *New York Times Magazine* in 1953. He recollects arriving in New York with $100 in his pocket, a flurry of dreams in his head, and a surge of fear in his heart. "From a porthole, then, I saw the city, and it horrified me. There was something monstrous about it—the tall buildings looming to the sky and the lights shining through the falling snow. I crept ashore—frightened and cold and with a touch of panic in my stomach." After pushing wheelbarrows of concrete at the construction of Madison Square Garden for a while, he recalls how his wealthy uncle got him a job on the *New York American* at $25 a week, a payment Steinbeck described as "a total loss." He admits he "didn't know the first thing about being a reporter. . . . They gave me stories to cover in Queens and Brooklyn and I would get lost and spend hours trying to find my way back. I couldn't learn to steal a picture from a desk when a family refused to be photographed and I invariably got emotionally involved and tried to kill the whole story to save the subject." Losing his job there, Steinbeck tried to get work as a laborer again, but the long weeks of loneliness had also drained his physical strength: "I could hardly lift a pick. I had trouble climbing the six flights back to my room. My friend loaned me a dollar and I bought two loaves of rye bread and a bag of dried herrings and never left my room for a week. I was afraid to go out on the street—actually afraid of traffic—the noise. Afraid of the landlord and afraid of people."[22] He returned to California in the summer of 1926, but with several completed short stories.

Perhaps the most revealing story of Steinbeck's brief stay in New York may have been written during the Christmas season of 1925, shortly after he arrived in the city. The despairing loneliness of the character, William, was very much Steinbeck's own. His loneliness is laid open like a wound.

In the tale, William wanders the streets of Manhattan and confronts three variations of "Merry Christmas." In the first encounter, the elevator operator, hand outstretched for a tip, offers William a reminder, "Merry Christmas." William tips him fifty cents and walks out to the cold streets. In the second encounter, a prostitute leers from a doorway: "Merry Christmas?" William offers her a dollar rather than his company. He has responded to each greeting in the way it was intended, a pragmatic transaction devoid of spirit. The third encounter is with himself. On the streets William sees the glowing tower of the Metropolitan Building lit like a new star in the east. This is the path we have taken from Bethlehem: following the light of the insurance companies. In his squalid little room, William confronts his own past, particularly the tyranny of his father, in the form of a pair of boots and a stuffed raccoon. He locks the boots in a closet and kicks the raccoon until it lies in tatters. William finds himself plunged uncertainly, and with vast loneliness, between the Christmas of his youth and the modern sense of Christmas as getting all you can when you can.

In years to come, Steinbeck was to return to that same speculation on the ability of greed to devour tradition and spirit. Frequently the Christmas season becomes the spur. In January 1931 he wrote George Albee, "Then Christmas eve we watched the workings of the god-given attitude, greed" (*SLL*, p. 33). Shortly before Christmas, 1959, Steinbeck wrote to Adlai Stevenson, speculating on two kinds of Christmas, one harboring a loving tradition, the other addled with greed:

Well, it seems to me that America now is like that second kind of Christmas. Having too many THINGS they spend their hours and money on the couch searching for a soul. A strange species we are. We can stand anything God and Nature can throw at us save only plenty. If I wanted to destroy a nation, I would give it too much and I would have it on its knees, miserable, greedy and sick. [*SLL*, p. 652]

Several weeks later, the subject was still on his mind. He wrote Elizabeth Otis on December 30, 1959, "True things gradually disappeared and shiny easy things took their place. I brought the writing outside, like a cook flipping hot cakes in a window. . . . I'll have to learn all over again about true things"(*SLL*, p. 657).[23]

Above all, however, this Christmas story of Steinbeck's incarnates a spirit of painful loneliness. It bears this haunting reflection of William: "I think I shall walk home in this storm. Perhaps I too may freeze. At least, I would if I were to take off this coat. And then even I might someday be adjudged literatesque. I do wonder then if all the reporters in the world will make pilgrimage to the street corner where my brass plate will be."[24]

That same feeling infiltrates his other New York stories. "The Nymph and Isobel" places a fantasy of nymphs among the grimy tenements and towers of lower Manhattan. The protagonist, Isobel, senses a fantasy world that lies beyond this grimness. If one were to look hard, one might find the echo of Gertie climbing the mountain in "Fingers of Cloud." "East Third Street" depicts the fearful Vinch, who somehow finds courage in a bottle and defeats the barroom bully. "The Days of Long Marsh," set in California, may have

been written during this period also. The story features an
old man with a totem-like shelf of shiny catsup bottles. He
rescues a hunter, who narrates the story in first person,
from the foggy marsh and reveals to him the symbolism of
the bottles. The old man says, "Now here's the Monday
vase before anything was. This is the beginning of all things.
The flowers in it are of the old days before Nellie. There's
ships in this Monday vase and big square sails to them.
There's men dying and not knowing or caring. There's me
tied to the shrouds and beat with a rope's end."[25] The bewildered hunter heads back to the marsh, having caught
sight for a moment of a surreal world of dreams bearing too
much reality.

"The White Sister of Fourteenth Street," the final New
York story, may serve as an example of some of Steinbeck's
artistic difficulties of the time. It is certain that during his
time in New York he felt severed from his own roots. New
York was an artificial environment to him then, foreign and
foreboding. The artificiality affects his work as well. The
shaping of the stories is uncertain and tentative. At his
best, Steinbeck revised boldly, adjusting sentences, slicing
verbs, phrases, and clauses not to his liking. Too many bad
sentences creep into these stories, as if he were clutching
to his work like a cherished thing. Nowhere is this more
pronounced than in the story of Elsie Grough, "The White
Sister of Fourteenth Street."

The artistic uncertainty is evident from the outset. In a
rare deviation from his artistic technique, Steinbeck ad-
dresses the reader directly in the story: "In spite of the
many catty explanations you may hear along Fourteenth
Street, this is the only authentic story of how Elsie Grough
lost her Wop-papa. (Wappapa it became of course)."[26] A
confident writer shows the reader, rather than announcing.
Here Steinbeck seems to struggle for the reader's attention:
"But to go on with Elsie. She liked to have boy friends, lots
of them, and there were several reasons why she was successful, her sweet, rounded legs for instance."

The narrator retains this sense of overt declaration, failing to trust the reader or the story he is telling. The descriptions are contrived: "When his black head, shiny as a shoe button was poked into her life, she began to languish, to read sentimental books and plan little coups d'amour." When Elsie is dancing at the Harmony Gardens, the narrator simply signs off: "So much for Elsie for a while." Elsie has a passion for dancing. She loves the motion and the music, the wilder the better. She longs to go out in Harlem. Instead she winds up at the opera with Angelo. This is a foreign world to her, one Steinbeck attempts to place by an embarrassingly belabored description: "The air was lousy with garlic. Take Elsie sitting in the fourth row, suppose she should write a dictionary. Lousy: noun, unsatisfying, bad, undesirable, Adj., full of, crowded with, i.e., man lousy rich, air lousy with garlic." The opera itself is foreign to her; but so too is the wave of passion that sweeps over Angelo: "This person was strange and wonderful and frightening. A new dignity made him seem tall, impressive, almost austere." In the wild applause after the opera, Elsie loses sight of Angelo and is left alone. She has discovered a world cut off from her, one she cannot participate in, and she is abandoned by it.

While the flaws in this story are pronounced, all the unpublished stories of the period are flawed to some degree. None of them would be truly representative of Steinbeck's later, published work. Their importance is largely private to the author: a testing of characters, language, and themes.

Steinbeck's one published short story of this time was "The Gifts of Iban," published under the name of John Stern in the first issue of a short-lived magazine, the *Smokers Companion*, in March 1927. For the fee of fifteen dollars, the magazine received full rights and apparently exercised them broadly in the editorial process. In 1928, Steinbeck wrote Katherine Beswick, "The only thing of mine I have ever seen in print was the old fairy story of Iban. An upstart magazine called the Smoker's Companion bought it from Brecht [Bill Brecht, story editor at Brandt and Brandt], and I got hold of it. They wrecked it so frightfully (I had of course conceded the right to edit) that I never wanted to see another."[27] Steinbeck seems to assume Beswick's familiarity with the story, which may suggest that it was drafted as early as the Stanford years.

The story is one of three during this period, along with "Fingers of Cloud" and "The Nymph and Isobel," to be heavily influenced by fantasy, a part of the romantic craze of the age and a trait also apparent in his novel *Cup of Gold*. Steinbeck had read widely in such romantic-fantasy literature and was particularly influenced by the novels of James Branch Cabell. Although he had read at least four of Cabell's novels, Steinbeck held a disparagingly low view of the author. To George Albee, Steinbeck wrote in 1931, "I consider a magnitude of concept and paucity in execution far more desirable than a shallow conception with preciousness. Cabell painted the logical conclusion of that."[28] Earlier than that, however, Steinbeck had written A. Grove Day, "I think I have swept all the Cabellyo-Byrneish preciousness out for good" (*SLL*, p. 17).

With such a view of the romantic fantasy, why did Steinbeck appropriate the genre? The answer is obvious. It sold. And he wanted to sell his work. To do so, he imitated Cabell. In this case, after a fashion, he succeeded in his aim. The *Smokers Companion*, subtitled "A National Monthly for Hearth and Home," was one in a long line of popular fiction magazines that appeared in the 1920s. The editor, Gerald Fitzgerald, labeled "The Gifts of Iban" as "A Charming Fantasy." Whereas in "Fingers of Cloud" Steinbeck mixed fantasy with realism, symbolism, and satire, creating a hodgepodge faintly held together by the wandering orphan Gertie, "The Gifts of Iban" succeeds in being exclusively fantasy. Moreover, it captures a later theme of Steinbeck's— the contrary pulls of the romantic dream and pragmatic reality.

The girl Cantha is caught between those two pulls. On the one hand, the romantic singer Iban offers her gifts of gold and silver. On the other, her autocratic mother directs her toward the wealthy but ugly and practical Glump. Enchanted by Iban's promised gifts, Cantha marries him in an "ivory house" in his forest. When she discovers, however, that the promised gold is simply the glow of sunbeams and the silver is merely moonlight, she petulantly rejects him:

"You have misled me, Iban, you have told lies about your fine things, and I think I can never forgive you for that. Of course they are very pretty, and I enjoy looking at them for a short while. Nature is always lovely, of course, especially when you know the names of things. But I wish I had married Glump, for then I should have real gold and silver instead of leaves and light. Gold and silver are truly fine things, Iban." [29]

Cantha challenges Iban to sing one of his magical songs, rejects the songs along with Iban, and leaves him lying heartbroken in the forest as she sets off in search of Glump.

"The Gifts of Iban" was probably the most successful of the stories of this time because of its very simplicity as a tidy little fable, well packaged in its own artistic terms. It provided Steinbeck with a fundamental dialectic of the dreamer in conflict with pragmatic demands, which would mark much of his later fiction. Jackson Benson observes,

The themes of the story—the isolation and defeat of the poet by society; the ideal (personified in the beautiful, unobtainable woman) which inevitably slips through the fingers of the quester; the destructiveness of material wealth and human pride—are much the same themes of his novel, which he finally completed in late January of 1928. *Cup of Gold* is not so much a historical novel as it is another fantasy-allegory. [30]

In fact, Merlin of *Cup of Gold* echoes the theme of Iban when he advises Henry Morgan:

You want the moon to drink from as a gold cup; and so, it is very likely that you will become a great man—if only you remain a little child. All the world's great have been little boys who wanted the moon; running and climbing, they sometimes caught a firefly.

But if one grows to a man's mind, that mind must see that it cannot have the moon and would not want it if it could—and so, it
catches no fireflies.[31]

Like Iban, Merlin celebrates the huge dream. In *Cup of
Gold*, civilization—pragmatic reality—destroys it. Near
the end of the novel Merlin ruminates, "Those who say
children are happy, forget their childhood. I wonder how
long he can stave off manhood."[32] In "The Gifts of Iban,"
Steinbeck crafted that same dream of childhood, dashed by
the realities of the pragmatic world.

In the era of flaming youth, John Steinbeck's desire to
write fiction seethed like a fire within him. In *Irrational
Man*, William Barrett observes, "With civilization, as with
individuals, the outer fact is often merely the explosion re-
sulting from accumulated inner tension, the signs of which
were plentifully present, though none of the persons concerned chose to heed them."[33] Steinbeck's writing, in many
ways, was an eruption of the heart, and few chose to heed
the signs.

Steinbeck's stories also erupted against the forms he
used. Conceptually the stories are full of promise. There
can be no doubt, reading back over those early passages, of
the man's genius. But it was all raw, untempered flame. If
"Fingers of Cloud" reveals a mind careening in several directions at once, the mind that charged along those contrary directions is clearly first-rate. The satiric framework
of "Adventures in Arcademy" can barely contain the explosive fireworks unleashed by the form. The genius is out
of control, firing words like a Gatling gun and destroying
everything in its path. "This mind is full of nervous promise," Steinbeck wrote in August 1934 (*LVN*). In the 1920s,
the promise is evident, but the nervousness is what emerges
on the page.

The huge conceptual ability pulses in the unpublished
stories as well. The ideas rampage on the page like uncaged
tigers; they only want a sure direction. "The White Sister of
Fourteenth Street" is richly styled, like an operatic move-

ment. "The Nail" turns scripture on its head to celebrate defiance. "East Third Street" reels through a world of darkness, choked with smoke and sanguine colors to evoke a Miltonic hell in lower Manhattan. "The Nymph and Isobel" lifts Crane's Maggie to a mythic world. "The Days of Long Marsh" concocts a symbology in catsup bottles that boggles the mind.

Perhaps there were too many influences on the young writer. He could not find his own way. Stephen Crane, whom Steinbeck had read by 1921, leaves his imprint upon the Manhattan stories.[34] Lillian Gish's performance in the film adaptation of Marion Crawford's *The White Sister* provides the impetus for Steinbeck's portrait of Elsie Grough. Rafael Sabatini's popular *Captain Blood* spurs the bloody seas of *Cup of Gold*. Steinbeck doesn't just imitate, however. He uses the sources as a spring board, a high dive. The problem was that he tumbled wildly once launched. He had to find his own way, his own story.

Joseph Epstein reflects in *Plausible Prejudices*, "I once wrote that the novels of the future would feature a group of genitals sitting around discussing fashionable ideas. I can now say, to wring a change on Lincoln Steffens, that I have seen the future and it doesn't work."[35] Had Steinbeck read the remark in the 1920s, he might have written the novel. It would have been full of fiery conception, hatching ideas with brilliant abandon, all the baby thoughts growing up and shuffling off in contrary directions. However they went, we would be forced to recognize his genius. Clearly Steinbeck had to find his own stories, ones that would embody his ideas but also domesticate them.

If the imitative quality is one mark of the inferiority of the work, the second is craft. Steinbeck manages to make nearly every possible error of narration, from shifting points of view, so slippery that they sometimes change page by page, to prose so heavily laden it wallows, to plots so indecisive they wander to foreign countries, irretrievably lost by the end of the story. Curiously, this problem would be solved by the solution to the first. In finding his own sto-

ries—rising from the people of his homeland rather than
peopled by his mind—Steinbeck also tempered the abandon of his prose.

Here is the huge transition at the end of the decade, no-
ticeable first in *The Pastures of Heaven*. Steinbeck turns,
like the restless soul he was in New York, to a search for a
usable past. He locates stories in the quiet foothills around
Salinas, and finds the stories strangely disquieting. Indeed,
they are full of tense drama and urgency. But the people,
these real people of his experience, also guide the telling.
The rhythms of the prose become tailored to the rhythms of
nature—descriptions of hills, skies, trees, animals—that
he saw before him. The rhythms of the prose also become
tailored to the rhythms of the people, capturing speech patterns that begin to ring with the awesome tone of reality
rather than artifice. The maker of fabrications is now made
a storyteller by his choice of subject matter.

There is a great deal more to the making of a fiction writer
than this, of course. The early thirties was also a struggle
to find that new artistic voice: the selection of stories and
the mode for telling them. But he had found a way in the
late 1920s. He turned from ideas to life. Joseph Epstein
comments,

What literature teaches, what it has taught me, is that life is more
various than any intellectual or political system can ever hope to
comprehend. Life, one learns from literature, is filled with sad-
ness and joy, tragedy and splendor, despair and dignity in despair, hatred and laughter, and more doublets of this kind than
any single sentence can hope to contain. Literature is about life,
which is commonplace; yet literature is also on the side of life,
which, if it too is commonplace, is frequently forgotten.[36]

This was also Steinbeck's singular discovery in the transition from the 1920s to the 1930s, and it was the discovery
that would invest his work with power and liberate his genius for all the years to come.

2

Sureness of Touch: The 1930s

THE EARLY 1930s was one of the odd eras of American history. Staggering under financial blows, reeling under the weight of the many homeless and the disinherited, the age seemed hopelessly afflicted. Misery lurked on the doorstep of every home, and might enter any morning. In shacks papered with newspapers the faces of hungry children peered into cameras. Upon seeing the photographs, one bitter father said, "A worker's got no right to have kids any more." For many the dream of the family lay shattered. Even the elements contrived against humanity. Nature dealt the nation blow upon blow of terrible weather; surging floods and blasting dust storms raked the country in turn; frigid cold and merciless heat raged through the skies.

Still, the nation was a factory of dreams. Harold Gray, who introduced Little Orphan Annie in 1924, was earning $100,000 a year marketing the chubby little redhead in the early thirties. "Yale-educated" Flash Gordon battled the evil genius Hans Zarkov in intergalactic showdowns. Problems were easily solvable when projected into space. Buck Rogers took readers to A.D. 2430 and displaced the threat of misery with his "disintegration gun" and "rocket pistol." Tom Mix and his wonder horse reeled through 180 feature films, in the process of which, as the official "Tom Mix Injury Chart" graphically shows, the hero endured twelve bullet wounds, twenty-two knife wounds, and a hole four inches square that was blown out of his back by a stick of dynamite.

Misery and the dream factory: here lay the curious contradiction of the early thirties, and so it was also for John Steinbeck. In his recollection "A Primer on the Thirties," he wrote,

Sure I remember the Nineteen Thirties, the terrible, troubled, triumphant, surging Thirties. I can't think of any decade in history when so much happened in so many directions. Violent changes took place. Our country was modeled, our lives remolded, our Government rebuilt, forced to functions, duties and responsibilities it never had before and can never relinquish. The most rabid, hysterical Roosevelt-hater would not dare to suggest removing the reforms, the safeguards and the new concept that the Government is responsible for all its citizens.[1]

He adds, "I saw it sharply because I was on the outside, writing books no one would buy." But not entirely on the outside, for his fiction of the thirties was also "terrible, troubled, and triumphant."

The age was rich with magazine fiction; the appetite of the public for stories seemingly endless. Magazine racks at any newsstand would display up to a hundred different magazines, most of them carrying fiction of one sort or another. Over twenty such, priced at ten cents apiece, carried exclusively western stories. Frederick Faust, writing under several different pen names because the magazines could not keep up with his torrid output, seems to appear in all of them. *Thrilling Western, Smashing Western, Sure-Fire Western, Lariat:* the popular western magazines were hot and dramatic fare. The detective story was also in high demand, running a close second to the westerns. Spliced in between random copies of sports journals and the growing number of Hollywood tabloids were the worthier periodicals carrying fiction: the *New Yorker, Redbook, McCall's,* the *Saturday Evening Post,* the *Atlantic Monthly.*

This was a great age, perhaps the golden age, of the American short story. The demand was incessant, the financial rewards quite possibly large. Faust earned enough off his American westerns to build an elaborate villa in

Italy, from which he continued to crank out stories at the
rate of thirty pages a day. One critic called it "brainless
drip," but the public soaked it up. The tabloids promised
recognition, fame, and a huge audience. It seemed the likeliest avenue for an aspiring writer in the early 1930s to
break into the big time.

It was a transitional period for Steinbeck. In January
1927, *Cup of Gold* had been accepted for publication by
Robert M. McBride and Company. By the time the book
appeared publicly, to muted sales, Steinbeck was heartily
tired of it, referring to it by the name of its hero, Henry
Morgan, as "the Morgan atrocity" (*SLL*, p. 15) and "an immature experiment" (*SLL*, p. 17).

In 1930 Steinbeck finished his series of sketches called
Dissonant Symphony, a 30,000-word mélange of related
pieces now lost to posterity. Although he wrote in October
1930 to Carl Wilhelmson of having burned a forty-page
start to a novel, "the most unrelieved rot imaginable," he
returned to *Dissonant Symphony* long enough in 1931 to
bundle the manuscript and send it to a contest sponsored
by Scribner's. He never heard from them.

Furthermore, *To a God Unknown* was going through a
series of frustrating versions and revisions, never seeming
to find the solidity of a final touch. By August 1931 he had
withdrawn it from circulation, intending to revise it later.
Some of the revision work was carried on during and after
the writing of *The Pastures of Heaven*. The cycle reached a
kind of climax with his unpublished mystery story, "Murder
at Full Moon by Peter Pym," a work that he described as full
of every shabby trick he knew, and one that he whipped out
in nine days of writing.

In all this, money became a pressing concern. On the
one hand, Steinbeck wanted desperately to shake off the
shackles of dependence upon his parents. On the other
hand, just as desperately, he yearned for a paying audience
that would provide a sense of validity to his work. Although
he would remark throughout his career that financial re-

wards were far from uppermost in his mind, it is clear that in the early thirties some financial stability from sales of his work was a powerful longing. Failure of sales signaled a failure of audience acceptance, and in turn, a failure of ability. In 1931 Steinbeck responded to George Albee's concern for his fragile financial condition by writing, "Everyone I have ever known very well has been concerned that I would eventually starve. Probably I shall. It isn't important enough to me to be an obsession" (*SLL*, p. 47). A few years later, in 1934, he wrote Albee, "In the matter of money, my conception doesn't extend beyond two or three hundred dollars," but he also mentions that "I am writing many stories now. Because I should like to sell some of them, I am making my characters as nearly as I can in the likeness of men" (*SLL*, pp. 93–94). He freely confessed to Amasa Miller in a December 1930 letter that he had written "Murder at Full Moon" expressly for financial reasons: "It is quite obvious that people do not want to buy the things I have been writing. Therefore, to make the money I need, I must write the things they want to read" (*SLL*, p. 32). The concern appears in his ledger notebooks also. In August 1934 he entered a note in the ledger notebook of the *Long Valley* stories: "Always the problem, who shall survive? Still we have no money. I've sent off story after story and so far with no result. Both of us are beginning to worry. I thought there might be a loss of one out of four but the loss seems to be all out of all."

Not infrequently, a sense of desperation incites a loss of artistic control in a young artist. That was precisely the case in "Murder at Full Moon." Remarkably, however, this press of extraliterary concerns turned Steinbeck to the methods and materials that he knew best. The two Stanford short stories represented, in a sense, the divergent paths his talent could take: recapturing the poignant scenes he knew from experience as in "Fingers of Cloud" or unleashing his intellect in the fierce satire of "Adventures in Arcademy." One could trace these two directions throughout

Steinbeck's fictional career. The remarkable event of the early thirties was Steinbeck's discovery of a usable past—the location of settings and characters in his personal experience that would also bear the weight of themes closest to his heart.[2]

Three forces, then, converged in the early thirties. His novel *Cup of Gold*, on which Steinbeck had staked so much hope and work, failed commercially and, in his estimation at least, artistically. Second, financial concerns gnawed at his pride. Although it was not unusual for young married couples to depend upon their parents' larder and largesse in the post-crash years, the fiery, independent Carol and John Steinbeck loathed it. Financial concerns thrust prison bars over their spirits, and they longed for freedom. Third, the love of the craft of short fiction writing compelled Steinbeck. He had received some of his earliest professional encouragement in short fiction. Edith Mirrielees had exhorted him to an independent imagination, and every fiber in Steinbeck, packed with imaginative stories, responded in the early thirties. What was born of exigency developed into artistry as he practiced his craft. Here, for the first time, we can begin to discern Steinbeck's artistic beliefs approaching coherence and clarity.

One guide to Steinbeck's developing sense of craft is simply to trace the directions of the stories themselves. But Steinbeck also provides valuable clues pocketed in his ledger notebooks and scattered through his letters of the period. In the notebooks he began a practice that would reach fullest expression in the daily journals for *The Grapes of Wrath* and *East of Eden*, however in a far less systematic fashion. The notes are a chronicle of an artist at work, clarifying his own process of making that art, and several of them were to mark Steinbeck's attitudes toward fiction for the rest of his life. Although a number of the ledger notes will be discussed in the context of the stories to which they relate, certain general patterns—sureness of touch, use of symbolism, and harmony or rhythm of prose—emerge.

One of the more significant notes relating to his developing artistic beliefs is in the *Tortilla Flat* notebook. Having struggled with several starts to "The Chrysanthemums," Steinbeck suddenly broke off writing with this note: "There's no sureness of touch in me today. I don't seem to be able to get at this story. I should not be writing this story this way at all. It should be a hard finish story." The composition of "The Chrysanthemums" gave Steinbeck more difficulty, perhaps, than any other story. It was often in his mind, went through several versions and false starts, and presented demanding challenges. The striking thing in this note is Steinbeck's insistence upon "sureness of touch." The term signified several things for him: confidence in his ability to write the story, a complete absorption of the story in his own mind (a sense of familiarity with it), and control over the technical craft.

Immediately following this interruption, Steinbeck stepped back from the story, invented a reader-adviser, and addressed a letter to him—"my dear little hypothetical turnip," named Ralph:

This morning I want to issue a warning against certain tendencies in the writing of short stories. I had a story, Ralph, and on a day when I did not feel like writing, I sat down to write it. Two days of work passed before I realized that I was doing it all wrong. And now it must be done again. Subconsciously I knew it was wrong from the beginning. But I blundered on, putting down words every one of which had an untrue ring. And so, Ralph, if you ever take up short stories as you no doubt will (everyone does) I implore you not to go on working when you have that untrue feeling in your bones. I cannot describe it. You will know it when you have it. My tendency, and no doubt yours, is to put more into a short story than belongs there. Keep out details that have no absolute bearing on your story. Keep out characterization that does not actually move the story on its way. I may and shall disobey the letter of this instruction, but don't you dare.

Shortly after this, Steinbeck returned to "The Chrysanthemums," starting from the beginning. This time he had that ineffable sureness of touch well in hand, producing one of his most masterful short stories. This sensibility of the artist, possessing confidence and control over all the materials of the story, perhaps strikes a modern critic oddly. It echoes a bit too much of the Romantic notion of inspiration. For Steinbeck, however, it forms an essential basis for writing. He felt that he had to possess the story powerfully—"in his bones"—before he could set it forth for others.

Part of this sureness of touch also lay in the revising process, both in the act of writing—confidently selecting and discarding certain options—and in rewriting. Although a number of Steinbeck's draft manuscripts appear deceptively clean, as if he sat down and rattled the story off straight through, actually he did far more conscientious and consistent revising than most people are aware. The process included going over the draft, often in pencil over the ink that he almost always wrote the first drafts of his short stories in, in order to change words, tighten rhetorical structures, and select more active verbs. The lesson in revision that Edith Mirrielees hammered home in her class in story writing at Stanford did find a home in Steinbeck's technique. In *Story Writing*, she repeatedly emphasizes a point that must have been a hallmark of her teaching as well:

> One of the unchangeable facts a writer always faces is that he can have only so many words in any story.
>
> How many "so many" may be differs from story to story, but one condition remains true in all but the rarest instances. The "so many" is never so many as in the beginning he feels he must use.[3]

Examination of Steinbeck's original manuscripts bears evidence of her dictum. Words are pared back, moved around, and substituted frequently.

The process also included a surprising number of deleted passages, and not infrequently a sense that the direction he had taken with a particular story was so wrong that he had to start all over. While working on the Bert Munroe story from *The Pastures of Heaven*, Steinbeck suddenly stopped

with the comment, "There are things so definitely wrong
with this story that I think it had better be remade. A large
part of it anyway" (*POH-1*). Steinbeck could be a ruthless
reviser, cutting flabby lines, even entire paragraphs that
were not essential. Much later in the *Tortilla Flat* notebook, Steinbeck again confronts the need to keep out su-
perfluous details and characterization: "Now I suppose I've
lost the pruning shears. I'm always doing something wrong.
I'm so sick of it." This pruning through revision was not a
new discovery for Steinbeck. In 1929 he had written Grove
Day, "I have tried to throw out the words that do not say
anything" (*SLL*, p. 19).

The notebooks indicate that Steinbeck may have been
one of his own harshest critics. Truly he loved the work of
writing. Indeed he often wrote in letters of his enduring
confidence in the quality of his work, regardless of the perception of others. But this joy and confidence were refined
in the crucible of nagging self-examination and doubt while
in the process of writing. While working on *The Pastures of
Heaven*, and again facing one of those periods in which he
did not feel the sureness of touch, Steinbeck poses his own
artistic problem: "These stories I have just finished. I know
what is the matter with them. They are not hard and central enough in theme. They waver. The characters only live
for seconds of a time. They leave no memory or call it taste.
That is the real trouble with them. They are *not* strong
enough" (*POH-1*). Good writing, in Steinbeck's estimation,
was produced by a marriage of feeling and craft. He writes,
"And yet of everything I finish, I think—this might be
good—somewhere in this might rest elements of greatness
because they were written with a great feeling, not with a
great technique. Such a feeling refutes itself. Great books
are not written with feeling but with ability" (*POH-1*).
When the touch is sure, when the writer has the flow of
story and craft and ability all working together, then a rare
and wonderful thing happens: "This other wonder comes
when I am working. The pencil moves of itself and writes

words which seem fine words to me. It is as though some person more wise, more practical and clever than I am held the pencil and put his thoughts on my paper. When this thing happens, I seem to be the reader rather than the writer" (*POH-1*). Sureness of touch captures the total feeling and practice of the act of writing, but Steinbeck also reveals specific techniques of his craft during this period. For example, he was beginning to discover his acute sensitivity for symbolism that rises naturally and unforced from the plot and characters of the story. Steinbeck believed that a story works best when it suggests things to a reader, as opposed to overtly declaring. The key to this suggestiveness lies in symbolism. While the symbolism of the major novels has attracted considerable critical attention, readers have been less aware of it in the short stories. Steinbeck's awareness and use of symbolism certainly became more refined and expert in later years, but it is clearly evident in this period. In the *Tortilla Flat* notebook, after writing a draft of "The Murder," Steinbeck entered a list of common symbols "that seem to tap a subconscious stream and cause a definite response." A singularly odd listing follows:

> In nature
>   mistle toe
>   octopi
>   caves & caverns
>   water in them
>
> phases of the moon
> particularly powerful
> strong winds
> Time conceived
> Solstice (winter)
>   Slow moving
>   insects
> mushroom poisoning
> reflections of

                    light in shiny
                    surfaces

          cats

          all necrophagi

Many of the symbols listed here, apparently derived from
the Jungian theory Steinbeck had been reading at the time
and from discourse with Ed Ricketts, would not be fully appropriated artistically until much later works, particularly
The Winter of Our Discontent, but the listing does suggest
Steinbeck's high awareness of symbolic qualities in writing.[4]

Although Steinbeck was conscious of symbolism as an artistic technique, he always saw it as subordinate to the realistic portrayal of a character functioning in a plot. When
drafting his failed short story "The Cow," Steinbeck described it as having "a hardness of reality and of symbol"
(*LVN*). A few days later, in August 1934, he added some
notes on the primacy of realism. Symbolism becomes for
him that supporting texture of feeling that changes "the
outline and the color of realities."

Shortly after completing the *Pastures of Heaven* stories
and while contemplating another draft of *To a God Unknown*, Steinbeck took the occasion to reflect upon some of
the foolishness of symbolism for its own sake—when reality
is subordinated to symbolism. He had just purchased several different colors of ink and while trying them out notes,
"An examination of this mss., should anyone ever be interested, should be of interest to the camp followers of literature. The change of ink colors, for example, might to those
students of influences in the life of an artist, be of the rarest
significance." Steinbeck playfully speculates on the symbolism one could find in the different colors. The ink begins
in purple, which, he points out, suggests "a mood rich with
the intricacy of style," and is linked to the soil. He comments, "My mood was rich with the blood of youth." Changing to green ink, he links the color to "old nature, bless
her," and "trees straining to lay their leaves in heaven."

Green, he observes, represents the growth of nature toward blue. In blue ink, he writes of the "blue of heaven—of the mysterious end—the finish—blue of philosophy of quiet maturity."

In one deft stroke, Steinbeck links the passage of time from youth to old age to the natural symbols, soil, tree, and sky, and the abstractions of idea, growth, and philosophy or wisdom. Before it gets entirely out of hand, however, he announces, "Indeed there is room for thought in all this. And lest some god dam fool should devote time to this subject which might be better employed in—say a concordance of Zane Gray, I shall explain" (*POH*-2). He then admits that the experiment resulted from a sale on ink at Holman's Department store—two bottles for five cents.[5] While Steinbeck was certainly aware of the suggestive power of symbolism in fiction, he was also wary of seeing it as an end in itself, superseding the reality of the story.

A third characteristic of Steinbeck's artistry during this period, a responsiveness to the sounds of language, is not announced overtly in the journals, but it is implied throughout them. In fact, one of his major artistic challenges during this period was controlling his diction. Many of the flaws of his 1920s work can be directly attributed to a penchant for purple prose, which distracts from or clouds both theme and character. This may be seen most noticeably in *Cup of Gold*, but also in the *Stanford Spectator* stories and in the unpublished tales.

Steinbeck's love for music touches the prose of his fiction, shaping phrases and sentences in a response to the emotional texture of character and plot development.[6] He himself was very much aware of this. In a 1929 letter to A. Grove Day, Steinbeck speculated on the musical tendencies in his writing:

I would continue to write if there were no writing and no print. I put my words down for a matter of memory. They are more made to be spoken than to be read. I have the instincts of a minstrel rather than those of a scrivener. There you have it. We are not of the same trade at all and so how can your rules fit me? When my sounds are all in place, I can send them to a stenographer who knows *his* trade and he can slip the commas about until they sit comfortably and he can spell the words so that school teachers will not raise their eyebrows when they read them. Why should I bother? There are millions of people who are good stenographers but there aren't so many thousands who can make as nice sounds as I can. [*SLL*, p. 19]

Although in part a recognition of his own tendency to ignore punctuation rules and misspell, the comment is nonetheless a very accurate self-assessment of the musical impulses of his craft.

Rather than simply a consciousness of the music of words, however, this musical quality of Steinbeck's prose seems to be a peculiar response to the feeling of the story itself as it evolved. It was the music of a harmony, of feeling at one with the work, sureness of touch manifested in the way words moved on the page. While Steinbeck could be a ruthless reviser of his own work, he insisted that the revision process follows the creative process. Concerns for revision should not disturb the rhythm of the first drafting. In a 1962 letter to Robert Wallsten, Steinbeck offered six points of advice, the second of which applies here:

Write freely and as rapidly as possible and throw the whole thing on paper. Never correct or rewrite until the whole thing is down. Rewrite in process is usually found to be an excuse for not going on. It also interferes with flow and rhythm which can only come from a kind of unconscious association with the material. [*SLL*, p. 736)

Contemporary critical theory has grown insensitive to the writer's delight in language, and Steinbeck's musical facility for the sounds of words has gone largely unappreciated. In his introduction to *Steinbeck's "The Red Pony": Essays in Criticism*, Warren French accurately assesses the situation:

In recent years, a distrust of language study has led to a minimalism in literature and an arid preoccupation with deconstructing it critically that has tended to reduce reading for sensory delight and shared experience to a middlebrow self-indulgence. Steinbeck, however, was one of a generation of writers like Thomas Wolfe, William Faulkner, and F. Scott Fitzgerald who were intoxicated with the music and color of words—writers who lost their powers when words lost their magical music. Their finest works must be reapproached on their own terms. [7]

While it may not be a fashionable scholarly pursuit currently, a substantial part of understanding Steinbeck's literary artistry consists of an appreciation for his musical sensitivity toward language.

In addition to Steinbeck's sense of sureness of touch, symbolism, and the musical qualities of prose, it is clear that he had a ready sense of the traditional components of fiction—development of character, coherence of plot, unity of elements, and point of view—to mention a few that will be examined more fully in the discussion of individual stories. While working on *The Grapes of Wrath*, he made a pointed reminder to himself in his journal: "The whole physical basis of the novel is discipline of the writer, of his material, of the language. And sadly enough, if any of the discipline is gone, all of it suffers." [8] The notes from the early 1930s are more remarkable, perhaps, for their revelation of Steinbeck's own growing sense of himself as a writer. At this early period he was acquiring a sureness of *his* way of writing.

The techniques and guiding principles discussed here should not be understood as a tablet of writing commandments that guided Steinbeck on his way. The remarkable trait of his artistry has always been its flexibility, a trait that also frustrated and sometimes angered his reviewers and critics. Throughout his life he feared technique as mere habit. In a September 17, 1954, letter to Elizabeth Otis, he defines the great challenge for a young artist as the mastering of technique: "When a writer starts in very young, his problems apart from his story are those of technique, of words, of rhythms, of story methods, of transition, of characterization, of ways of creating effects. But after years of trial and error most of these things are solved and one gets what is called a style" (*SLL*, p. 497). Steinbeck might very well have been describing his own transition in the early 1930s from learning technique to perfecting a style.

But the reliance upon a certain style also made Steinbeck nervous. When technique solidifies into style, the writer is tempted to simply go through the exercise of writing. While some people, Steinbeck observes, might see this as the ideal situation for a writer, he confesses "a sense of horror about this technique." Artistic craft—what he calls "technique" here and what he was learning in the early 1930s— is a stabilizing but also an inhibiting influence:

The tail of the kite is designed to hold it steady in the air but it also prevents versatility in the kite and in many cases drags it to the earth. Having a technique, is it not possible that the technique not only dictates how a story is to be written but also what story is to be written? In other words, style or technique may be a straitjacket which is a destroyer of a writer. [*SLL*, p. 497]

This observation and Steinbeck's conclusion that he wanted "to dump my technique, to tear it right down to the ground and to start all over," could only be made by an accomplished but flexible stylist. Already in *The Pastures of Heaven*, one observes the remarkable variety of stories that Steinbeck could produce, his ability to peer into several different lives or into one life from several different angles. During the early 1930s, however, the greater challenge for Steinbeck was the discovery of a technique that, to use his metaphor, would sail with the kite of the story, one fluid expression soaring easily.

In the opinion of a number of scholars, Steinbeck never found that elusive solidity of technique in short story writing. Such a view may be represented by Brian M. Barbour in his essay "Steinbeck as a Short Story Writer," one of the very few essays devoted to Steinbeck as a writer of short stories, albeit exclusively in relation to *The Long Valley*. In Barbour's estimation, Steinbeck's failure as a short story writer was finally a failure of technique:

> It is impossible to plot any kind of growth or development for Steinbeck in the thirties. His artistry is inconsistent and his movement is by fits and starts. Stories written in 1938 are less successful than stories written four or five years earlier. The pieces of this puzzle make sense only if we keep in mind two postulates; that Steinbeck was a very intuitive writer whose success depended on modes of feeling he could not always understand or direct, and that he lacked the critical sense, making him an insufficient judge of his own work.[9]

The redeeming quality of the short stories, for Barbour, was Steinbeck's discovery of "a means for focusing his generous vision of humanity."

Indeed, uneven quality marks the short stories of the 1930s, and it would always be a secondary form for Steinbeck, more confining for his particular thematic, artistic, and moral vision than the novel. Nonetheless, careful assessment of the stories makes it difficult to accept a view as denigrative as Barbour's. The short stories served as a necessary apprenticeship for Steinbeck, and many of them are marked by enduring greatness. If nothing else—and they are a great deal more—they opened the necessary gateway for the young writer to the major novels.

3

The Pastures of Heaven

IT COULD HAVE BEEN any valley at all. Fiction creates its own worlds. But the peculiarities of this one valley a few miles southwest of Salinas very much shaped the fictional world of *The Pastures of Heaven*.

The Corral de Tierra is an oblong valley rimmed by a gritty road uncoiling over humps of land. One can circle the entire valley in an hour or so. The speeds on the road haven't changed much since Steinbeck's time. It has been graveled, but it twists over the same ridges in the same areas. It is a valley in a "fence of earth."

At the north end, groves of live oak hold a perpetual mistiness. Their branches are draped with spirochete, their thin veils masking the landscape with a light green sheen. The grass is so lush and emerald green that one seems to walk through a living blanket. The eerie quiet is broken occasionally by the raucous barking of a crow, the sudden swoop of a hawk, the low of cows by the stream.

The valley rises through a tangle of hills toward its southern extremity. The air lightens, grows piercing and keen. Severed from each other by a maze of rills and rock, the farms hold their distance. The valley contains that interplay of light and shadow, a geographically symbolized good and evil, that was to intrigue Steinbeck for years.

The faces of the hills are pocked by a peculiar tan, stippled rock. It is a land uniquely held between two extremities—at once the Corral de Tierra, the land barely formed, dark, primeval, bearing the scars of an evolutionary shaping by sea and wind, but also the Pastures of Heaven, the

48

land lifting upward toward the light and airy spaces. It captures perfectly the essential tension Steinbeck strove for in his stories of *The Pastures of Heaven.*

The Pastures of Heaven may well have been one of the critical turning points in Steinbeck's fictional career. His work had been wandering, aimless and footloose. The affirmation of this work lay both in theme and setting. He could, the work assured him, write about the characters he knew in the places he knew and find expression for his fictional themes through them. With that affirmation, a way was fixed in his mind. For the entire decade of the 1930s, he wrote about the places he knew, one work leading surely to another, from *The Pastures of Heaven* in 1932 to *The Grapes of Wrath* in 1939.

According to Jackson Benson, Steinbeck first came across the ideas for the sequence of stories through Beth Ingels in the winter or spring of 1931.[1] Ingels, a native of the Corral de Tierra region, had planned to write her own sequence of stories on her experiences there. During informal meetings with Steinbeck, she related her stories, and there was some talk of Steinbeck's having stolen them from her for his book. While Steinbeck was quick to pick up a good source, as in Edith Wagner's influence on "How Edith McGillcuddy Met R. L. Stevenson," the stories are indisputably and uniquely his own. He had been thinking about writing a related sequence of stories from his native region for at least a year previously.

The concept of related stories began with the failed manuscript *Dissonant Symphony,* which Steinbeck described in early 1930:

I am putting five hours every day on the rewriting of this one [*To a God Unknown*] and in the evenings I have started another [*Dissonant Symphony*]. I have the time and the energy and it gives me pleasure to work, and now I do not seem to have to fight as much reluctance to work as I used to have. The start comes much easier. The new book is just a series of short stories or sketches loosely and foolishly tied together. There are a number

of little things I have wanted to write for a long time, some of
them ridiculous and some of them more serious, and so I am putting them in a ridiculous fabric. [*SLL*, p. 22]

It is clear, however, that *Dissonant Symphony*, while
perhaps giving Steinbeck the germ of the idea for *The Pastures of Heaven*, should be considered a separate work. In
a 1931 letter, after he had begun writing *The Pastures of
Heaven*, Steinbeck describes the new manuscript as "the
companion piece" to *Dissonant Symphony*, because he had
thought for a time of combining the two. By this point,
however, *Pastures* had acquired its own singular life. In
August 1931 Steinbeck wrote his new agent, Mavis McIntosh, "Mr. Miller will hand you a manuscript of about thirty
thousand words [*Dissonant Symphony*]. It is an impossible
length for marketing. I had thought perhaps it could be included under one cover with the ten stories which will
make up The Pastures of Heaven. . . . The Pastures stories
proceed rapidly, perhaps too rapidly. They should be ready
to submit by Christmas" (*SLL*, pp. 45–46). The clearest indication that *Dissonant Symphony* is a separate work, now
lost, comes in a letter to McIntosh in January 1933. After
The Pastures of Heaven was published, Steinbeck requested
a return of the *Dissonant Symphony* manuscript: "The manuscript called Dissonant Symphony I wish you would withdraw. I looked at it not long ago and I don't want it out. I
may rewrite it sometime, but I certainly do not want that
mess published under any circumstances, revised or not"
(*SLL*, p. 68).

When *Dissonant Symphony* failed to jell as a complete
work, Steinbeck approached the *Pastures of Heaven* stories
with the same artistic concept of a thematically and geographically related series. In early 1931 he wrote to Amasa
Miller, "It is a fairly original plan (the new book) and quite
a vital story or really series of stories" (*SLL*, p. 40). Apparently the writing had begun at this point, for in May 1931
Steinbeck wrote George Albee, "I am rewriting one more

short story to send out and then I shall go back to The Pastures of Heaven" (*SLL*, p. 41). By May 1931, Steinbeck had the conceptual framework for the narrative fully in mind. In one of the longer expositions he ever provided for a work, he described the project in detail to McIntosh:

The present work interests me and perhaps falls in the "aspects" theme you mention. There is, about twelve miles from Monterey, a valley in the hills called Corral de Tierra. Because I am using its people I have named it Las Pasturas del Cielo. The valley was for years known as the happy valley because of the unique harmony which existed among its twenty families. About ten years ago a new family moved in on one of the ranches. They were ordinary people, ill-educated but honest and as kindly as any. In fact, in their whole history I cannot find that they have committed a really malicious act nor an act which was not dictated by honorable expediency or out-and-out altruism. But about the Morans there was a flavor of evil. Everyone they came in contact with was injured. Every place they went dissension sprang up. There have been two murders, a suicide, many quarrels and a great deal of unhappiness in the Pastures of Heaven, and all of these things can be traced directly to the influence of the Morans. So much is true.

I am using the following method. The manuscript is made up of stories, each one complete in itself, having its rise, climax and ending. Each story deals with a family or an individual. They are tied together only by the common locality and by the contact with the Morans. Some of the stories are very short and some as long as fifteen thousand words. I thought of combining them with that thirty-thousand word ms. called Dissonant Symphony to make one volume. I wonder whether you think this is a good plan. I think the plan at least falls very definitely in the aspects of American life category. I have finished several and am working on others steadily. They should be done by this fall. [*SLL*, pp. 42–43]

The work fired his imagination, virtually overwhelming him with the sheer excitement of the telling. Steinbeck often spoke of his pleasure in the writing, as in this comment to Albee: "The story I am working on charms me more than any of the others. I wish to heaven you could read these things" (*SLL*, p. 40). In another letter to Albee, he adds, "Sometimes I think these stories are very fine. There's material for ten novels in these stories. That was the method, you remember. In the last story of thirty pages I covered three generations. You can see how packed they must be. . . . I'm fairly convinced that I can't get a publisher for them. They make too much use of the reader and readers don't like to be used" (*SLL*, p. 50).

Writing continued through the summer of 1931. By late fall 1931 the work as a whole was completed, and much to Steinbeck's satisfaction. He wrote to Miller in December 1931:

The Pastures of Heaven I sent off last Saturday. It should be there by the time you receive this. If the reader will take them for what they are, and will not be governed by what a short story should be (for they are not short stories at all, but tiny novels) then they should be charming, but if they are judged by the formal short story, they are lost before they ever start. I am extremely anxious to hear the judgment because of anything I have ever tried, I am fondest of these and more closely tied to them. There is no grand writing nor any grand theme, but I love the stories very much. [*SLL*, pp. 51–52]

The initial reaction by McIntosh, however, was not favorable. Steinbeck wrote to Miller on February 16, 1932: "Miss Mc. dismissed the ms. by saying the form doesn't interest her, but it may interest someone else. The Pastures has begun its snaggy way" (*SLL*, p. 53). The temporary setback was followed in February 1932 by an acceptance by Cape and Smith.[2] Steinbeck was delighted, and took special pleasure in his parents' delight with his achievement. He had proven his ability as a writer to them, but, more importantly, he had proven a level of artistic craft and theme to himself.

While early reviewers and critics were inclined to see

The Pastures of Heaven as a collection of short stories framed by a narrative prologue and epilogue, careful study reveals a finely wrought unity among the individual stories. Steinbeck's idea was to take a series of impressionistic tales, as if suddenly peering in upon one family at a time, and by their conflation attain a whole picture of the valley. If the valley is the unit, Steinbeck demonstrated that in this case, at least, we can know that unit best by intensive portraits of the individual organisms—the families. While Steinbeck wanted a wholeness in each story, the composite of these units creates the novelistic world of *The Pastures of Heaven*. That Steinbeck had a sense of the whole from the outset is evident when he announced the work in his notebook. He provides his working plan as follows:

The Pastures of Heaven

I

Pasturas

A curious story of which at least half—or one third of the space is taken up with dramatis personae. The first chapter will deal with the valley itself: and following that will be nine or ten chapters devoted to nine or ten families. Then will come the entrance of the McCoys.

I	The Discovery of the Valley
II	The Battles
III	The Munroes
IV	Shark Wicks
V	Tularecito
VI	Raymond Banks
VII	The Maltbys
VIII	Mrs. Van Deventer & Daughter
IX	Miss Morgan
X	Blind Frank
XI	Howard & the Spinach [*POH-1*, p. 2]

The individual stories are in fact scattered through two notebooks, and completed stories are liberally interspersed with notes, rough beginnings, and sketches. According to primary works and Steinbeck's titles, the first notebook contains, in order, "Sharks Wicks," "The Battle Farm" ("Bert Munroe"), "Tularecito," "The Munroes" (joined with "The Battle Farm"), a rough beginning of "Raymond Banks," and "The Maltbys" (draft). The second notebook contains "Mrs. Van Deventer and Daughter," "The Maltbys," "The Lopez Sisters," "Story of the Battle Farm," "Molly Morgan," "Raymond Banks," "John Whiteside and His House," and "Pat Humbert." The unfinished story of Mizpah, which does not appear to be a part of *The Pastures of Heaven*, follows.

The stories are not, then, a random accumulation of odds and ends from a writer's scrapbook. They were envisioned together as one piece. While lacking the organic unity of novelistic plot, nonetheless unifying characteristics mark the disparate pieces. The most evident—and commonly observed—of these is the frame of the prologue and epilogue. The two function historically and thematically. Their ironic tone suggests the central theme of the stories: a fallen Eden in which we all, like sheep, have gone astray.[3]

In the prologue, "a group of twenty converted Indians abandoned religion during a night." Their religion consisted of nothing more than a rigid body of rules enforced by the troops of the Carmelo Mission. In fact, they labored like slaves in the clay pits to make bricks for the mission. Thus, the soldiers ardently pursue the Indians "to give the poor neophytes a chance at repentance." From the outset we have a rule-dominated religion, highly persecutory, from which a people flees to the valley. The conflict between rules and individual freedom also serves as a central theme in the stories of *The Pastures of Heaven*.

The Spanish corporal, in pursuit of the Indians, actually discovers the valley. At once an enforcer of rules and a sufferer under military rules, he is so struck by the serene beauty of the pastures that he stands in awe:

In a few minutes he arrived at the top of the ridge, and there he stopped, stricken with wonder at what he saw—a long valley floored with green pasturage on which a herd of deer browsed.

Perfect live oaks grew in the meadow of the lovely place, and the hills hugged it jealously against the fog and the wind. [p. 2]

Here is the magic of the valley, imaged in the herd of deer. Wayward human sheep, straying from the iron staff of rules, will also wander to the valley and there meet the beneficent paradise of its lush pastures. Inviolate freedom stretches before them; however, they bring with them the memory of the staff and the whip. It is an Eden to which the wanderers come; the wanderers, however, are decidedly fallen.

This first pilgrim, shepherding his flock of captive Indians in the prologue, is perfectly paralleled in the epilogue by the modern-day sightseeing bus. This bus leaves from the center of modern civilization in the region, Monterey, and must first arch down to Carmel to retrace the corporal's early route. The soldiers on horseback are replaced by tourists on a bus.

The bus also arrives at a narrow ridge, the driver announcing, "This is as far as we go, folks." The passengers step out to survey the pastures that greeted the corporal two centuries before. But the vision is slightly different. In lieu of the browsing deer, they survey a mélange of farms:

They climbed stiffly from their seats and stood on the ridge peak and looked down into the Pastures of Heaven. And the air was as golden as gauze in the last of the sun. The land below them was plotted in squares of green orchard trees and in squares of yellow grain and in squares of violet earth. From the sturdy farmhouses, set in their gardens, the smoke of the evening fires drifted upward until the hillbreeze swept it cleanly off. [p. 240]

Eden has been domesticated. The herds of grazing deer are replaced by cows wearing bells.

In the prologue, the corporal's throat tightens with longing. At the farther end of time, in the epilogue, the newer pilgrims are stirred by that same vision as the Pastures calls to them. But each pilgrim also holds back, not quite daring to test the vision. Steinbeck poses four representatives of modern civilization peering earnestly into the possibilities of the place. Each of them, for a moment, is stirred by the allure of the valley; each of them retreats to the security of a present way of living. Promise and danger seem to hover side by side over the tangled green fields. The pilgrims board the bus and return to their own little places in civilization. The magic lingers, however. The great dream of Eden reaches out and touches their imaginations for a moment as it also touches each of the residents of the Pastures of Heaven in Steinbeck's revelation of their lives.

If the Pastures is a newer-day Eden—this little world almost, but not entirely, cut off from civilization—its inhabitants are in the process of discovering their fallen nature. Eden, perhaps, measures what we once were, what we once had. This Eden of the Pastures measures what its inhabitants could be—there is that sense of rich promise rising from the land—but more decisively, what they are. They are mere mortals discovering the fallenness of human nature, not sons of God.

An essential framework for this discovery is the curse of the valley. The Edenic curse recorded in Genesis, chapter three, primarily represents the dissociation from close harmony with God that leads to enmity with neighbors. In *The Pastures of Heaven*, the curse will be revealed in the conflicts between individuals, and between individuals and social structures.

Second, the biblical curse entailed a human knowledge of evil as personal experience.[4] The Bible gives the example of pain in childbirth, and this fundamental human experience in perpetuating the lineage suggests how ineradicably and universally the knowledge of evil has infiltrated human life. If it is a part of the very act of being born, then no human creature escapes it. The thematic unity of *The Pastures of Heaven* is the inevitability of evil in human life. No one escapes it here either.

Third, the curse is represented biblically by exile from the rich beneficence of Eden to a lifetime of toil upon the earth. No longer does the rich fruition of Eden prevail; instead, "Cursed is the ground because of you; in toil you shall eat of it all the days of your life; thorns and thistles it shall bring forth to you" (Gen. 3:17–18). The Pastures is a valley of farmers, working the land into submission, carving out a small patch of Eden whose vestiges of beauty remain, but always battling against the crookedness of nature.

The Pastures of Heaven is not well read as a biblical allegory, however, surely not in the way that sections of *East of Eden* have been. Instead, its aim is a generalized revelation of human struggle in that broad dialectic signified by its title: these pastures (physical, earthy, human) of heaven (spiritual, divine, incomprehensible). Thus, the curse of the Battle farm, the curse that touches every story, should be understood metaphorically as humans struggling with their own inevitable patterns of good and evil in this present world.

That knowledge of good and evil occurs in different ways, but it is inescapable for all. There is no Eden left on this earth. There are merely mortals making the best, and sometimes the worst, of things according to their individual natures. The curse of the Battle farm is by no means limited to the Munroes. As T. B. Allen says, "Maybe your curse and the farm's curse has mated and gone into a gopher hole like a pair of rattlesnakes. Maybe there'll be a lot of baby curses crawling around the Pastures the first thing we know" (p. 20). What Melville described in *Billy Budd* as "the reactionary sting of the serpent" is experienced here in different ways. Each pilgrim bears his or her burden. This is most evident, perhaps, in the disproportionately high number of mentally defective characters. Myrtle Cameron Battle suffers from epilepsy and goes insane. Her son, John Battle, who inherited her epilepsy, is demon-crazed. Alice Wicks is retarded, a radiant beauty bearing an inward flaw, her very nature a metaphor for the valley. Manfred "Mannie" Munroe is retarded from an abnormal adenoidal condition. Tularecito, that strangely gifted person, is committed to the insane asylum. Helen Van Deventer's neurosis dissociates her from reality in a world of tragic endurance until reality snaps through at the point of a shotgun. Her schizophrenic daughter Hilda escapes everything but reality. These may be the notorious examples. Their shadow reaches throughout the valley, however. All experience the knowledge of evil, sometimes in others, sometimes in themselves. All struggle to find their place in the world with this knowledge. For some, such as the Lopez sisters or Junius Maltby, the knowlege insists that they leave the valley. Yet, for all that, the valley is not a slough of despond. Often touched with remarkable courage, sometimes with radiant humor, these pilgrims demonstrate, finally, that even with the knowledge of evil, the Pastures, if no longer Eden, can yet be a happy valley. For it is also very much a book about grace. Human nature receives a rare dignity under Steinbeck's touch. Because one bears knowledge of evil, he demonstrates, one is not necessarily malign. Humanity has the capacity to fight back. Love is a weapon.

The Edenic quality of the book is supported by the narrative point of view. Appropriately for a book titled *The Pastures of Heaven*, Steinbeck adopts the omniscient point of view. This is his kingdom, and he looks upon it with the eye of a god. That point of view functions importantly in the stories. It provides the reader not only with a narrative coign of vantage, but also with a keen sense of both the pathos and the comedy of human nature. The story of Helen Van Deventer turns entirely upon what the reader and the narrator, but no one else in the story, see: "She climbed up on a chair, unlocked the gun case and took down a shotgun." Here the one sentence captures entirely the theme of tragic endurance. In the delightful story of the Lopez sisters, on the other hand, the omniscient point of view admits us to a world of human comedy. Alone with the narrator, we observe Maria harnessing the ancient Lindo for the ride into Monterey. The scene bears the deft, comic touch of *Tortilla Flat:*

The buggy sagged alarmingly when Maria clambered into it. She took the line gingerly in her hands. "Go, my friend," she said, and fluttered the lines. Lindo shivered and looked around at her. "Do you hear? We must go! There are things to buy in Monterey." Lindo shook his head and dropped one knee in a kind of curtsey. "Listen to me, Lindo!" Maria cried imperiously, "I say we must go. I am firm! I am even angry." She fluttered the lines ferociously about his shoulders. Lindo dropped his head nearly to the earth, like a scenting hound, and moved slowly out of the yard. [pp. 122–23]

We look upon this world through the narrator, but also see inside the lives encompassed by it.

Beyond the secrets of these private lives, the omniscient narrator also drops us, occasionally, into the minds of the characters. We learn their inner thoughts, motives, fears. The point of view is developed thoroughly and masterfully in "Molly Morgan," wherein the narrator reports the conversation of John Whiteside's interview while dipping us into Molly's recollection. Thereby we witness a coalescence of past and present, swimming together in the stream of the interview, and revealing a depth and complexity to the character of Molly.

It is a remarkable place, this valley. Like the pilgrims on the sightseeing tour, the reader stands for a moment and wonders, "What if . . ." The answer lies in the characters who inhabit the valley, for as they in aggregation compose a picture of fallen humanity finding its way in a latter-day Eden, so too we stand alongside them finding our way.

THE CURSE: BERT MUNROE AND JOHN WHITESIDE

After the founding corporal's descendants held sway in the valley for nearly a century, a transition occurred in 1863 when the Battles arrived from upstate New York. Financed and accompanied by his wealthy mother, who died at sea on the passage to California, George Battle built a little kingdom before he died at sixty-five in 1910.[5] He married Myrtle Cameron, a wealthy spinster from Salinas, and fathered one child, the demon-crazed John. In 1921 the deserted farm was taken over by the Mustrovics, and finally by the Munroes with their three children, Mae, Jimmie, and Manfred.[6]

Although the Whitesides had settled earlier, in 1850, the Battle farm carries the weight of modern history in the valley, for it bore the curse. It is suited for Bert Munroe, who leaves behind his personal curses by coming to the farm, but who transmits it to others in the valley. While Mrs. Myrtle Battle spends her waning days in the Lippman Sanitarium "crocheting a symbolic life of Christ in cotton thread," her demented son, John, flails the brush for demons. He too is in a kind of insane asylum, but it is the farm itself:

John's life was devoted to a struggle with devils. From camp meeting to camp meeting he had gone, hurling his hands about, invoking devils and then confounding them, exorcising and flaying incarnate evil. When he arrived at home the devils still claimed attention. The lines of vegetables went to seed, volunteered a few times, and succumbed to the weeds. The farm slipped back to nature, but the devils grew stronger and more importunate. [p. 7]

The Mustrovics, who arrive at the farm as mysteriously as the wind, battle against the decay with the same terrible energy with which John had allowed it to go to ruin: "At any hour he could be seen working feverishly, half running about his tasks, with a look on his face as though he expected time to stop before a crop was in" (p. 9). Upon their disappearance, the legend of the Battle farm curse arose: the frenzied conflict of order versus disorder, of community life in the Pastures versus personal demons.

Bert Munroe enters to set the farm in order and lay the curse to rest: "Bert himself cut down all the vines, and all the trees in the yard, to let in the light. Within three weeks the old house had lost every vestige of its deserted, haunted look. By stroke after stroke of genius it had been made to look like a hundred thousand other country houses in the west" (p. 13). But he comes from a disordered past that he must also lay to rest: "Bert Munroe came to the Pastures of Heaven because he was tired of battling with a force which invariably defeated him. . . . Bert saw all the accidents together and they seemed to him the acts of a Fate malignant to his success" (pp. 16–17). For Bert, the Battle farm is a liberation. He can exorcise his personal demons by laying straight the land, but legends are not as easily put to rest as the land. As T. B. Allen says, the curse is simply respawning into a host of curses.

Here, then, is the tension of the Pastures: Can one exercise dominion over the land and the personal curse each person carries, or will the land and the curse respawn to fly into disorder?

The pattern of exercising dominion over the land is figured in different ways, physically and metaphorically, throughout the book. The early history of the Battle family tells of subduing the land. George Battle, "bent with work, pleasureless and dour," has a farm that springs with beauty, "a poem by an inarticulate man." It is a wonder of order that frames the antithesis to his internal disorder.

When demon-driven John Battle returns, he ignores the land altogether. And when he dies, stung mortally by the serpent, the land goes dissolute with abandon: "There was something fearsome about the gaunt old house with its staring, vacant windows. The white paint fell off in long scales; the shingles curled up shaggily. The farm itself went completely wild" (pp. 8–9). In the Battle family, one can find no intrinsic harmony between person and the land, which are at war.

For the Mustrovics, working the land seems a purgative ritual. Mr. Mustrovic's frenzied labor is a kind of personal exorcism also, although Steinbeck doesn't tell us what demons he carries. Nonetheless, under his frantic efforts, the land grows beautiful again. But there is no harmony. Dominion is not simply subduing; rather, it constitutes a harmonious relationship. When the Mustrovics leave, the land devolves to untended squalor.

The labor of the Munroes is more calculated and assiduous. They start from the home out, signifying a relationship between person and land. The land lifts a personal curse from Bert Munroe: "The moment he had bought the farm, Bert felt free. The doom was gone" (p. 18). The land becomes a beneficent provider for him. A harmony between spirit and land is achieved.

The pattern of person and land in a state of discord or dominion continues throughout the stories. One can tell a great deal about the characters by how they manage the land: whether they let it grow coarse and wild, as does Junius Maltby; whether they impose a kind of tyrannical order, as do Helen Van Deventer and Raymond Banks; or whether they achieve a degree of harmony, as does John Whiteside. The Pastures are full of gardens and orchards. Often they are twisted and grotesque, signifying this crooked and fallen world. At times the land responds bountifully to the human touch. In either case, the curse lies buried just out of sight.

Wherever the curse arises, the Munroes seem to be involved. They are not willfully evil. Indeed, they seem to grow in grace and peace throughout the work. Nonetheless, they are accidents for the curse. Shark Wicks's agony arises from his fear of Alice's meeting Jimmie Munroe. It is on Bert Munroe's land that Tularecito exercises his tragic quest for gnomes. Bert Munroe happens to be the one paying the courtesy call on Helen Van Deventer, which triggers Hilda's escape. Mrs. Munroe insists on giving Robbie Maltby new clothes, thus destroying the Maltby idyll. Bert Munroe, innocently joking about the Lopez sisters to his wife, initiates a reaction in the valley that drives those happy women to San Francisco. Bert's hired hand, sleeping drunkenly in his car, brings the past crashing upon Molly Morgan, and she flees the valley. Raymond Banks's orderly life is twisted by Bert's imaginings. Pat Humbert's dream for Mae Munroe is crushed by her engagement. And John Whiteside, following Bert's advice, fires the brush and watches with Bert as the Whiteside house burns.

One would be mistaken, however, to see Bert Munroe as

a Satan figure. There is no deliberate malice in the man.
Steinbeck made quite specific his intention in this regard.
In a letter to Amasa Miller he described the Munroes:
"They were just common people, they had no particular
profundities or characters except that a kind of cloud of un-
intentional evil surrounded them. Everything they touched
went rotten, every institution they joined to broke up in
hatred. Remember, these people were not malicious nor
cruel nor extraordinary in any way, but their influence
caused everybody in the valley to hate everybody else."
They simply brought, as Steinbeck says, an awareness of
"this nameless sense and power of evil."[7]

The story of the Pastures, then, is one of characters coming into a knowledge of evil. One could as well blame Shark
Wicks as Jimmie Munroe. One must admit that Tularecito
is genuinely threatening to Bert. Hilda Van Deventer is indisputably schizophrenic. The Maltbys are hopeless dreamers. The Lopez sisters are doing a lively business in the
bedroom as well as in the kitchen. Molly Morgan's father
will haunt her until she comes to terms with his absence.
Raymond Banks has never confronted the human reality of
hanging—the fact that these are humans, not chickens. Pat
Humbert's dream severs him from the reality of his past.
And John Whiteside finds himself at the tragic end of a legacy. For these circumstances, Bert is the catalyst, not the
cause. The curse that accompanies his coming is one that
falls upon all humanity, and the isolated valley demonstrates that, finally, no one escapes it.

Just as the prologue and epilogue frame the stories as a
whole, the Munroe and Whiteside stories frame the thematic pattern. They represent beginnings and endings; the
curse, the dream, and human relationships with the land.
It is a matter of artistry as much as geography that the two
farms adjoin: they are thematically adjunctive and counterparts. The curse buried on the Battle farm burrows under-
ground and rears its head on the Whiteside farm.

The stories reveal different relationships with the land,
but they also reveal a cycle of beginning and ending along

with a transference of the curse. Bert Munroe arrives at the Battle farm a failed man coming to a failed land. Yet, the curse lifts, and the land blesses him. It is appropriate that he becomes fast friends with John Whiteside and that Bert is at his side during the destructive fire. Richard Whiteside arrives in prosperity, but for him the cycle is a negative one, the tragic fall from grace when his great house goes up in flames. A legacy has ended. Or perhaps it has only passed hands: John Whiteside loans Bert his treasured volume of Thucydides, the same that his father Richard had read to him. Bill Whiteside, the third generation, will have none of it. At the end of the story, Bert has not returned the volume, and John and Allie Whiteside go to live with Bill. It suggests that history passes hands, for the two stories are very much about lineage and human history.

Arriving in 1850, Richard Whiteside is contrasted with the gold seekers of the era. They saw the land with pragmatic immediacy, wondering what they could get here and now. Once finished using the land, they moved on, unaffected by it. Richard, on the other hand, sees the land as a living history and wonders what it can give in the future. He sees the land not as a supplier, but as a sustainer.

With his huge sense of posterity, Richard sets himself first of all to building a home. The action parallels Bert Munroe's later work of first setting the home in order, then exercising dominion over the land. But Richard also sees the land itself as a home: "Richard knew that he had found his home. In his wandering about the country he had come upon many beautiful places, but none of them had given him this feeling of consummation" (p. 202). Then he sees his house—the future—on that land: "Richard saw a beautiful white house with a trim garden in front of it and nearby, the white tower of a tank house. There were little yellow lights in the windows, little specks of welcoming lights. The broad front door opened, and a whole covey of children walked out on the veranda—at least six children" (p. 203). When a neighbor reproves him with the advice that he should test the land first, Richard insists that he will become one with the land. A sense of future will guide him: "I don't want to move. . . . That's just what I'm building against. I shall build a structure so strong that neither I nor my descendants will be able to move" (p. 205). What he does not know, of course, is the curse squirming through the very soil that he builds his dream upon.

Steinbeck invests a subtle twist of naming into this theme of lineage and posterity. When Alicia Whiteside becomes pregnant, Richard sends to San Francisco for a little bronze replica of Michelangelo's *David*. It becomes a kind of totem for the expectant parents: "Alicia blushed at its nakedness, but before very long she became passionately fond of the little figure. When she went to bed it stood on her bedside table. During the day she took it from room to room with her as she worked, and in the evening it stood on the mantel in the sitting room. . . . She was thoroughly convinced that her child would look like the *David*" (p. 208). And both parents fully expect to name their child David.

Biblically, David was the progenitor of the royal race, the king of God's own choosing. Out of his lineage the Messiah is predicted, and the genealogy of Jesus recorded in Matthew identifies Jesus as "the son of David, the son of Abraham." David stands prophetically, then, as the father of a royal priesthood. If the child were so named, Richard would be the Abraham to his David, and the great patriarch was, of course, biblically renowned for God's promise to him in Genesis 17:5–6: "I have made you the father of a multitude of nations. I will make you exceedingly fruitful; and I will make nations of you, and kings shall come forth from you." It is not surprising, then, that when the child is born, Alicia says "Yes, he looks like the statue. I knew he would, of course. And David will be his name, of course" (p. 211).

When the time for the child's christening comes, however, Alicia insists upon a new name: "I want to have him called John. That's a New Testament name." Alicia immediately thrusts reasons at Richard—it is her father's name; she doesn't want the child named after a statue. But there is also the clear suggestion of the end of a lineage. In the New Testament, John appears as the last of the prophets, the forerunner to Christ, and none will come after him to prepare the way. Thus, the change in names signals the fulfillment of the Whiteside lineage in this story. The one who will come after, Bill Whiteside, will go out into all the world. In the words of Isaiah 53:8, he will be "cut off out of the land of the living."

The expectation of lineage, the hope of posterity that so possessed Richard Whiteside, grows dim with John Whiteside. There is promise, to be sure. Bill marries Mae Munroe. But Bill is the pragmatist, the businessman who buys into a Ford dealership, and he has no love for the land.

John Whiteside, the middle generation between the dreamer Richard and the pragmatist Bill, feels a keen sense of things slipping away. He cannot share his father's huge, romantic dream. His failed attempt to write Virgilian poetry typifies his inability to capture his father's spirit. His failure to understand Bill ("Do you think he has any intelligence?") typifies his inability to adapt to the pragmatic realities of his time. He is a man caught between two contrary pulls. Steinbeck writes, "Most lives extend in a curve. There is a rise of ambition, a rounded peak of maturity, a gentle downward slope of disillusion and last a flattened grade of waiting for death. John Whiteside lived in a straight line" (pp. 223–24). With no compelling dreams or impelling desire, the straight line goes without variation to its inevitable end.

Steinbeck has ably undergirded the process symbolically. Most notable is the coloration of the meerschaum pipe. Richard Whiteside, whose love for the accoutrements of civilization is huge, enjoys the pipe as part of his picture of himself as a country squire in a house rumbling with children: "I'm founding a dynasty. I'm building a family and a family seat that will survive, not forever, but for several centuries at least. It pleases me, when I build this house, to know that my descendents will walk on its floor, that children whose great grandfathers aren't conceived will be born in it. I'll build the germ of a tradition into my house" (p. 205). Part of that tradition is the meerschaum. The pipe is first described as "turning from its new, chalky white to a rich, creamy yellow" (p. 207). It is getting nicely broken in. The dream is still full and rich with promise. Along with the house and works of the three great authors—Herodotus, Thucydides, and Xenophon—John Whiteside also inherits the pipe from his father: "The meerschaum pipe was reddish brown by now, delicately and evenly colored" (p. 218). The pipe is a constant friend to John, a part of the legacy. But its color darkens. It actually become foreboding: "The big meerschaum pipe was very dark now, almost a black in which there were red lights" (p. 220). A mature meerschaum is at its prime when the color is a creamy brown, perhaps with an amber tinge. When it shades to black, the vibrancy of the meerschaum dies. The black meerschaum of John Whiteside has reached its ending, yet it remains a fond friend: "John sat in his chair caressing the big meerschaum. Now and then to oil it he stroked the polished bowl along the side of his nose" (p. 222).

Toward the end the pipe is jet black. Because John understands that Bill is utterly unlike him, he resorts with increasing frequency to his sitting room: "John's leather chair and his black meerschaum and his books reclaimed him again from the farm" (p. 227). That sitting room is the last thing to go up in the flames: "The leather chairs shivered and shrank like live things from the heat. The glass on the pictures shattered and the steel engravings shriveled to black rags. They could see the big black meerschaum pipe hanging over the mantel" (p. 236). The legacy ends.

The Whiteside house itself functions as a symbol of the dream and the legacy in the story. From the outset, it is more than just a residence; it is a repository of dreams and great expectations. Before he has cleared the land to see if it will support a family, Richard Whiteside builds his house. The crowning touch—last to be put on in the building process, last to collapse when the Whiteside world ends in fire—is the heavy slate roof, its sign of permanence. Because of the roof, the neighbors also believe in the dream:

This roof was an important and symbolic thing to Richard. To the people of the valley the slate roof was the show piece of the country. More than anything else it made Richard Whiteside the first citizen of the valley. This man was steady, and his home was here. He didn't intend to run off to a new gold field. Why—his roof was slate. [p. 206]

The house is symbolic of steadfastness, but in Richard's mind it also symbolizes room for his expected lineage. Once before the Whiteside family had lived in a house for several generations, spread across 130 years. Seventy-three children were born in that house. Then it burned down. Richard permits himself to believe "the curse is removed" (p. 208). But like a premonition, even as he mouths the words, "an ember had rolled out of the fireplace and off the brick hearth" (p. 209).

For Richard, the house becomes a living spirit: "There's something mystic in the house, Alicia, something marvelous. It's the new soul, the first native of the race" (p. 210). As in Poe's "The Fall of the House of Usher," the house and lineage are identified as one. The House of Whiteside becomes the symbol of the Whiteside presence in the valley. And when John is born, Alicia remarks, "The family is safe, Richard." To which Richard responds, oddly enough, "The house is safe. I'm going to begin reading Herodotus to him, Alicia."

When John Whiteside takes over the house, it retains its symbolic qualities. But the fact that he becomes so closely identified with the house, rather than a lineage, begins to suggest an ending to the lineage: "The house of Whiteside was John's personality solidified. When the people of the valley thought of him, it was never of the man alone in a field, or in a wagon, or at the store. A mental picture of him was incomplete unless it included his house" (p. 227). The sense of finality is complete when Bill announces that he and Mae are going to move to Monterey, there to live in a new home and start a new lineage.

Ironically, as the circle comes around to the curse once more, John has just painted the house, "although it did not need it very badly" (p. 231). He admits that he has not paid attention to the land, but that renewed attention is the very thing that breeds the fire. He and Bert Munroe decide to burn the overgrowth of brush. When Richard Whiteside arrived at the valley, he begged a sign that this was the appointed place to live. In response a little gust of wind "picked up a few leaves and flung them forward," which Richard declares is his answer. Here at the end of things, the wind once again responds with a sign: "At that moment a little autumn whirlwind danced down the hill, twisting and careening as it came. It made a coquettish dash into the fire, picked up sparks and embers and flung them against the white house" (p. 234). The curse has come full circle.

John's closing remark carries a sense of finality. He says, "I wish I could have saved my pipe." Bert Munroe responds, "Yes, sir. That was the best colored meerschaum I ever saw. They have pipes in museums that aren't colored any better than that. That pipe must have been smoked a long time." In the end, it was just a pipe after all.

The Munroe and Whiteside stories provide a historical frame for the book, a beginning and ending. But they also provide a thematic frame of beginning and ending. In the first, the curse is unleashed, but in the end, John Whiteside lets it go. Rather than battle the flames, he sits with Bert Munroe and watches them devour his stolid, four-square house. In her study of the allegorical framework of *The Pastures of Heaven*, Melanie Mortlock suggests that John Whiteside is a kind of hero in his acceptance of the inevitable:

What makes John Whiteside the most heroic character in *The Pastures of Heaven* is that unlike the other characters, he has no illusions, delusions, and fantasies or innocent beliefs. What he does have is a dream; and when the dream is destroyed, he is wise enough to let it go and strong enough to carry on, to survive. Realistically, John Whiteside has been an example of virtue for the community; he has taught them how to cope with political and social problems. Allegorically, he is an example of how to cope with the human predicament: he dreams, but he is capable of living with broken dreams.[8]

The truth of the curse has been revealed to him, but he does not rage against the roaring of the light. He merely reflects that it is time to change, pull up stakes, and go live with Bill and Mae Whiteside, thus completing a cycle in which the nurtured becomes the nurturer. That is the saga of human existence in the Pastures of Heaven—the compromise between divine yearning and human reality.

THE CONFLICT WITH CIVILIZATION: TULARECITO, JUNIUS MALTBY, AND THE LOPEZ SISTERS

In the epilogue to *The Pastures of Heaven*, Steinbeck momentarily places the travelers from the tour bus at the rim of the valley. Each senses a deep call from the land stirring the heart; each retreats to a claim that the larger structure of civilization has upon their lives. Throughout his literary career, Steinbeck perceived "civilization" as the power structure in society, often, as in *Cannery Row*, depicting it as a rapacious beast that chews up individual lives. Individuals who don't fit neatly into its power structure because they dream huge dreams, are a bit abnormal, possess unusual gifts, or openly defy it are crushed by its force.

Each of the characters in the Pastures has fled from this force, and each has found temporary refuge in this valley whose hills cut off the symbolic winds and fogs of civilization. As the founding corporal observes, "The hills hugged it jealously against the fog and the wind." Occasionally, however, that force leaks into the valley and clashes dramatically with the way of life there. Such instances occur with Tularecito, Junius Maltby, and the Lopez Sisters.

The story of Tularecito, titled "Coyote Tularecito" in the ledger, exemplifies the conflict between the artistic gift and civilization.[9] An outcast by virtue of his misshapen body and limited intelligence, Tularecito nonetheless has the gift of making art. At first his gift seems merely "amusing." But Steinbeck also describes it in terms that he will use for Elisa Allen's repressed artistry: "He had planting hands, tender fingers that never injured a young plant nor bruised the surfaces of a grafting limb" (p. 49). As his gift emerges more frequently in artistic designs, the hired hand Pancho perceives it as a supernatural thing: "Pancho, who had never quite considered the boy human, put his gift for carving in a growing category of diabolical traits definitely traceable to his supernatural origin" (p. 49).

At the age of eleven, but with the intelligence of a five-year-old, Tularecito starts school. He does not belong there. He is impervious to learning in the traditional sense of a civilized order. But he does have the gift of art-making, which the effusive Miss Martin calls "a great gift that God has given you." Upon so designating its divine origin, Miss Martin, like an avenging angel, wipes it off the board. After applying the ritual beating to Tularecito, which Miss Martin insists upon—for it is the proper thing to do in the civilized order—Franklin Gomez says, "You say he is an animal, but surely he is a good animal. You told him to make pictures and then you destroyed his pictures" (p. 53).[10] Gomez holds the view that Tularecito is not crazy, but "one of those whom God has not quite finished" (p. 53). Miss Martin's view, representing civilization's intolerance for anyone who doesn't fit into its neat little categories, runs counter: "This creature is dangerous."

Molly Morgan, whose succoring nature forms the counterpart to Miss Martin's officious rigidity, provides a brief liberation for Tularecito. She gives his artistry opportunity for expression, recognition, and definition. But she also opens to Tularecito a wholly other world—the realm of fantasy. In the world of gnomes, Tularecito sees his true home. Failing to find a place in the civilized structure of life,

Tularecito has to locate an impossible world. People like
Tularecito, Steinbeck would insist, must find a place in this
world. To try to separate them is to destroy them, but also
ourselves. Called like a warrior to defend his fantasy kingdom, Tularecito is beaten and carted off "to the asylum for
the criminal insane at Napa."

Molly Morgan demonstrates that a Tularecito is harmless
to society when his gift is recognized and he is given the
opportunity to exercise it freely. Society, however, insists
otherwise. Unless the gift can be neatly categorized, the
gifted person will be ostracized. The story certainly captures some of Steinbeck's personal frustration as an artist as
well. Rejections of his work had reached the flood-tide
stage. In characters such as Tularecito and, later, Elisa Allen, Steinbeck demonstrates the tragedy of society's failure
to recognize and value the artistic gift.

If Tularecito demonstrates civilization's inability to find a
place for the gifted or unusual individual, Junius Maltby
demonstrates the individual's difficulty finding a place in
society. Generally, Steinbeck's characters who are in conflict with civilization fall into three categories. The first
category includes those oddities of human nature that society simply doesn't understand. Some, such as Tularecito
or Elisa Allen, are of artistic temperament, possessing gifts
that civilization rejects or scorns as being of no account.
Some, such as Tularecito or Lennie Small, are physically or
mentally abnormal, and civilization treasures nothing quite
so much as normality. A second group includes those who
willfully or by accident of circumstance violate civilization's
standards of social decorum. Some, such as the paisanos of
Tortilla Flat and Mack and the boys of *Cannery Row*, simply create their own little worlds beneath the jaws of the
tiger. Some, such as Steinbeck's hookers, live quietly apart.
Some, like Cathy Ames, are moral monsters who clash the
gears of mechanized civilization itself. A third category, and
perhaps the largest for Steinbeck, is the group of dreamers.
A recurrent theme from his earliest work to the latest is the
individual dreamer in conflict with civilization. We find it

in the great dream of the Joads, the dream of Juana and Kino, even Steinbeck's dream in *Travels with Charley* of rediscovering his manhood, his home, and his nation. We find it also in Junius Maltby. Civilization has no patience with dreamers, for it insists upon the supreme value of the pragmatic enterprise. It insists upon results, not hopes. Its god is the ledger, its altar the bank, its worship the nine-to-five job. Civilization insists especially upon no individualism; sadly enough, artists, dreamers, those who violate the norms of decorum are individuals. These civilization devours as fuel for its relentless appetite for sameness.

The allure of the Pastures is that it is a world set apart from civilization; yet, the tentacles of the devourer reach into this valley also. That is part of the curse. The very act of exercising dominion over the earth by ordering and laying straight the crooked places is an act of civilization. For what purpose? For gain, of course. To build a new civilization. The pity of the matter is that each inhabitant comes here fleeing civilization, and that the Pastures, of all places, ought to be free from its marauding touch. "Junius Maltby" demonstrates the inevitability of that touch.

Reeling from a series of failures in San Francisco, including failed physical health, Junius cuts the strings to his past and, armed with $500, heads for the Pastures of Heaven in 1910: "He felt that the name meant something personal to him, and he was very glad, because for ten years nothing in the world had been personal to him" (p. 86). He arrives bereft of personality, one more cog spat out by the machinery of civilization. His excuse for chronic laziness is the need for convalescence, but laziness, he discovers, is his nature. Marrying the Widow Quaker in 1911, Junius finds himself with a farm and a willing worker in his new wife. Junius retreats to the fallen sycamore, dangles his feet in the river, and lets Stevenson's *Kidnapped* carry him away. Within the space of six years, his two foster sons and his wife die, and Junius inherits a dilapidated farm along with the infant Robbie, named after Robert Louis Stevenson.

Junius is not mean-spirited in his laziness; nor is he untouched by the events around him. He offers his family the only consolation he knows in their dying hours. He reads them *Treasure Island*. The simple fact is that Junius lives in a different world from the one determined by the pragmatic stringencies of civilization.

As the years pass, Junius grows in happiness in reverse proportion to the dissolution of his farm. He eschews certain standard articles of clothing, such as shoes, along with labor. Jakob Stutz wanders onto the farm, is hired to labor, and does nothing. Junius himself provides the best assessment of his own character: "There are long-visioned minds and short-visioned. I've never been able to see things that are close to me. For instance, I am much more aware of the Parthenon than of my own house over there" (p. 91). The long view sees beyond civilization, which insists upon the pragmatic short view.

In Junius, Steinbeck also has an interesting mouthpiece for some of his own views. His personal spokesmen are nearly always outsiders, cut off from civilization and thereby free to think their own way. In later works we find such types in Doc Phillips of *In Dubious Battle*, Jim Casy of *The Grapes of Wrath*, Sam Hamilton of *East of Eden*, Dr. Winter of *The Moon Is Down*. Here we find the prototype of such characters: the man with the freedom to speculate. Junius states some decidedly Steinbeck-like opinions. His speculation on water and dryness, which is also echoed by Sam Hamilton, is lifted directly from Steinbeck's notes of the time and his budding interest in marine biology.

Junius, Jakob, and Robbie speculate together—and they are equals in such speculation. While Tularecito's mind stopped growing at age five, Robbie's mind was never young. Sitting by the river they consider, naturally enough, water. Jakob says, "Good things love water. Bad things always been dry" (p. 94). The discourse continues:

> "But water," Jakob broke in. "Do you see about water too?"
> "No, not about water."

"But I see," said Junius. "You mean that water is the seed of life. Of the three elements water is the sperm, earth the womb and sunshine the mold of growth." [p. 94]

Similar comments riddle Steinbeck's notes and letters, culminating, of course, in *The Log from the Sea of Cortez*. While working on *Tortilla Flat*, for example, he jotted an entry in his ledger: "Man is so little removed from the water. When he is near to the sea near the shore where the full life is, he feels terror and nostalgia. Terror because the life is voracious and homophagus [sic], nostalgia because the quiet pools and the dim caves under the rocks are home. Come down to the tide pool, when the sea is out, and let us look into our old houses, let us avoid our old enemies" (*TFN*). In this story, Junius's fascination with such speculation and his proclivity to rest along the river mark him as the outcast of society.[11]

The story proper, however, focuses more upon Robbie than Junius, for it is Robbie who is required to confront civilization. At a certain point in time, the authorities call him to school. When Robbie protests, Junius remarks,

I know. I don't much want you to go, either. But we have laws. The law has a self-protective appendage called penalty. We have to balance the pleasure of breaking the law against the punishment. The Carthaginians punished even misfortune. If a general lost a battle through bad luck, he was executed. At present we punish people for accidents of birth and circumstance in much the same manner. [p. 96]

Robbie is destined to become, instead of an outcast, the school leader. His differences are lionized and imitated. He brings imagination and daring to the school. Since he has the good fortune to have Molly Morgan for a teacher, he flourishes in the attitude. But not everyone in the Pastures bears the conciliatory attitude that makes room for those who are different.

Ironically, Mrs. Munroe, so closely associated with the valley curse, is the one who brings the demise of the dream.

Out of good-heartedness, she wraps a bundle of clothes for
Robbie. The very thing that has marked Robbie, and freed
him, is cast in jeopardy. Molly tries to fight back. John
Whiteside insists, "Embarrass him to have decent clothes?
Nonsense! I should think it would embarrass him more not
to have them" (p. 111). Molly is reduced to pleading, "I
wish you wouldn't. I really wish you wouldn't do it." She
recognizes full well the significance of the gift: It will tame
Robbie according to civilization's standards. It will strip
away the fabric of the dreamer, and deck him in sameness.
Seeing the abashed and defeated look on Robbie when he
opens the package, Molly says, "I don't think he ever knew
he was poor until a moment ago" (p. 112).

At the advent of Christmas vacation, two woebegone pilgrims are found on the road to the shining city of San Francisco. One is reminded of Yeat's words: "What rough beast
. . . slouches towards Bethlehem to be born?" Jakob has
fled to the hills. Robbie and Junius are driven from them.

For a time, Robbie and Junius frolicked in a new Eden.
But to them also came the knowledge of good and evil. This
is civilization's tutoring: they are evil in the eyes of the god
decorum. They don't fit. And so they wander into exile,
bound once more for the city of San Francisco, where
Junius will try to earn a living by the sweat of his brow, toil-
ing over account books where earnings of others are plowed
into straight rows.

Some years later, upon completion of the first draft of *In
Dubious Battle*, Steinbeck penned an odd little note to
himself: "It is some years now since Junius Maltby and
Robbie climbed on the bus to go back to San Francisco to
get a job. I've often wondered about him, whether he got it
and whether he kept it" (*IDBN*). Apparently the speculation stayed in his mind, for shortly after that he wrote an
addendum to the story and retitled it "Nothing So Monstrous," publishing the whole in a pamphlet-book in December 1936. The opening paragraph of the addendum begins with nearly the same words, adding, "He was strong in

spirit when he went away. I for one should find it difficult
to believe he would go under." [12]

Clearly, Steinbeck wanted to see some survival of the
idyll that Junius and Robbie enjoyed. In the addendum he
speculates on their eventual return to the Pastures:

I think rather he might have broken away again. For all I know he
may have come back to the Pastures of Heaven. Somewhere in
the brush-thick canyons there may be a cave looking out on a
slow stream, shaded by sycamores. And in the cave Junius may
live and Robbie with him. This cave would be secret, mind you,
and curtained with vines, the entrance concealed. And to this
cave young farmers who were little boys when Junius was here
before, may come secretly, slipping through the brush, splashing
across the stream in the night. Yes they may leave their warm
comfortable wives in bed and creep out to sit in Junius' cave, a
whole raft of them around a little fire. Each man would fill his
hand with the dry sand of the floor and let the sand sift out of his
closed palm while Junius talks, and each man would study his
hand and not see it. [*IDBN*]

In his speculation, Steinbeck portrays Junius spinning his
stories and fantasies from ancient history. The great books
live on. Well after midnight, the farmers slip back home
like little boys, leaving a kind of Huckleberry Finn fantasy
world. Steinbeck concludes, "I don't know that this is true.
I only hope to God it is."

The reader is left with much the same hope, but not the
expectation. The reader is left, instead, with the certain
knowledge that one little dream, which flowered so briefly
and so harmlessly, lies destroyed because of the insistence
that the dream be subordinated to civilization's standards.

"The Lopez Sisters," while ending in the two ladies'
flight from the valley, nicely demonstrates that the Pastures
is not finally a vale of tears. It is a refreshing comic interlude in the text, a delightful revelation of human nature.
Although possibly first written as an early part of *To A God
Unknown*, the revised version of the story captures well

the ironic tensions of *The Pastures of Heaven*, for it demonstrates how "in the end the flesh conquered" (p. 115). The lusty flesh of the good-hearted sisters conquers spiritual imaginings; the nastier flesh of vindictive people conquers their happy compromise. The sisters depart for San Francisco where, as prostitutes, they will no longer serve enchiladas, only the sensual needs of the flesh. Civilization intrudes upon their happy world, brands them as bad women, and sends them forth on the same road traveled by Tularecito, Junius, and Robbie.

This sharply crafted story of huge hungerings and human satisfaction is also important to the spiritual geography of the Pastures. The valley farms lie in the eternal conflict of order and disorder, human dominion and natural rampage. The dark, fertile soil, the thick trees and brush spring easily from the soil. But with them springs a Hieronymous Bosch *Garden of Earthly Delights*. As in the painting, the delights of this garden are often perverse. Crookedness thwarts the best efforts of the laborers; the garden goes completely wild with their worst efforts. But the Lopez sisters reside on the arid heights, victims of stony soil and gritty waste, also slightly above the eternal warfare of the lusher gardens. Their own weapon is their spirituality and indomitable spirits.

Curiously enough, it is the high, arid land that Steinbeck associates with the life of the spirit in his stories. In "Flight," Pepe faces his ultimate spiritual revelation in the high, barren places. In *East of Eden*, the enduring heroism of Samuel Hamilton prevails over the stony ground, even as he looks down upon a valley tortured with darkness. While Sam Hamilton plods over the land on scraggly old Doxology, the Lopez sisters have their counterpart in the ancient mule Lindo. Somehow these characters, exiled to the barren soil, ascend to a spirituality that is majestic.

It is also comic, this contention of spirit and flesh in the high places. Above all, we notice that the Lopez sisters "were too fat and too jolly to make martyrs of themselves over an unreligious matter like eating" (p. 115). Deeply religious, their lives are ones of simple compromises to honor their spiritual tradition. They are not flagellants, these sisters, bowed under the weight of spiritual burdens. Life surges too powerfully in them; their native wit works too quickly with imaginative compromises. Because business doesn't come with a rush to their kitchen, advertised as "TORTILLAS, ENCHILADAS, TAMALES AND SOME OTHER SPANISH COOKINGS, R. & M. LOPEZ," they add a little spice to their cooking. The good sisters will offer the delights of their ample flesh to hungering customers, construing "other Spanish cookings" in the broadest possible terms. There is, of course, no end to such appetites, as Steinbeck was also to show in his lineage of hookers in subsequent books. So it is that when Maria offers herself, a living sacrifice, to a customer, he has a sudden urge for enchiladas also: "It is necessary to encourage our customers if we are to succeed. And he had three, Maria, three enchiladas! And he paid for them" (p. 118). There is no measurable sense of guilt over the inducement, simply a vague sense that some homage should be paid: "I think, Rosa, I think our mother would be glad, and I think your own soul would be glad if you should ask forgiveness of the Mother Virgin and of Santa Rosa" (p. 118). Indeed, throughout the development of their business, the sisters remain hugely devout. They sin pragmatically and are pragmatically shriven:

They remained persistently religious. When either of them had sinned she went directly to the little porcelain Virgin, now conveniently placed in the hall to be accessible from both bedrooms, and prayed for forgiveness. Sins were not allowed to pile up. They confessed each one as it was committed. Under the Virgin there was a polished place on the floor where they had knelt in their nightdresses. [p. 119]

In fact, it may be said that their flesh offering is a religious exercise for them, humbly given to the needs of a starving humanity that beats an ever-deepening trail to their doorway. Their temporal reward consists of increasing quantities of sweets from Monterey to assuage their own appetites. All in all, it is a happy situation: "For these sisters knew how to preserve laughter, how to pet and coax it along until their spirits drank the last dregs of its potentiality" (p. 119).

Never would the sisters admit that their sex was for sale, a solely commercial venture relegated in their peculiar theology to fallen women. The one poor buffoon who offers money for the transaction and is unable to devour three enchiladas receives Rosa's most livid rage. Sex for sale! It would disgrace their proud lineage. This is the appetizer for their meal, not the main course. So too it is an illusion they have fabricated, and thus very much in keeping with the illusions that curse others in the valley. But it is a harmless one, high in moral standards and convenient religious absolution. The flesh will be served.

Their good intentions are their very undoing. Riding in the buggy behind the windmill motions of ancient Lindo, Maria sees Allen Hueneker, "The ugliest, shyest man in the valley." The good-hearted Maria offers him a ride. The whole scene is set in a wonderfully comic tone: "Maria tugged on the lines as though she pulled up a thunderously galloping speed" (p. 124). She calls to Lindo, "Steady, Lindo! Be calm!" when the most excitable motion Lindo is capable of is a desultory sweep of his tail. The description of Maria making room in the buggy has a circus-like touch: "She rolled aside to make room for him, and then oozed back" (p. 124). Maria "remembered how polite it was to encourage conversation." Allen glares and refuses to speak. But the horror is about to happen.

Bert and Mrs. Munroe clatter by in their old Ford and observe the odd couple. "'Say,' Bert cried. 'It'd be a good joke to tell old lady Hueneker we saw her old man running off with Maria Lopez'" (p. 126). The curse of the wagging tongue, the vile poison of rumor, is unleashed in the valley. Who can stand against it? Surely not Maria, who "in a riot of extravagance" buys four candy bars to fortify her bulk against the onslaught of the world.

Even the catastrophic showdown receives a comic touch, however. The sheriff comes to serve notice. But Maria construes this as a mark of social acceptance. They are established now: "Now Maria fairly chattered with excitement. 'The sheriff, he came? Now we are on the road. Now we will be rich. How many enchiladas, Rosa? Tell me how many for the sheriff?'" (p. 128). A subtle series of ironies invades her comment. She has just remarked to Allen Hueneker, "I have heard very rich men say it is good to travel." She tells Rosa, "Now we are on the road." It is indeed true. They will travel. They will be on the road. The irony is darkened, however, by the sudden reversal from great expectations: "My poor little sister. . . . Now we cannot ever sell any more enchiladas. Now we must live again in the old way with no new dresses" (p. 128).

The sisters are so broken by the tragic reversal of their fortunes that they are left with but one option to pursue— the hunger of the flesh: "See, Maria! I will go to San Francisco and be a bad woman." Maria evidences the monumental depth of their fall by dropping to her knees and praying fifty Hail Marys, ten times the standard penance for an immoral act. They stand in tears, ready to undertake the long road to San Francisco, not rich to be sure, but traveling nonetheless.

"The Lopez Sisters," very much in keeping with the pattern of the valley, exemplifies the irony of the book's title. Read by several critics as the odd story of the collection, the misfit with an implausible ending and atypical setting, the story actually fits very well with the human drama of the book.[13] The Pastures is not a vale of sorrow. It is also shot through with grace and laughter. Certainly it bears the touch of tragic fallenness, and the sudden reversal of the Lopez sisters' fortunes admirably captures that tension.

Taken together, the three stories of Tularecito, Junius Maltby, and the Lopez sisters establish a theme that Steinbeck would return to often. Civilization, the power structure of society, holds little value for the outcasts of its standards. Yet, these are the very people in whom Steinbeck takes enduring delight and whose stories he sets forth with poignancy and grace even while aware of the tragic pressures that civilization brings upon them to conform to its order. Even in the Pastures, filled as it is with the oddities of human nature, these wayward sheep are driven out to the world of wolves.

CONFRONTATION WITH THE SHADOW: MOLLY MORGAN

"Molly Morgan," one of Steinbeck's more ambitious tales of this period, indicates a growing self-confidence in his artistry. The complexity of the tale resides in the overlapping of present and past, and their coalescence through the omniscient narrative point of view. Furthermore, the deep probing of Molly's psychology posed an artistic challenge for Steinbeck that he would confront again in Elisa Allen and Cathy Ames, two women, albeit with decidedly different results, who also struggle to liberate themselves from the psychological conditioning of their pasts.

In *Steinbeck's Re-Vision of America*, Louis Owens argues that "Molly Morgan" is a piece of the larger Pastures of Heaven framework in Molly's insistence upon manufacturing an illusion to live by: "Molly lives in a world filled with illusions, as is shown by her need to romanticize the outlaw Vasquez."[14] Such illusions, in Owens's view, are a part of the curse of the valley and are destructive to the individual who insists upon clinging to them: "While Molly's desire to maintain an aura of romance in every day life might ordinarily be applauded, it is a destructive force in her life, paralleling the illusion she desperately clings to about her father, who was, in Bill's words, 'kind of an irresponsible cuss.' The necessity to maintain the illusory vision of her father drives Molly from the Pastures and the happiness she had discovered there."[15]

It is true, as Owens observes, that Molly participates in a pattern of illusions, as do so many in the valley. However, understanding Molly Morgan at that level alone fails to do justice to the rich and complex psychological portrait Steinbeck has made of her. In this early work, Steinbeck was fashioning one of his intricate studies of the female heroine that would reach fruition in characters like Juana of *The Pearl*, Ma Joad of *The Grapes of Wrath*, and Abra Bacon of *East of Eden*. While Molly is afflicted by illusion, she also grapples magnificently with the crushing burden of reality, finding her own way through conflicting emotions of love and fear. The thematic development of this pattern provided Steinbeck with one of his most demanding artistic challenges to date, and his resolution of it marks the story as a worthy achievement in his canon.

In his original plotting of the story sequence for *The Pastures of Heaven*, Steinbeck scheduled "Molly Morgan" to follow "Mrs. Van Deventer." Perhaps in the sequence we can deduce one clue to the thematic pattern of confronting illusion. Helen Van Deventer's life is indeed cast in illusion, as she clings frantically to her idea of noble endurance in the face of tragedy, willfully shutting out the clear, realistic voice of Dr. Phillips until reality shatters her illusions with the blast of a shotgun. Molly Morgan similarly treads a tightrope between the illusion that her father is still alive and noble and full of love and the reality of the drunken sot in Bert Munroe's car. But we do not know if the drunk is Molly's father; indeed, there is no evidence that he is, simply Molly's fear of the reality that he might be, and so she flees. A natural pairing between Helen and Molly exists, then, but two quite different persons are acting out the drama of illusion versus reality.

The published sequence of stories, however, was quite different from the order of composition. The story of Molly Morgan appears in the second *Pastures of Heaven* notebook. After the Lopez sisters story, Steinbeck entered the title "Molly Morgan," crossed it out, and entered "Story of the Battle Farm." The Molly Morgan story follows directly after this. There were also a few telling revisions in the manuscript. A scene recounting Vasquez's death was deleted entirely, thus subduing the heavily romantic tone of Molly's vision of the outlaw. And in a brief alternative to the

closing dialogue between Whiteside and Molly, Whiteside
initiates the conversation:

"You mean you think he might be ———?"
"No," she cried. "No I don't. I'm sure I don't."
"Can't you tell me," he asked.
"I'm afraid," she cried. "Can't you see I'm afraid?"

The lines state a bit more strongly the climactic disclosure
of Molly's fear to John Whiteside a few lines previously:

John Whiteside nodded very slowly.
"No," she cried. "I don't think that. I'm sure I don't."
"I'd like to do something, Molly."
"I don't want to go, I love it here—But I'm afraid. It's so im-
portant to me."

Steinbeck's attempted revision of the final scene lends
emphasis to Molly's fear of confrontation with herself—her
dream of her father and the reality of her father. Thematically it also emphasizes the meaning of love in the story.
The psychological drama of the story occurs in Molly's disclosure to herself of what it means to love and what threatens love, and the terrible fear that occurs when one stands
uncertainly between the two.

One means of understanding that internal struggle, and
especially Molly's comment, "Now I'm killing myself" as she
faces the reality of her father, is through Jungian psychology. Although once a highly speculative field of influence
study, there now seems to be no question about the considerable attraction Jung's ideas had for Steinbeck. It may
be observed in works such as *To a God Unknown* and the
unpublished "Murder at Full Moon" from the early 1930s,
and even more dramatically in *The Pearl* and *The Winter
of Our Discontent*.[16] By 1930 Steinbeck had been reading Jung's works for some time. Jackson Benson observes,
"Aspects of Jungian theory, particularly the collective unconscious, found fertile ground in Steinbeck's interests in
myth and evolutionary theory."[17] In his catalogue of Steinbeck's reading, Robert DeMott lists nine separate works by

Jung.[18] DeMott states that Steinbeck arrived at Jung's works independently of Ed Ricketts during the early 1930s.[19]

One of the most compelling elements of Jung's psychological theory for Steinbeck was his concept of one's confrontation with the shadow. The theory, elucidated in over a dozen separate works by Jung, may nonetheless be condensed in terms of "the mask" and "the shadow."

The fundamental premise undergirding Jung's theory of the shadow is that the conscious and the unconscious are necessarily in conflict. Even when one adopts a mask, what Jung calls the "persona," for the conscious part of one's nature—the part we present to others—the unconscious part of one's personality will afflict that persona: "The shadow personifies everything that the subject refuses to acknowledge about himself and yet is always thrusting itself upon him directly or indirectly."[20] The unconscious will not be denied, and the effort to deny it results in psychological imbalance. To achieve psychological harmony, one must confront the reality of one's unconscious. This confrontation Jung describes as "the meeting with the shadow."

The shadow must first be understood, then, in distinction from the public "mask" of the persona, for the customary, social mask avoids confrontation. The mask would assure us that everything is well with the world, when in fact it is not. The shadow insists that it is not. The shadow hides those parts of our personality that are not socially acceptable; they are locked away, repressed, cast into psychological darkness. Such a repression constitutes the tension of Jung's dialectic: "A conflict of duty forces us to examine our conscience and thereby discover the shadow."[21] It also constitutes the tension of "Molly Morgan." As Jung demonstrated psychologically and Steinbeck reveals artistically, the longer the unconscious is locked away, the more dangerous the confrontation becomes.

Molly enters the story as the naïf, at once eager and fearful of what lies before her in the valley. Her fear is evident from the start. Pat Humbert pulls over in his Ford truck to offer her a ride and, detecting her uncertainty, says, "Well, get in, then. Needn't be scared. I'm Pat Humbert. I got a place in the Pastures" (p. 131). Despite Pat's reassurance that John Whiteside is "a fine old man," Molly feels her fear surging: "When he put her down in front of the big old house of John Whiteside, she was really frightened. 'Now it's coming,' she said to herself. 'But there's nothing to be afraid of. He can't do anything to me'" (p. 131).

The Whitesides function in this story as the polar opposites to Molly's own mother and father. Mrs. Whiteside is witty, full of good cheer, brimming with love. She accepts others immediately, rejects no one, and yet has a keen, intuitive understanding of others. Molly's own mother was a pinched nerve of lovelessness, an empty vessel claiming love as a kind of debt. John Whiteside provides that sense of steadfast presence, working out of his home office, that Molly never knew in her absentee father. While her father would periodically drop in to regale the children with nonstop gifts and stories, John Whiteside offers the gift of his presence, listening to Molly rather than filling her ears with din. Moreover, the Whiteside household is filled with wit. Already Steinbeck had this sense that healthy people laugh, most often at themselves. Laughter, as he would demonstrate in his delightful *Tortilla Flat* or the great farce *Sweet Thursday*, is healthy and restorative. Language frolics along with the emotions here in the Whiteside household, as Steinbeck demonstrates in this punning repartee:

> Molly laughed happily. "You have children," she said. "Oh, you've raised lots of children—and you like them."
>
> Mrs. Whiteside scowled. "One child raised me. Raised me right through the roof. It was too hard on me. He's out raising cows now, poor devils. I don't think I raised him very high." [p. 133]

In the light of Mrs. Whiteside's radiant personality and John Whiteside's calm presence, Molly begins to see her own fears objectively.

When Molly is ushered into John Whiteside's study, he

is immediately depicted as a kind of deity—a confessor figure: "There was an old-fashioned roll-top desk, and behind it sat John Whiteside. When he looked up, Molly saw that he had at once the kindest and the sternest eyes she had ever seen, and the whitest hair, too. Real blue-white, silky hair, a great duster of it" (p. 134). Guided by his kindness, "Molly dropped her mind back into the past." Thus begins the narrator's revelation of her past, carefully orchestrated to the present of Whiteside's questions and Molly's answers. If Whiteside is a kind of deity here, before whom all things are made known, Steinbeck permits the reader the shared intimacy of that knowledge through the omniscient narrator. Several of Molly's important attributes are disclosed in the revelation of her past. Growing up in a family with two rambunctious brothers, Tom and Joe, governed by a mother whose desperate need is ever evident, she becomes the giving figure in the household. She succors others. One can see her in a fictional line that leads to Ma Joad and Juana. In Molly's reverie, her mother calls, "Molly come in and stay with your mother. I'm so tired today." Molly obediently goes into the house, but not before threatening the stick doll with which she has been playing: "Molly stood up the stick in the deep dust. 'You, miss,' she whispered fiercely. 'You'll get whipped on your bare bottom when I come back.' Then she obediently went back into the house" (p. 135). The doll, imagined by Molly as "a tall lady in a dress," functions as a totem of her mother, a means for Molly to vent her anger at having to be the nurturing figure in the home. She is desperately uncomfortable before her mother's demands: "Her mother sat in a straight chair in the kitchen. 'Draw up, Molly. Just sit with me for a little while. Love me, Molly! Love your mother a little bit. You are mother's good little girl, aren't you?' Molly squirmed on her chair. 'Don't you love your mother, Molly?'" (p. 136).

Her mother's insistent need and Molly's sacrifice of herself to that need arise from George Morgan's prolonged absences. An inveterate wanderer guised as a traveling salesman, Molly's father is known more as a long absence and great expectancy than as a father. Occasionally he visits, showering the children with presents in lieu of his presence, spieling stories of great adventures that only make the children more impatient with their impoverished captivity. Precisely because of his inaccessibility, he is "a glad argonaut, a silver knight. Virtue and Courage and Beauty— he wore a coat of them" (p. 141).

Cursed with an absentee father, young Molly is forced psychologically to deify him to vindicate his absence. If he is a kind of remote god, whatever he does must be all right. On the other hand, John Whiteside represents the father figure as nurturer, and he satisfies Molly's lifelong yearning for someone present to love her, or simply to hear her. Thus the conflict between the actual father, who is present only in illusory dreams and a long expectation, and the figurative father, who is nonetheless present, sharpens in the story, compelling Molly to her confrontation with her own dreams and realities.

After Molly's brothers ran away to join the navy, Molly entered San Jose Teachers' College, boarding with Mrs. Allen Morit. Molly's mother died while Molly was at college, and Mrs. Morit proved a poor substitute. Stern and unyielding, she foreshadows but is the antithesis to Fauna, indomitable matron of the Bear Flag in *Sweet Thursday* with her chart of Gold-Star girls. For Fauna, etiquette is the avenue of marriage. For Mrs. Morit, it is an end in itself. Etiquette affords her the pleasure of nagging, the consolation of rules. The mother starved for attention is replaced by the domineering mother of rules, one who has no room for affection.

A third kind of mother enters upon the conclusion of Molly's interview with John Whiteside. Molly suddenly announces that she wants to board at the Whiteside home. Mrs. Whiteside responds, "Couldn't think of it. We never take boarders. She's too pretty to be around that fool of a Bill. What would happen to those cows of his? It'd be a whole lot of trouble. You can sleep in the third bedroom upstairs" (p. 144). Molly is adopted into the Whiteside home, amply supplied with those things missing in her own home—a father who is present and a mother who succors her.

For a time, Molly's teaching career in Pastures of Heaven is a smashing success. Despite the haunting fears of her past, her present is stripped clean of illusions. She becomes the vital core of school board meetings and the repository of knowledge in the valley. In the classroom, her students respond with uncustomary diligence and undisguised enthusiasm. Her teaching is described in "Tularecito":

> Miss Morgan, the new teacher, was very young and very pretty; too young and dangerously pretty, the aged men of the valley thought. Some of the boys in the upper grades were seventeen years old. It was seriously doubted that a teacher so young and so pretty could keep any kind of order in the school.
> She brought with her a breathless enthusiasm for her trade. The school was astounded, for it had been used to aging spinsters whose faces seemed to reflect consistently tired feet. Miss Morgan enjoyed teaching and made school an exciting place where unusual things happened. [p. 54]

Whereas Miss Martin drove in knowledge like nails into stone, under Molly's tutelage classes become exciting, knowledge accessible, learning kindled.

It has been suggested that Molly's handling of Tularecito represents her ultimate illusion.[22] The claim seems adequately contravened by the story itself. It is Miss Martin, not Molly, who operates under illusion in the classroom. Miss Martin praises Tularecito's artistry, exclaiming that it is a gift from God, then busily erases God's gift from the blackboard, throwing the classroom into an uproar. She has the strict and narrow view of life that permits no reality of individual differences to intrude. Molly's alternative recognizes individuality. It is unfortunate to consider Molly the *cause* of Tularecito's imprisonment in the insane asylum.

The fault clearly lies with the larger society, which can permit no room for the individual dreamer. Molly and Franklin Gomez offer the positive alternative of acceptance, encouragement, and understanding.[23] The Molly-Tularecito scene gave Steinbeck artistic problems. In his initial draft of the story he made Molly an exponent of all the current educational-psychological theories. Steinbeck deleted this sentence: "Miss Morgan had taken all the new fangled courses in normal and abnormal psychology, and the training periods in teaching methods" (*POH-2*). He replaced it with the paragraph now beginning "She brought with her a breathless enthusiasm for her trade" (p. 54). Clearly, he wanted to shape her character as a nurturer.

Similarly, when Molly first discovers Tularecito's rare gift for making art, Steinbeck originally depicted her as an amateur psychologist. In the ledger a deleted passage reads, "Miss Morgan sent a sheaf of the drawings to her old professor of psychology and received back a larger sheaf of special mental tests to be given the boy. Tularecito refused to take the tests. He was engaged on a stalking tiger and could not take the time" (*POH-2*). Steinbeck replaced the deletion with the simple observation that "she knew all about him, had read books and taken courses about him" (p. 54), and ends the paragraph with the positive assertion, "Every day he labored over his drawing board, and every afternoon presented the teacher with a marvelously wrought animal. She pinned his drawings to the schoolroom wall above the blackboards" (pp. 54–55).

The effect of these revisions is to enhance Molly's levelheaded sensibility in "Tularecito." She is a dreamer, surely, even a bit of the romantic, and that can be dangerous in an age so pragmatically set against the dreams of individuals. In a sense, society's refusal to find a place for the Tularecitos of society parallels Molly's inability to find her place in the Pastures of Heaven.

Molly's role in the Junius Maltby story also testifies to her success as a teacher. One finds the sensitive, nurturing quality as she instructs Robbie Maltby in writing. But she also finds herself irresistibly drawn to old Junius: "Of course Miss Morgan had heard all the bad stories of Junius, and in spite of them had approved of him. But now she began to have a strong desire to meet him" (p. 100). Junius, like her father, lives an adventure in defiance of social norms.

Upon visiting the Maltby farm, instead of squalor, she sees it like this: "'How run-down and slovenly,' she thought. 'How utterly lovely and slipshod!'" (p. 104). She enters the yard as Junius and Jakob enact a burning at the stake for the schoolboys: "'Such things don't happen,' she insisted. 'You're dreaming. Such things just can't happen.' And then she heard the most amiable of conversations going on between the two men" (p. 105). Once over the initial shock, Molly joins delightedly in the game. It is her kind of adventure. She even takes off her shoes, dangling her feet in the river, as she joins the boys for Junius's discourse on "cannibal societies among the Aleutian Indians."

During this period, Molly's teaching excels, and she is given the respect she merits. After a board visit, John Whiteside tells her, "'We've never had a teacher who kept better order,' he said kindly. 'I think if you knew how much the children like you, you'd be embarrassed'" (p. 110). Her expertise in teaching is also marked by common sense. She alone stands up to the well-intentioned but misguided people who thrust their standards of social decency upon Robbie Maltby.

If "Tularecito" and "Junius Maltby" are accurate measures of Molly's halcyon period, they demonstrate the restorative effect that the Whiteside household and her career have upon her. Her fears temporarily drop behind her, but they cannot disappear. In fact, in Jungian psychology this is the point of greatest danger. The happiness Molly experiences has displaced the painful memory of her father but cannot dispel it. Locked in the shadow of her unconsciousness, the memory battles for release. Jung states that one "tries to repress the inferior man in himself, not realizing that by so doing he forces the latter into revolt."[24]

The shadow will insist upon breaking out. Jung states the tension like this: "A man who is possessed by his shadow is always standing in his own light and falling into his own traps."[25] The traps in this case are twofold: the adventure to Vasquez's cabin and the drunken hired hand of Bert Munroe. Together they force Molly into confrontation. Molly has never relinquished the illusion of her father as a conquering hero, imagining that he would return home once more to sweep his little girl off her feet. A deep pathos underlies the laughter in Molly's classroom. Sitting with Bill Whiteside one evening, Molly tells him about her father: "She told him about the visits, and then about the disappearance. 'Do you see what I have, Bill?' she cried. 'My lovely father is some place. He's mine. You think he's living, don't you, Bill?'" (pp. 145–46). Bill's response, one expected from this plain, pragmatic man, cuts her: "From what you say, he was a kind of an irresponsible cuss, though. Excuse me, Molly. Still, if he's alive, it's funny he never wrote" (p. 146). This, the narrator tells us, "was just the kind of reasoning she had successfully avoided for so long." Here is Molly's dilemma: to cling to the father of her dreams or to confront the reality signified by his perpetual absences. This tension causes the resurgence of her old fear.

Feeling the tug of her father's footsteps, Molly finds them leading to the Vasquez cabin. Molly insists upon going alone, for, as she says, "I want to have an adventure. . . . If Bill comes along, it won't be an adventure at all. It'll just be a trip" (p. 147). Having traced the long, lonely path up to the cabin, she has also traced the route to a confrontation with her father and that bit of her father indisputably residing in her. Steinbeck makes his aim unmistakable: "Molly sat down on the slope and rested her chin in her cupped hands. Young Vasquez was standing beside her, and Vasquez had her father's gay face, his shining eyes as he came on the porch shouting, 'Hi, kids!' This was the kind of adventure her father had" (p. 148).

With that romantic experience of her father's adventures, Molly decides, "Now I want to go back to the first and think it all over again"—that is, to see the romantic picture realistically. Bill, who functions throughout this story as a pragmatic realist, thrusts the reality forcefully upon her: "Funny old box, isn't it? Just an old woodshed. There are a dozen just like it down here. You'd be surprised, though, how many people go up there to look at it. The funny part is, nobody's sure Vasquez was ever there" (p. 149). Bill calls the very presence of Vasquez at the cabin into question, and also the nature of the man himself: "Everybody thinks Vasquez was a kind of a hero when really he was just a thief" (p. 149).

This is precisely the crux of Molly's confrontation. Bill's comment, suggesting that Vasquez (and implicitly her father) was simply no good, is incarnated in the bum in Bert Munroe's car. Here lies, in a drunken stupor, the counterpart to her romantic ideal. Bert's initial description of the hired hand evokes parallels to George Morgan: "Now I've got him, I find he isn't worth a cent as a hand, but I can't get rid of him. That son of a gun has been every place. You ought to hear him tell about the places he's been. My kids wouldn't let me get rid of him if I wanted to. Why he can take the littlest thing he's seen and make a fine story out of it" (p. 150). Suddenly, Molly sees head on the reality of her own father. She is terrified of confronting that reality, not so much the possibility that the bum might actually be her father. And the old fear erupts in her heart once more: "She was dreadfully afraid someone would ask the man's name" (p. 151). Molly assures herself that "there isn't a chance in the world," but the fear is nonetheless real.

The terror overwhelms her; her normal vitality dissipates to wan pallor. At the next board meeting, Bert Munroe has the drunk, freshly hauled from a gutter in Salinas, sleeping in his car. Fear impels Molly to the car. The confrontation with the shadow of herself is overwhelming. As she approaches, she thinks, "Now I'm killing myself." Indeed. She is killing the dream that has sustained her and her place in the happy valley of the Pastures of Heaven. Cut by a "blubbering, drunken snore," Molly spins around and runs back to the house. She cannot face the moment of truth.

After the men leave, Molly begs Whiteside to find a substitute for her. She insists upon leaving the valley that night: "I told you my father was dead. I don't know whether he's dead or not. I'm afraid—I want to go away tonight" (p. 153). Molly thrusts a puzzling comment at Whiteside: "Once I'm away I'll be able not to believe it." She has to distance herself from her own fear of discovery to discover herself. The sense of adventure, the romantic dream, struggles in her own nature with her crushing recognition of reality. Both of these rage in Molly now. She recognizes it and fears it.

Molly has reached the dangerous point of confrontation with her shadow. Her tension and unrelenting fear must be understood not simply as a knowledge of her father, but ultimately as a knowledge of herself. In Jungian theory, the power behind the shadow, the force that drives the person to self-confrontation, is a kind of counterperson, which Jung calls the "anima" in males, since it is also a sexual counterperson, and the "animus" in females. So too, Molly's confrontation is not so much with her father as an independent person in her life as with the father within her.

This tension will also color the way we see the ending of the story. The common perception is that Molly flees the valley forever. But Steinbeck doesn't suggest that. She wants to get away for a while, perhaps not forever. She asks for a substitute teacher, not to be released from teaching. She affirms that she wants to get away to come to understanding. Jung observes,

If we are able to see our own shadow and can bear knowing about it, then a small part of the problem has already been solved: we have at least brought up the personal unconscious. The shadow is a living part of the personality and therefore wants to live with it in some form. It cannot be argued out of existence or rationalized into harmlessness. This problem is exceedingly difficult, because it not only challenges the whole man, but reminds him at the same time of his helplessness and ineffectuality.[26]

Molly arrives, at the end of the story, at precisely that point. She is able to see her own shadow and can bear knowing about it. In fact, the shadow has insisted upon it. But now she has to get away for a time to resolve the shadow into her personality.

The enigmatic ending, then, can be understood two ways. Molly says to John Whiteside, "Once I'm away I'll be able not to believe it." On the one hand, this may signify that she will leave the confrontation and the valley for-ever—that she will be able not to believe it because she will have time to bolster her illusions about her father. On the other hand, the comment has a note of hope. The pro-cess of confrontation has begun. She will be able not to be-lieve it—that is, that the drunken sot is not her father—because she will have assimilated her father, her animus, finally into her own being.

The ending is deliberately ambiguous, much like the endings of *In Dubious Battle* and *The Grapes of Wrath.* Steinbeck's comments on the ending of *In Dubious Battle* might also apply to "Molly Morgan":

I hope when you finish it, in the disorder you will find a terrible kind of order. Stories begin and wander out of the picture; faces look in and disappear and the book ends with no finish. A story of the life of a man ends with his death, but where can you end a story of man-movement that has no end? No matter where you stop there is always more to come. I have tried to indicate this by stopping on a high point but it is by no means an ending. [*SLL*, pp. 105–06]

Like that ending, the ambiguity of "Molly Morgan" in itself signals hope. A dramatic confrontation has been made. That has been the painful process. The restorative process is left as a question mark.

"Molly Morgan" is an ambitious story that provides a gripping revelation of the dark sore that festers in a person's subconscious. Its very pain, however, insists upon the per-son's attention and action. One cannot evade it. The story

succeeds artistically through Steinbeck's use of the omniscient point of view. At once he holds before the reader the
unfolding present and the resurging past. However painful
the story is, it also taps out a drumbeat of hope. The act of
confrontation in itself initiates the process of restoration.
Having made that confrontation, Molly is in a position to
reconsider the conflicting sides of her personality and personal experience. She has the opportunity to rise above
them, like the omniscient narrator, to see life steadily and
whole.

FANTASY AND REALITY: SHARK WICKS AND RAYMOND BANKS

Both Shark Wicks and Raymond Banks possess a secret
world, one to which they turn to step momentarily out of
this world of sharp realities. Other than their sharing a fantasy world, however, the two men are altogether dissimilar.
Shark Wicks's fantasy world of an empire of wealth becomes
an alternate reality for him, so much so that his present
world of pragmatic reality seems more the deceptive dream.
Reality will not have it so, of course, and the devastation
of Shark's fantasy demonstrates his tragic inability to live
in reality. On the other hand, Raymond Banks, successful
farmer and friend to the valley, is hardly aware of the full
implications of his retreat world in the hangings at San
Quentin. Not until Bert Munroe paints a monstrously imaginative picture in Raymond's mind does the chicken farmer
begin to see the implications of his other world. He reels
before it, staggered by Bert's portrait of horror. Both Wicks
and Banks find themselves toeing a line between fantasy
and reality, a dangerous line with all sorts of traps poised on
either side.

That basic conflict had been a staple theme of Steinbeck's
for some time, reaching back, perhaps, to "Fingers of
Cloud." Here, however, in the conflict between human
and divine, earthly and spiritual in The Pastures of Heaven,
he found a stronger framework for his theme. Humans will

dream, he insists, and almost invariably that dream will cast
them into conflict with social standards.

Unlike Raymond Banks, with his ebullient good cheer
and ruddy complexion, Edward Wicks is a strange, ferret-
like little man. He lives in a "small, gloomy house" like a
nocturnal animal. His features are vaguely reptilian: "Edward Wicks had a blunt, brown face and small, cold eyes
almost devoid of lashes. He was known as the trickiest man
in the valley" (p. 21). And he has a powerful secret. While
posturing to the valley as a wealthy man, so successfully
that he earns the nickname "Shark," his finances are all
based upon his secret ledgers and amount to no more than
the ink and paper that he surreptitiously draws down to cal-
culate his imaginary gain: "Shark's greatest pleasure came
of being considered a wealthy man. Indeed, he enjoyed it
so much that the wealth itself became real to him" (p. 22).

The immense value of this imaginary world for Shark is
the complete freedom it provides over time and reality.
With complete insouciance, Shark can change the past.
When he learns of a stock failure, he can enter a retroactive
note that he had sold out just in time, reaping a considerable fortune by his good foresight. Each such imaginary
transaction, however, diverts him further from present reality. Real people lose considerable amounts of money in
the present.

Shark's inability to live in reality is demonstrated also in
the two women in his life. At nineteen he marries Katherine Bullock, not out of any idea of love or romance, but because she is a serviceable piece of property for his farm, an
implement that frees him to exercise his dream. Simply
put, Katherine is for him a piece of livestock: "He governed
her with the same gentle inflexibility he used on horses"
(p. 25). Katherine is, admittedly, a good investment. Doc-
ile and hard laboring, she singlehandedly works the farm,
transforming it into a working operation and leaving Shark
to wander his peach orchard and his fantasies.

The second woman in Shark's life is less tractable. Their
daughter, Alice, is born a beauty, perceived as a gift from

the gods in much the same way that Tularecito is perceived as a curse from the devils. Like Tularecito, Alice's mind is retarded, but her beauty is her asset. It is a beauty so pristine, so striking, that Shark believes it must be unsullied by reality. He sets his aim at protecting her from reality's touch, and thereby she becomes the physical adumbration of his fiscal fantasy. The inevitability of a fall from grace is sure in the Pastures, however. The fall of Alice, albeit in Wicks's mind, will parallel the fall of his fantasy fortune. One cannot have heaven in the human world of the Pastures.

Shark's protection of Alice begins with fears for the loss of her virginity, but in a perversely abnormal sense of separating her from reality as a kind of sacred grail of purity:

To him it was not a moral problem, but an aesthetic one. Once she was deflorated, she would no longer be the precious thing he treasured so. He did not love her as a father loves a child. Rather he hoarded her, and gloated over the possession of a fine, unique thing. Gradually, as he asked his question—"Is she all right?"— month by month, this chastity came to symbolize her health, her preservation, her intactness. [p. 29]

The fear becomes an obsession; in time he will not even permit her near young men who might deflower her. The neurotic protectiveness over Alice grows precisely in proportion to his ever-increasing paper fortune.

In this valley with its crawling curse, however, reality cannot be so avoided. In this particular instance, the dramatic confrontation is incited by the person of Jimmie Munroe, who becomes the repository of all of Shark's worst fears:

Before the Munroe family moved into the valley, Shark suspected all men and boys of evil intent toward Alice, but when once he had set eyes on young Jimmie Munroe, his fear and suspicion narrowed until it had all settled upon the sophisticated Jimmie. The boy was lean and handsome of face, his mouth was well developed and sensual, and his eyes shone with that insulting cockiness high school boys assume. [p. 31]

When Shark commands Alice never to see Jimmie, the adjuration simply sparks her interest: "After a number of repetitions of this order, a conviction crept into the thickened cells of Alice's brain that she would really like to see Jimmie Munroe" (p. 33). She becomes the unsullied Eve wistful for the forbidden fruit.

Shark is called away to Oakland to attend his Aunt Nellie's funeral on the same weekend that Tom Breman invites Katherine and Alice Wicks to the school dance. Katherine has never tasted the freedom of making her own decisions before, and it bears a sweet taste to her. The tempter in the garden of the schoolhouse dance is Jimmie Munroe. At the dance Jimmie moves in on the beautiful Alice, casually whisks her outside, and tutors her in the art of kissing, an art she finds most attractive.

Steinbeck took pains in this section of the story to depict Jimmie as the accident, rather than the villainous perpetrator, of the figurative fall from grace. In his initial draft of the story, he presented Jimmie as really quite an evil rake, a masterly seducer. The Shark Wicks story itself endured considerable stylistic revision in which phrasing is smoothed or substituted. The revision involving Jimmie Munroe is clearly substantive, however. His character is decisively softened, even made charming. In the ledger, the original passage reads as follows:

Jimmy was a town boy. He overcame obstacles by scoffing at them. It was the rule of his life never to let anything amaze him. Consequently when the lonely Alice entered the school house it took him only a fraction of a second to convince himself that he had spent his life in impudent converse with beautiful women. He swooped like a lazy hawk. . . .

"It's hot in here. Let's go outside," he suggested and led her out under the willow trees in the school yard. There he folded her in his arms and kissed her long on the lips. "We're going to get on," he said as he released her.

Alice backed away, frightened and pleased, "Now, now will I get a baby?" she asked dully. For a moment Jimmy look[ed] with amazement into her cloud[y] eyes and then he saw—of course he saw. He laughed shrilly and put his arm around her waist and strained her against him. "You're just wasting your time her[e]," he said. "You ought to come into high school." "Pa won't let me, said Alice. "Don't know as I blame him. God! That's a good one. Baby, I knew I was hot, but nobody every told me I was that hot. Goin' to have a baby. God! That's a good one." [*POH-1*]

In the final version, the entire passage is cut back to two brief paragraphs that allow the reader to fill in any untoward activity:

> Jimmie found that Alice danced badly. When the music stopped, "It's hot in here, isn't it? Let's stroll outside," he suggested. And he led her out under the willow trees in the schoolhouse yard.
> Meanwhile a woman who had been standing on the porch of the schoolhouse went outside and whispered in Katherine's ear. Katherine stared up and hurried outside. "Alice!" she called wildly. "Alice, you come right here!" [p. 37]

In the revised draft, the reader experiences the scene through Katherine, rather than by watching Jimmie with Alice. Moreover, Alice herself reports what happened. The effect of the revision is to humanize the scene. Rather than seeing Jimmie as the demonic intruder upon Shark Wick's Eden, the reader sees Shark's Eden collapsing within itself simply because he tried to separate it from reality and, finally, because he cannot.

Thus, when T. B. Allen reports the evening's events to Shark Wicks, the ultimate fall from fantasy is Shark's own doing: "While he glared at T. B. Allen, his brain fought with the problem of his daughter's impurity. It did not occur to him that the passage had stopped with a kiss" (p. 41). Going with his rifle to confront Jimmie, Shark is arrested and forced to post a peace bond. So it is that the secret of his fantasy comes out; he hasn't the money to post bond.

Shark is a ruined man, and the story might well have ended there. The fantasy dream cannot survive in its ancient warfare with reality. That has been demonstrated. But Steinbeck gives the story a peculiar twist that allows it to end in solace rather than suffering. Here is the rest of the story in the passage east of Eden: human comfort allays the whiplash of reality and makes life endurable.

Out of the ashes of Shark's dream and out of the abject sterility of her own years on his farm, Katherine rises with the resources of her own dream: "She did a thing she had never contemplated in her life. A warm genius moved in her. Katherine sat down on the edge of the bed and with a sure hand, took Shark's head on her lap. This was instinct, and the same sure, strong instinct set her hand to stroking Shark's forehead" (p. 44). She is the nurturer in a fallen world, expressing a flood of humankindness that washes away the gritty residue of broken hopes. In an image evoking the tenderness of Rose of Sharon in *The Grapes of Wrath*, Katherine grows large in her expression of love: "Katherine stroked his head gently and the great genius continued to grow in her. She felt larger than the world. The whole world lay in her lap and she comforted it. Pity seemed to make her huge in stature. Her soothing breasts yearned toward the woe of the world" (pp. 44–45). Shark and Katherine awaken from a nightmare to the realization of the power of love in human reality. Shark's skinny body jerks into life: "Her genius passed into him." The concluding comments signify a new start: "'I'll go soon,' he cried. 'I'll go just as soon as I can sell the ranch. Then I'll get in a few licks. I'll get my chance then. I'll show people what I am'" (p. 46).

The conclusion of the Shark Wicks story is ambiguous. It can be read as the birth of one more fantasy. Will Shark be able to show people what he is? One might argue that he has just done so. The revelation was of a weak dreamer, a man incapable of dealing with reality. It might also be read as a redemptive action, however. Shark's source of strength emanates, in this case, not from some perverted fantasy but

from the human source of Katherine, precisely the resource he had neglected in his prior fantasy world. The
conclusion seems more properly read as redemptive. It
demonstrates a way of combating the curse rather than
being beaten by it. Shark has placed his heel on the serpent's head, realizing as he does so that his own eyes stare
out at him under that heel. If he is driven out of Eden,
however, he now finds the steadfast support of Katherine
by his side.

Raymond Banks seems, upon first glance, the antithesis
to Shark Wicks. Earthy, ruddy, brimming with good cheer,
he is a man of huge, good-hearted energy. It is surprising to
find a little bit of Shark Wicks dwelling within him. Shark
Wicks awakens to the reality of the valley he lives in. Raymond Banks awakens to the fact that real human beings,
complete with systems of fear and pain, are hung from the
gallows at San Quentin. While Shark's fantasy is a paper
fortune that denies present reality, it may be argued that
Raymond's fantasy is the present reality, which denies the
world of emotion and imagination.

Raymond Banks's farm, the jewel at the crowning north
end of the valley, is a shrine of compulsive cleanliness and
order. From the neat tally of "five thousand white chickens
and one thousand white ducks," to the immaculately whitewashed chicken house, to the whitewashed Banks's home,
we find the human hand exercising dominion over the land.
In this pristine world of glowing whiteness, Raymond Banks
rules like a ruddy king: "Every exposed part of him was
burned beef-red by the sun, his heavy arms to the elbows,
his neck down into his collar, his face, and particularly his
ears and nose were painfully burned and chapped. Thin
blond hair could not protect his scalp from reddening under
the sun" (pp. 156–57). The clash of red against white is por-
tentous, as much so as the sudden squirt of blood down the
white chicken's throat. It is very much a story about the discovery of a seething undercurrent of red emotions under a
whitewashed veneer.

The initial portrait of Raymond Banks also conveys an essential tension in him. Steinbeck pairs paragraphs, back to back, as if giving a dual perspective on the man. There are two sides to him, one of which he has not yet discovered. In the first paragraph the portrait is vaguely foreboding. An exceedingly strong man, with "thick, short arms, wide shoulders and hips and heavy legs," Raymond exudes a kind of primitive force. The portrait is accentuated by eyes "black as soot" and a "villainously beaked nose." In the mirror paragraph that follows, Banks is described as the people of the valley see him—exuberant, boisterous, jolly. He does not speak so much as emit a hearty roar of good cheer. He lifts spirits, sets people laughing:

He said things, even the commonest of things, as though they were funny. People laughed whenever he spoke. At Christmas parties in the schoolhouse, Raymond was invariably chosen as the Santa Claus because of his hearty voice, his red face and his love for children. He abused children with such a heavy ferocity that he kept them laughing all the time. [p. 157]

If Raymond is Santa Claus, Cleo Banks is Mrs. Claus: "She was so jolly. She made people feel good. No one could ever remember that she said anything, but months after hearing it, they could recall the exact tones of her laughter" (p. 160).

The complex pattern of colors, the jarring contrast of the whiteness of the farm and the red cheer of Raymond and Cleo, and the strange darkness of Raymond's eyes and his villainous nose in a face as raw as hamburger capture the sense of internal conflicts that human nature bears.[27] It would be a mistake to see Raymond Banks, however, as a secretively villainous person with a macabre attraction to the violence of the hangings he so willingly attends. Just the opposite. The hangings, first of all, give him his only vacation, a chance to get together two or three times a year with his boyhood chum, now the prison warden. Moreover, Raymond has no intrinsically perverse attraction to killing. Indeed, Steinbeck denies this attitude by his careful depiction of the surgical precision with which he kills his chickens. With young children watching, he carefully warns them against trying it:

> He refused to let the boys help with the killing, although they asked him many times. "You might get excited and miss the brain," he said. "That would hurt the chicken, if you didn't stick him just right." [p. 159]

Yet, the hangings do stir something within him, something belied and displaced by the order of his farm and his daily routine:

> The hanging itself was not the important part, it was the sharp, keen air of the whole proceeding that impressed him. It was like a super-church, solemn and ceremonious and somber. The whole thing made him feel a fullness of experience, a holy emotion that nothing else in his life approached. Raymond didn't think of the condemned anymore than he thought of the chicken when he pressed the blade into its brain. No strain of cruelty nor any gloating over suffering took him to the gallows. He had developed an appetite for profound emotion, and his meager imagination was unable to feed it. [p. 161]

To this point, his imagination has steadfastly sublimated the primitive urge toward violence or evil in human nature. It is stirred into recognition by Bert Munroe.

While the Munroe family is indirectly tied to every bad event in these stories because they bring the "cloud of evil," for the most part their tie to such events is coincidental or peripheral. The Munroes, too, are making the best of their way in a crooked world. They are not malign people, not moral monstrosities of the same order as Cathy Ames in *East of Eden*. The one exception to this pattern lies in this story, for it is Bert Munroe who fills the unimaginative head of Raymond Banks with the grotesque writhings of his own memories. Bert's vivid imagination, filled with a childhood horror, concocts a world of fears in Raymond Banks. While it is a catharsis for Bert, it is an infection for Raymond. This is a clear case of the displacement of the curse from one to another.

"Before he ever saw Raymond, Bert Munroe pictured him as a traditional executioner, a lank, dark man, with a dull, deathly eye; a cold, nerveless man. The very thought of Raymond filled Bert with a kind of interested foreboding" (p. 162). As in the narrator's earlier paired descriptions of Raymond, Bert is surprised to find the outward appearance of such ordered calm and joviality: "The very health and heartiness of Raymond seemed incongruous and strangely obscene. The paradox of his good nature and his love for children was unseemly" (p. 163). Possessed by his own Imp of the Perverse, a secret craving for violence and danger, Bert confesses his secret desire to see a hanging. His civilized self does not want to see this thing, yet he cannot stop himself from willing it.

Bert's increasing irritability and nervousness begin to infect Raymond. Like a contagious disease, the dark germ of pain and fear infiltrates Raymond's mind. The transmitting event lies in killing chickens. Raymond dispatches his chickens with painless precision and celebrates by entertaining the neighbors. But for Bert, killing chickens evokes a painful childhood memory, and he is unable to eat chicken or participate in the festivity. Each time, the memory of an old man hacking at the chicken with a hatchet, finally severing his own finger, surges up in gruesome detail. Bert secretly hopes to purge his horror by witnessing a hanging. Despite Raymond's protests about the clinical sureness of the hangings, Bert finds himself obsessed by an imagined horror. He recalls a case in Arizona where a woman's head was pulled off. He imagines himself in the place of the condemned person, waiting the awful moment when the knot tightens.

When Raymond angrily denies such feelings, Bert jabs him at his weak point: "If you had any imagination, I wouldn't have to tell you. If you had any imagination, you'd see for yourself, and you wouldn't go up to see some poor devil get killed" (p. 174). The accusation bears a certain truth. Raymond is singularly lacking in imaginative qualities, but now, for the first time, he feels the disquieting squirm of that quality in his mind. He writes the warden that they will not be coming. A new world has been opened for him, and he finds the terrible possibilities of it overwhelming. Raymond Banks's orderly white world lies threatened by the red wound of suffering. He had been able to inure himself to its reality by a neat routine and a singular lack of imagination. Prompted by Bert's "death row" confession, the reality of the imaginative world threatens every routine he knows.

In *The Wide World of John Steinbeck*, Peter Lisca argues that Bert Munroe takes a kind of perverse pleasure in tainting Raymond's mind:

> With Bert Munroe, however, it is clear that the attitude toward violence is morbid. He enjoys shivering at the horrible images of suffering which his mind readily conjures up. And it is obvious that he enjoys describing to Raymond in detail the incident from his youth and the possibility of a person's being strangled instead of having his neck broken. . . . It is obvious that Steinbeck intends to show that Raymond has the healthy attitude and that it is Bert Munroe who has the sick one.[28]

It seems more reasonable to see the action as cathartic for Bert. Rather than "enjoying" it, he agonizes over it: "The choked feeling of illness was becoming a strange panting congestion of desire. The desire puzzled Bert and worried him. He didn't want to go to San Quentin. It would make him unhappy to see a man hanged. But he was glad he had asked to go. His very gladness worried him" (p. 167).

Such a view would be more consistent with the book as a whole. The Munroe family spreads a curse, but they are not deliberately perverting their neighbors. Steinbeck made his intentions in this matter perfectly clear, and it would seem clear enough in the text also. Joseph Fontenrose perceives the pattern accurately when he observes, "What the Munroe act provided for each principal was a moment of truth, when he clearly saw the emptiness of his condition."[29] Such is precisely the case with Raymond Banks. Bert shows him an imaginative realm wholly lacking in him before, a moment of truth that was to alter his perception of reality. The story gives a poignant and unusual twist to a theme that Steinbeck would use often in future years. Often he sees the artistic imagination and the individual dream at odds with pragmatic reality. But the dream itself, he shows here, can also be a destructive thing to the untutored imagination. Early in the story, when the reader first sees the glistening white farm sprawled against the green pastures, a red-tailed hawk suddenly dives over the panicked chickens. Bert triggers the shotgun and frightens the hawk away. The chickens spread out once more, oblivious to the threat that has now passed. Human nature will not have matters quite so neat. No one stands with a shotgun to blast red fear from the orderly patterns of a mind. Yet those fears persist in coming, diving suddenly out of nowhere. In the case of Raymond Banks, it leaves an ineradicable scar against the neat order of his emotional life.

ESCAPE FROM THE PAST:
HELEN VAN DEVENTER AND PAT HUMBERT

In the "Descent into Hell" from *Joseph and His Brothers*, Thomas Mann observes, "Very deep is the well of the past. Should we not call it bottomless?" When we allow the mind to plumb that well, it finds hazards lurking in the depths. Recoiling before them, humanity attempts to reshape its own past in order to live in the present. It cannot be so, of course. The bottomless well of the past cannot be fully known, nor reshaped, nor escaped.

Yet humanity persists in the impossible dream of a new beginning. Like the corporal at the beginning of *The Pastures of Heaven* or each of the inhabitants in the years following, people make their way to the valley trailing a past from which they hope to escape, only to find it rising up to greet them in the most unexpected ways. There can be no new Eden; they bear in them the inextricable past of that first Eden, the long lineage of human suffering at their backs, marking every step of the present. Nonetheless, the characters in *The Pastures of Heaven* strive to shape a new world in which they might escape the past. Helen Van Deventer and Pat Humbert represent two means of doing so, both of them failed means in the end. Helen attempts the steely gaze of tragic endurance; Pat attempts the phoenix-like rebirth from parental dominion. One discovers that tragic endurance is met by enduring tragedy; the other learns that he cannot shake off the ashes of the past and that the fires of his parents' grip upon him will consume him.

Helen Van Deventer, like Helen of Troy, is a woman born for tragedy. While some people bear the burden of tragedy with nobility and never let it darken their souls, Helen's experience of tragedy is intrinsic to her nature: "She hungered for tragedy and life had lavishly heaped it upon her." With painful regularity, the wheel of fate deals her tragedies in six-month cycles. She mourns for her Persian kitten six months. Her father died six months after the kitten, instituting a new cycle of mourning. Her husband Hubert hunts six months of the year, and three months after their marriage fatally wounds himself in a hunting accident. Her daughter, Hilda, her final tragedy, was born six months following. At age six, Hilda is diagnosed as mentally troubled, an illness that deepens into the psychosis of schizophrenia in the years to come. Tragedy is a regular beat in Helen's life, pulsing blows at her in regular cycles.

Helen's reaction to these blows is, in itself, tragic. She walls herself in the world of tragedy, accepting it obdurately and blindly as an irrevocable world. When Dr. Phillips challenges her to see life whole, Helen is adamant in her insistence: "We take what is given us. I can endure. I am sure of that, and I am proud of it. No amount of tragedy can break down my endurance" (p. 66). Like the fourth-century Stoics, Helen assumes the inevitability of fate. For the Stoics, virtue was an action of the internal will, a disposition of

the soul that makes one superior to external events. Helen's
stoic countenance will shatter, however, when she takes
her own fate into her hands at the close of the story. Steinbeck does not permit the escape into stoic determinism.
In keeping with her fatalism, Helen's retreat to the Pastures is not an effort to flee tragedy or reorder her life but
to perpetuate her scenario of tragic endurance untouched
by larger realities. The house she builds is a prison of the
soul, reflecting a kind of iron will imposed upon life. While
Hilda's dreams rage into a world of fantasy and Helen lan-
guishes in a world of blind acceptance, the Van Deventer
grounds bear the imprint of a cruel order. Bert Munroe reports, "Every log is perfect, and what do you know, you've
got gardeners working there already" (p. 71). It is as if present reality does not exist, as if one can make one's own kingdom by an act of the will.

Life isn't like that, Dr. Phillips points out. Life has little
patience with iron wills and will melt them in the heat of
tragic onslaught. To be whole, to be human, requires the
ability to bend and flow with the patterns of life. Helen's
adamancy lies in contrast to some of Steinbeck's later hero-
ines, women who have the ability to bend with life and
thereby endure. Ma Joad, in her moment of crisis, reflects,
"Woman can change better'n a man. . . . Woman, it's all
one flow, like a stream, little eddies, little waterfalls, but
the river, it goes right on. Woman looks at it like that. We
ain't gonna die out. People is goin' on—changin' a little,
maybe, but goin' right on."[30] Similarly, in the dramatic confrontation between Juana and Kino in *The Pearl*, Juana reflects how "the mountain would stand while the man broke
himself," and how, therefore, a man had need of the woman
whose qualities of reason, caution, and preservation would
help him endure.[31] Helen Van Deventer is more like the
man, blindly beating his head against the stone mountains.

When Dr. Phillips advises her, "You simply cannot go on
as you are. It isn't fair to yourself," Helen responds, "I can
endure anything, but I cannot send her away" (p. 70). Angered at her insistence, Dr. Phillips points out, "You love

the hair shirt. . . . Your pain is a pleasure. You won't give up any little shred of tragedy" (p. 70).

While it might be tempting to see Helen Van Deventer as a hero of tragic endurance, in Steinbeck's design she is not. She has cut herself off from reality as surely as Hilda's schizophrenia has cut her off from reality. Although thoroughly painful, Helen's world is ultimately a fantasy world, severed from life and bearing its inevitable judgment.

Nowhere is the fantasy more evident than in Helen's evocation of her dream of a ruined past, wrought into the very construction of her home. The home itself comes to represent the prison of tragic endurance. In the living room, she has designed a shrine to her dead husband: "In her design for the living room of the cabin Helen felt that she had created a kind of memorial to her husband. She had made it look as much as possible like a hunting lodge" (p. 76). The point of it is to retain, if not to change altogether, the past: "Helen felt that she would not completely lose her husband as long as she had a room like this to sit in" (p. 76).

If, according to Thomas Mann, the past is a bottomless well from which we can never fully extricate ourselves nor plumb its vast depths, it is also true that the past is an elusive thing. Like Shark Wicks with his retroactive manipulation of his fantasy fortune, we tend to reshape it to fit the convenience of our present. If Helen's living room is patterned after the drawing room in San Francisco, where in seance-like reveries she evokes the ghost of the past, it is altogether clear that she is recreating the past in her mind to fit her concept of herself as a creature of tragic endurance in the present. She fails to understand, as Dr. Phillips so urgently encourages her, that each action of the present has the potential of liberation from the past.

Oddly enough, the tragedy of this story occurs just as Helen begins to feel the stirrings of present life in her again. The Pastures seems to work its strange magic upon her spirit. Walking among her well-kept gardens one day, she feels "foolishly happy." Suffused by a "new, delicious peacefulness," the sight of a rabbit makes her "quiver with pleasure." The house is just possibly a haven, the gardens a kind of paradise walled against the past by the beneficent ring of hills about the Pastures. Helen reflects, in a spirit she has never permitted herself before, "I haven't looked forward to anything for ages. Isn't that funny? Or is it sad? But now I'm looking forward to something. I'm just bursting with anticipation. And I don't know what the something can be" (p. 79).

At this moment, Helen begins to feel the awesome weight of the past recede slightly: "She realized that she didn't want to think of Hubert any more." Hilda relates her strange fantasy, stirred by Bert Munroe's visit. Two fantasy worlds are about to collide: Helen's tragic forebearance and Hilda's schizophrenic dissociation. Fighting her way through to a clearer recognition of reality—that she doesn't have to be dominated by the past, that her daughter is hopelessly ill—Helen finds the sad ghost of Hubert slipping away: "She was not building the figure of her husband. He was gone, completely gone. For the first time in years, Helen put her hands to her face and cried, for the peace had come back, and the bursting expectancy" (p. 82). Free of the ghostly presence that has haunted her, she realizes now that the Pastures is a life-bringer: "She leaned out of the window and listened. So many little noises came from the garden and from the hill beyond the garden. 'It's just infested with life,' she thought, 'It's just bursting with life'" (pp. 82–83).

At that very moment, however, she also hears the rasping of the saw as Hilda breaks through the wooden bars on her window. Helen can escape the tragic legacy of the past in only one way. With "her face paled and her lips set in the old line of endurance," she walks to the living room, takes down Hubert's shotgun, and sets out after Hilda.

For a moment, only a moment, Helen escaped the past. A bright direction shone, however fleetingly, in the moonlit garden. When Dr. Phillips comes to her after the shooting, he finds, "She didn't look afraid. In her severe, her almost savage mourning, she looked as enduring as a sea-

washed stone" (p. 83). There is nothing left for Helen but
the stoic endurance that has shaped her: "'By this time I
know what my life expects of me,' she said softly. 'Now I
know what I have always suspected. And I have the strength
to endure, Doctor. Don't you worry about me'" (p. 84).

As Helen Van Deventer witnesses a moment of freedom,
only to have the past come crashing down upon it, so too
Pat Humbert tries desperately to escape the past of his parents' hold upon him. Helen cannot shake off Hubert's ghost;
his shotgun is used to kill Hilda. Pat Humbert cannot shake
off his parents' ghost; their eyes watch him. Both stories are
gripping psychological portraits of a mind in bondage to
the past.

The theme of "Pat Humbert" is stated early: "Youth was
a clumsy, fumbling preparation for excellent old age. Youth
should think of nothing but the duty it owed to age, of the
courtesy and veneration due to age. On the other hand, age
owed no courtesy whatever to youth" (p. 177). The parents
rear Pat in hatred of youth, raising him to be an austere old
man from the cradle on. Thus, two levels develop in the
story. In the first, Pat is born an adult, never having had
time or a place for childhood. At the second level, Pat, as
an adult, becomes the child, attempting to deny his parents
and to create the fairy-tale kingdom that eluded him in his
youth. He will be the prince; Mae Munroe, the princess.
The fairy-tale world also has its wicked witch: the eyes of
Pat's mother. This regression and the tensions produced by
it creates the psychological drama of the story.

Pat's parents die within a month of each other when he is
thirty years old.[32] Even as his mother dies, however, "her
eyes still accused him." They never stop. Steinbeck pin-
points their accusation: "Toward the end of their lives, they
really hated Pat for being young" (p. 178). He has never
had a chance to be young, or to grow up to be his own person. Their deaths, then, signal a reversion in Pat as he attempts to recapture a lost youth.

At the cemetery he stands before the grave like a bewildered child: "He didn't know what to do now there was

no one to demand anything of him" (p. 180). When he finds his way back home, the house creaks with his parents' admonitions: "'There'll be frost,' his father said. 'I hate the frost worse than rats.' And his mother chimed in, 'Speaking of rats—I have a feeling there's rats in the cellar. I wonder if Pat has set the traps this year past. I told him to, but he forgets everything I tell him'" (p. 182). Only a "cold sense of duty" drives him to the tasks. With the morning light, however, the little boy that has never broken free revolts within him. Like a three-year-old, defiant in his first sense of individuality, Pat denies the call to duty:

"Why should I go in there?" he demanded. "There's no one to care, no one even to know. I don't have to go in there if I don't want to." He felt like a boy who breaks school to walk in a deep and satisfying forest. But to combat his freedom his mother's complaining voice came to his ears. "Pat ought to clean the house. Pat never takes care of things."

The joy of revolt surged up in him. "You're dead!" he told the voice. [p. 184]

While the "spirit was still strong in him," he locks the ghosts in the parlor, throws the key into the weeds, and nails the shutters over the windows.

Pat has locked duty away, but in his childlike state he can find no replacement. Starved for company, Pat is attracted to any place in the valley where two or three are gathered together, simply to enter the converse of human life. He volunteers for activities with an avidity born of loneliness. For ten years Pat pursues his lonely way, gripped by a "terror of being solitary." So consuming is his loneliness that he loses a perception of others as anything else than assuagement for it: "He did not often think of people as individuals, but rather as antidotes for the poison of his loneliness, as escapes from their imprisoned ghosts" (pp. 188–89). Until he meets Mae Munroe.

Pat has a dream to pursue then, and like the prince smitten with love for the fairy-tale princess, he builds his Vermont-styled cottage to woo her. In a flurry of energy he ransacks the locked room, tossing out his parents' belongings, including the huge old Bible, which represents the rigidity and order of their rule. The bonfire he lights is a kind of ritual destruction of the past, a cleansing of the ghosts of his parents from his memory: "'You *would* sit in there all these years, wouldn't you?' he cried. 'You thought I'd never get up the guts to burn you. Well, I just wish you could be around to see what I'm going to do, you rotten stinking trash'" (p. 194). From the ruins he constructs his dream home.

Like an adolescent dreamer, Pat stages his love drama in his new house, imagining little scenes where he reveals the shining dream to Mae. He practices snatches of romantic dialogue. He has wooed and won her a thousand times in his dreams. The problem, of course, is that he is dreaming, not acting. And while Pat plots his desperate assignations of Mae Munroe, the princess of his fairy tale is being sedulously courted by another.

The plot stops short of the prince carrying the princess over the threshold. In his first thirty years, Pat never had time for childhood. In ten years he has reverted to childhood, from infant-like fear and uncertainty, to a toddler's revolt in the obdurate "no" to his parents, to a pubescent fantasy world and dream-like sexuality, and now to adolescent confusion. He approaches manhood and cannot act on it. He cannot force himself to take the risks of maturity, and so his dream stalls: "Now that he was ready, a powerful reluctance stopped him. Evening after evening passed while he put off asking her to come" (p. 199).

Forcing himself at last to confront his fairy bride, Pat Humbert arrives at the Munroe household on the very evening that they are celebrating Mae's engagement to Bill Whiteside. In subtle contrast to Pat, Bill is the consummate pragmatist. He has already been shown in the Molly Morgan story to be incapable of romantic dreams. His cutting remarks about Molly's absent father dash her dream. He refuses to see anything romantic in the outlaw Vasquez—simply another cheap crook. Bill is a man good with cattle, with trade and profit. Ironically, he will carry Mae off to his own castle, but it will be outside the Pastures: he decides to buy into a Ford dealership in Monterey and build his own home there. Pat Humbert simply has never considered this realm of practical reality in his dream world. Never allowed to dream when he grew up, his dream possesses him when his parents die.

Pat returns to his dream cottage that night, but it no longer bears the radiance of the fairy tale. In fact, it bears precisely the same description it did when he returned from his parents' funeral ten years prior. Then Pat returned to hear his mother's querulous voice ordering him around: "The house was black and unutterably dreary when he arrived" (p. 183). Now he heads home once again to find that "the rambling house was dark and unutterably dreary when he arrived" (p. 201). Pat has had one brief, little dream between two prolonged darknesses. This time he cannot even enter the house, as he could not enter the parlor before. He turns instead to the barn to sleep, for inside the house the ghosts of his parents gaze "wistfully into the ghost of a fire" (p. 201).

Pat Humbert's story thrusts the crushing weight of the past and the fleeting dream of the present into dramatic conflict. This is the curse he bears: the voices of his parents creaking in the dry timbers of the house. While Helen Van Deventer tries to destroy the past by a shotgun blast, Pat tries to escape the past by building a fairy-tale kingdom. Neither suffices.

Because of that, the two stories remain the bleaker portraits in *The Pastures of Heaven*. To Bo Beskow in September 1950, Steinbeck wrote, "I have not grown up. And I am only two years short of 50. I have very little time. I would like to be an adult part of that time. There are too many disappointments for a child. The world will not give the party he has designed and so he loves no party" (*SLL*, p. 410). He reflects, furthermore, "It is the first symptom of adulthood—I cannot be God" (*SLL*, p. 411). In a sense, the same observation might apply to Helen Van Deventer and Pat Humbert. Both are children playing at being God, thinking that they can design and effect the order of their lives. But the world will not have it so. If the world comes to the party they have planned, it comes with fearful surprise—a crushing revelation that strips away the childlike gaiety and forces recognition of the darker side of reality.

4

The Red Pony: "The Desolation of Loss"

WHEN IN FEBRUARY 1932 the firm reorganized as Jonathan
Cape and Robert Ballou, Inc., issued a contract for *The Pastures of Heaven*, it also signed the next two novels Steinbeck
produced: "There are three contracts, one for The Pastures
of Heaven and one each for two later mss which are simply
named by their succession. The publisher binds himself to
publish the things sight unseen" (*SLL*, p. 61). Although the
Great Depression was about to make these "binding" prom-
ises little more than dreams, the rare praise spurred Steinbeck's work. His first action was typical for a writer: What
do I have on hand? The unwieldy carcass of *To a God Unknown* had been lying around in unsettled stages for several years. For the first half of 1932, Steinbeck again wres-
tled with the manuscript to prepare it for publication.

By mid-1932, however, his mind was running to other
stories he wanted to tell. In June 1932, Robert Ballou, now
with the firm of Brewer, Warren and Putnam, requested
biographical data to be used for publicity. For Steinbeck,
the request evoked memories of the past and his personal
stories. He was still hovering between writing of the people
and places he knew, as in *The Pastures of Heaven*, and
writing of the great mythic concepts that fired his imagination, as in *To a God Unknown*. The request pointed a direction, and Steinbeck reflected in reply,

Immediately there arises a problem of emphasis. Things of the
greatest emphasis to me would be more or less meaningless to
anyone else. Such a biography would consist of such things as—

117

the way the sparrows hopped about on the mud street early in the morning when I was little—how the noon bell sounded when we were writing dirty words on the sidewalk with red fuchsia berries—how Teddy got run over by a fire engine, and the desolation of loss—the most tremendous morning in the world when my pony had a cold. [*SLL*, pp. 62–63]

For the first time, the possibility of the story of the red pony arises. With it arose his greatest challenge of a writer: making those "things of greatest emphasis to me" and perhaps "meaningless to anyone else" meaningful to anyone else by the alchemy of art.

By early January 1933, Steinbeck had finished work on *To a God Unknown* and was now looking for a new subject. In a letter to Mavis McIntosh, he lists in remarkable detail a series of possible short stories. Each of them evolves directly from his own past. Writing them, however, was stalled by the sudden illness of Steinbeck's mother in March 1933. Paralyzed by a massive stroke, she was hospitalized until June when she returned to the family house on Central Avenue, where John, as the only child free from the rigors of a regular job, moved to tend her. There he began writing the *Red Pony* stories, living once more in his childhood home and tending his ill mother and increasingly bewildered father. The reversion to the childhood stories of Jody, as Jackson Benson points out, "gains an extra measure of poignancy when placed within the circumstances of its composition."[1]

Steinbeck wrote George Albee at this time, "I have the pony story about half written. I like it pretty well. It is more being written for discipline than for any other reason. I mean if I can write any kind of a story at a time like this, then I can write stories" (*SLL*, p. 71). He goes on to describe the action and style of the first story:

It is a very simple story about a boy who gets a colt pony and the pony gets distemper. There is a good deal in it, first about the training of horses and second about the treatment of distemper. This may not seem like a good basis for a story but that entirely depends upon the treatment. The whole thing is as simply told as though it came out of the boy's mind although there is no going into the boy's mind. It is an attempt to make the reader create the boy's mind for himself. An interesting experiment you see if nothing else. [*SLL*, p. 71]

The backdrop of a confrontation with his own past while living again in the family home, the prolonged dying of his mother, and the recollection of childhood provide a rich thematic context for these stories. They are very much about the realization of lost youth, maturity through understanding of death, and the loss of innocence.

The writing itself was anything but an easy passage. Fractured by incessant demands, it seemed an erratic diversion rather than a concentrated effort. Steinbeck recounts the effort in a letter to Albee:

The pony story, you can understand has been put off for a while. But now I spend about seven hours a day in the hospital and I am trying to go on with it, but with not a great deal of success, because partly I have to fight an atmosphere of blue fog so thick and so endless that I can see no opening in it. However, if I can do it, it will be good. Anyone can write when the situation is propitious. [*SLL*, p. 73]

A few days later he again wrote Albee, this time telling how he was trying to type the second draft of the story while being constantly interrupted to tend his mother: "One paragraph—help lift patient on bed pan. Back, a little ill, three paragraphs, help turn patient so sheets can be changed" (*SLL*, p. 83). Steinbeck made a poor nurse. He openly confessed to a "fear and hatred of illness and incapacity which amounts to a mania" (*SLL*, p. 83) and often returned to the typewriter feeling nauseated and emotionally drained. Yet, the story developed steadily and deliberately.

This period also marked the growth of Steinbeck's intense interest in his phalanx theory. In a June 21, 1933, letter to Carlton Sheffield, Steinbeck relates the group organism concept to his mother's illness: "Half of the cell units of my mother's body have rebelled. Neither has died, but the devolution has changed her functions. That is cruel to say. . . . She, as a human unit, is deterred from functioning as she ordinarily did by a schism of a number of her cells" (*SLL*, p. 76). He also announces that "when the parts of this thesis have found their places, I'll start trying to put them into the symbolism of fiction."

At this point, in June, Steinbeck had not yet seen a link between the *Red Pony* stories and the phalanx. Having finished writing "The Gift" in late June 1933, he wrote, "It was good training in self control and that's about all the good it is. Now I have my new theme to think about there will be a few loopholes in my days. I can think about it while helping with a bed pan" (p. 78). Steinbeck's intention with the stories was to keep them narratively pure, free from the philosophical burden that weighed down *To a God Unknown:* "It is an unpretentious story. I think the philosophic content is so buried that it will not bother anybody" (*SLL*, p. 85). Nonetheless, as the writing continued over the summer of 1933 and the phalanx ideas developed simultaneously, if largely through his correspondence, one begins to observe an overlap between the two. There are huge, amorphous patterns in this life that one cannot fully control, that seem to develop a force and life of their own. One such pattern is death itself. How we deal with the force, submitting blindly to it or battling against it and maturing through it, determines our own place in life.

The stories were also a bit like a phalanx, acquiring a life of their own that forged steadily onward. Writing continued into the fall of 1933, when Steinbeck started the first writing on *Tortilla Flat* in the notebook containing some of the *Red Pony* stories. The *Tortilla Flat* draft, with the central character identified as Bennie, then Benny, covers roughly eighty pages of the ledger in a complete draft. The "Beans and Tortillas" story of Señora Terrasina Cortez follows, to be incorporated into the revised novel, then the first draft of "The Murder" and several drafts of "The Chrysanthemums."² At the end of the ledger, in early 1934, Steinbeck returned again to the *Red Pony* stories.

By May 1934, now working in the ledger notebook that would contain stories for *The Long Valley*, Steinbeck had apparently exhausted the *Red Pony* stories. He announces,

I think I'll get to some short stories. I feel that I should be able to do one story a week. In two or three months I would have enough for a volume or more and maybe it could come out. I don't know. But I must work like a dog. I do know that. And why not after all. There's no reason why if I do my work every day—see few people, think, walk some, I shouldn't get a good series out. Things are ticking along in my head all ready." [*LVN*]

He comments that he had written five stories of "Jody, or in which Jody was the eyes." The fifth story, if it was written, has not survived. Perhaps the fifth existed only in Steinbeck's mind, for following the note he outlines a *Red Pony* story in which Jody and his mother go to church, Carl Tiflin having refused to accompany them. Apparently the story would test matters of belief versus pragmatism, focusing upon Jody and his mother's seeing a ghost. Carl, who has little patience for either the imagination or faith, rejects the experience. In Carl's view, it is against "the law," and for him the law is the world of pragmatic reality. But Steinbeck cut the outline short:

After all, why should I go on with the stories of Jody—forced stories. I have two of them in New York now. If they want more, I'll send them when they've used up what I sent. Meanwhile why shouldn't I write some for a possibly more expensive market. There's nothing holding me to these stories save an apparent willingness on the part of the magazine to buy them. Let's do something else for a change then. Something more to liking. Something it isn't necessary to force. That shouldn't be too hard. I know, I'll tell the story of the raid in Watsonville. [*LVN*]

Apparently, the stories were finished as a series, and his attention turned to the new activity of the stories that would eventually comprise *The Long Valley*. They did, however, open the door to a paying market. By the end of the summer of 1933, McIntosh and Otis had placed two of the *Red Pony* stories, "The Gift" and "The Great Mountains," with *North American Review*, a periodical with a limited circulation but excellent prestige. They appeared in the November 1933 and December 1933 issues. Subsequently, the periodical purchased three additional stories, "The Murder," "The White Quail," and "The Raid" for between forty-five and fifty dollars each. "The Promise," written in the winter of 1934, was turned down for publication by the *North American Review* but was eventually published in *Harper's Magazine* in August 1937. "The Leader of the People," written in late winter or early spring of 1934, was first published in the British periodical *Argosy* in August 1936.

Written during a period of acute psychological duress, the *Red Pony* stories have a richness of narrative texture and theme that has made them a treasured addition to anthologies and a treasure trove to critics. They possess a belying simplicity of tone and point of view, but one that is extremely difficult to capture fictionally. The contrast between the youthful innocence of Jody and the pragmatic vision of his elders has made the stories enduring favorites at the high-school level. The forceful grappling with death and the rich stylistic qualities have enamored scholars.

Accepting Steinbeck's fundamental premise of a young boy's initiatory experiences, several critics have divided that experience into psychological categories. Joseph Fontenrose views the story as a "passage from naive childhood to the threshold of adulthood through knowledge of birth, old age, and death, gained through experience with horses," the whole of which he likens to Faulkner's "The Bear."[3] Joseph Warren Beach likens it to Marjorie Rawlings's *The Yearling*,[4] and Arnold Goldsmith observes a resemblance to Hemingway's Nick Adams stories.[5] The comparison with Hemingway is also developed by Mimi Gladstein in her analysis of Jody's growing into a "person," which she signifies by use of the Yiddish word "mench."[6] In order to focus the initiation pattern, R. Baird Shuman applies the framework of Mircea Eliade's *Rites and Symbols of Initiation* to the story.[7] Several studies have explored symbolic properties of the tales. Frederic I. Carpenter suggests that "the red pony is also the physical symbol of the old American dream,"[8] a view that Peter Lisca deemed "possible by simplifications amounting to distortion."[9] In their exchange on the idea of westering in "The Leader of the People," Donald E. Houghton and Robert E. Morsberger demonstrate that the American dream motif is, at least, very much an issue in the final tale.[10] In his study "The Black Cypress and the Green Tub: Death and Procreation in Steinbeck's 'The Promise,'" Robert S. Hughes, Jr., argues that there is a great deal more symbolism in the stories that we observe by a casual reading.[11] His study is one of the few to provide a lucid explication of their patterns of imagery.

All these permutations of the scholarly mind are certainly important to a full appreciation of the work. As Hamlet said, "There are more things in heaven and earth, Horatio, / Than are dreamt of in your philosophy," so too any artist crafts more patterns into his work than he is consciously aware of. It is also true, as Warren French observes, that "Steinbeck was a more self-conscious narrative architect than has always been recognized, but even he in his cyclical works, like *The Pastures of Heaven, Cannery Row*, and *The Red Pony*, created more subtle patterns than he may have deliberately contemplated in providing an overall meaning for seemingly heterogeneous elements in an episodic narrative."[12]

While standing independently of each other, the *Red Pony* stories share an organic structural unity as a whole through several patterns. The first of these is a natural time progression beginning in Jody's tenth year and ending in his twelfth. "The Gift" begins in late August, with the start of the school year, and concludes with Gabilan's death shortly before Thanksgiving, at the start of the rainy winter season. "The Great Mountains" begins in midsummer of the following year, and the entire story covers less than twenty-four hours. The rage that Jody vents at the end of "The Gift" by smashing a buzzard's head carries over to the beginning of "The Great Mountains," when he kills a thrush with a stone and cuts off the bird's head. "The Gift" ends with Jody smeared with the blood from the buzzard; in "The Great Mountains," Jody "drank from the mossy tub and washed the bird's blood from his hands in cold water" (p. 240).[13]

"The Promise" begins in the spring of the following year and ends on February 2 with the death of Nellie and the birth of the black colt. "The Leader of the People" begins in the spring, when Billy Buck rakes together "the last of the old year's haystack." The stories, then, follow an annual cycle, covering events in two years of the life of Jody Tiflin.

Other subtle patterns lend a structured unity to the whole. While the first story begins at daybreak, suggesting the youth and innocence of Jody, subsequent stories begin on "a midsummer afternoon," "mid-afternoon of spring," and a "Saturday afternoon." The rhythmical pattern may be extended, as Arnold L. Goldsmith observes in "Thematic Rhythm in *The Red Pony*": "Steinbeck follows the violence of the first story with the tragic quiet of the second, with this same pattern repeated in the third and fourth sections. Where the first and third stories are about the violent deaths of horses, the second and fourth are about the twilight years of two old men."[14] The entire pattern, Goldsmith points out, represents "the neverending rhythm of life and death to which Jody is continually exposed."[15]

Throughout the cycle of changes, however, Steinbeck persistently identifies Jody, at the beginning of each story, as a youth. In "The Gift" we meet him as "only a little boy, ten years old, with hair like yellow grass and with shy polite gray eyes, and with a mouth that worked when he thought" (p. 202). In subsequent stories he is introduced each time as "the little boy Jody." Thus the larger theme emerges: A little boy is finding his place in the larger rhythmical patterns of life and death, of passing time, of dreams and responsibilities.

Steinbeck made his thematic intentions for *The Red Pony* quite clear. In addition to the notes and letters of the time, we have a remarkably candid retrospective statement in "My Short Novels":

> *The Red Pony* was written a long time ago, when there was desolation in my family. The first death occurred. And the family, which every child believes to be immortal, was shattered. Perhaps this is the first adulthood of any man or woman. The first tortured question "Why?" and then acceptance, and then the child becomes a man. *The Red Pony* was as attempt, an experiment if you wish, to set down this loss and acceptance and growth.[16]

The pattern of "loss and acceptance and growth" furnishes the basic theme for the tales and culminates very successfully in the much-disputed "Leader of the People."

The maturation of Jody is developed in several minor patterns that complement and sustain the major pattern of the experience of death. The most notable of these is the relationship with his father, Carl. From the start Carl Tiflin demonstrates three qualities that provide a framework for Jody's adolescent spirit of rebellion: stern discipline, incipient cruelty, and pragmatic realism.

A stern, unbending man, Carl possesses a rigid sense of ordered discipline. This is all that Jody has known—an unyielding framework of rules. He obeys his father "in everything without questions of any kind" (p. 203). Rules are produced by Carl with the aim of order, but also of training Jody to his high sense of dignity. Thus, he suspects Jody's own careful training of Gabilan because it might produce a "trick horse." Watching Gabilan working on the long halter, Carl observes, "He's getting to be almost a trick pony. . . . I don't like trick horses. It takes all the—dignity out of a horse to make him do tricks. Why, a trick horse is kind of like an actor—no dignity, no character of his own" (pp. 217–18).

What Carl fails to see is the association between Gabilan's training and his own training of Jody. It has never occurred to him that his own rigid discipline threatens Jody's independence, almost transforming him into a trick boy. So it is also that Jody's sense of revolt at Carl's rules becomes closely allied with Gabilan's spirit, for Jody is very much a young boy in rebellion, finding his own ways to assert his independence. Walking through the vegetable garden, "He paused for a moment to smash a green muskmelon with his heel, but he was not happy about it. It was a bad thing to do, he knew perfectly well" (p. 205). This minor act of defiance is a part of the general rebellion at the start of the school year: "There was still a spirit of revolt among the pupils" (p. 206). Jody's independent spirit is mirrored in Gabilan, whose eyes shine with "the light of disobedience."

Carl's character is marked by a kind of aloof and stern dignity, but he can also be a cruel man. His incipient cruelty is openly manifested with old Gitano. While hating the brutality he shows to Gitano, he nonetheless turns on the old man:

"It's a shame not to shoot Easter," he said. "It'd save him a lot of pains and rheumatism." He looked secretly at Gitano, to see whether he noticed the parallel, but the big bony hands did not move, nor did the dark eyes turn from the horse. "Old things ought to be put out of their misery," Jody's father went on. "One shot, a big noise, one big pain in the head maybe, and that's all. That's better than stiffness and sore teeth." [p. 249]

The cruelty carries to Grandfather as well, for here too is an "old thing" that ought to be put out of his misery. Ironically, Carl's own cruelty defeats him. Thinking that Grandfather is out of earshot, Carl berates the old man mercilessly. Terribly shamed by his outburst, Carl stalks out of the kitchen, but Jody has witnessed the unraveling of his father's stern dignity:

Jody glanced in shame at his mother, and he saw that she was looking at Carl, and that she wasn't breathing. It was an awful thing that he was doing. He was tearing himself to pieces to talk like that. It was a terrible thing to him to retract a word, but to retract it in shame was infinitely worse. [p. 301]

The tyrannical order of sternness has crumbled, and in its wreckage Jody comes of age. With his father's harshness shattered by shame, and bearing in mind Carl's attitude toward "old things" as worthless clutter, Jody steps into the role that rightfully should be Carl's.[17] Having lost heart for the gratuitous violence of killing the mice in the haystack, Jody ushers Grandfather into the house and makes him a glass of lemonade, the right action toward an old thing whose only sin has been to run out of room for his great dream of westering. Jody becomes the leader of the party.

To describe Carl Tiflin in such a way is not to imply that he is a mean or malicious man. Indeed, many readers have assumed that because he is the foil for Jody's maturation and for the key role-reversal in "The Leader of the People," Carl is something of the villain in the story. Billy Buck, in this view, operates as surrogate father to the boy, providing nurture and understanding. It would be more accurate, however, to characterize Carl as a victim of his own pragmatic concerns. Twice before the climactic shaming before Grandfather, he has his own attempts at capturing some larger vision thwarted. When Gabilan is dying, Carl attempts to cheer Jody by telling stories:

He told about the wild man who ran naked through the country and had a tail and ears like a horse and he told about the rabbit-cats of Moro Cojo that hopped into the trees for birds. He revived the famous Maxwell brothers who found a vein of gold and hid the traces of it so carefully that they could never find it again. [p. 229]

Asking for some response from the silent, withdrawn Jody, Carl reacts with hurt and anger. He has no other resources. The scene foreshadows "The Leader of the People," wherein Carl himself ignores Grandfather's stories.

In "The Great Mountains," after cruelly demeaning

Gitano, Carl again feels remorse: "Jody sat and secretly watched his father. He knew how mean his father felt" (p. 251). In this instance, Carl has failed to participate in Gitano's vision of a transcendent power in life, again foreshadowing his reaction to Grandfather. Stern he may be, even cruel at times, but Carl Tiflin represents nothing quite so much as a pragmatic authority locked in a prison of his own making.

"The Leader of the People," which brings the conflict between Jody and Carl to a culmination, gave Steinbeck considerably more difficulty than the other *Red Pony* stories. He seemed to want a sense of closure to the tales and to the thematic pattern of Jody's revolt and Carl's sternness. In an early draft the focus of the conflict centered upon the haystack, which served as an omen of tragedy:

From the very first the haystack in the lower field was ill fated. In July when the pole was set up and the loaded header had creaked up beside it, the big Jackson fork slipped and drove a tine through Billy Buck's foot. The little boy Jody, watched Billy pull off his shoe and pour blood out of it, and jerk off his sock to prevent the poisoning of black dye. Billy was laid up then. Jody himself led the horse that pulled the Jackson fork tackle. At last the tall yellow stack was made and Jody's father thatched it carefully to keep the rain water out. That very afternoon Jody slid down the stack a few times and ruined the thatching so that it had to be done over again. This piece of badness on Jody's part not only brought instant punishment but had a far-reaching and sharp effect on the following Christmas for Jody's father Carl Tiflin was an irreparable punisher [last two words blurred]. [*TFN*]

The scene sets a conflict between Carl and Jody Tiflin, but it also depicts Jody as still a very immature child, rambunctious to be sure, but also willfully destructive for his own pleasure. It lacks the sense of growth Steinbeck had been aiming at.

In a second start to the story, under the title of "Grandfather," Steinbeck begins with Jody's being punished in school for shooting a needle through a reed blowgun into the woodwork around the blackboard. The teacher treats the offense promptly, but with a certain degree of lightness. This scene leads into the revised haystack scene, in which Carl catches him sliding down the haystack: "This piece of badness not only brought an instant punishment but had a far-reaching effect on the following Christmas, for Jody's father Carl Tiflin was a stern punisher and a keeper of his threats." The same conflict is there, and we never do learn the effect on the following Christmas. In this version, however, Jody vents his anger at being punished upon the mice in the haystack: "Those sleek, fat, smug mice who had lived all winter in the warm hay stack were good objects of revenge for all the evil of the stack. And Billy Buck had said the moldy straw was fairly crawling with fat frightened mice. Jody licked his nervous lips."

The mice hunt, which had appeared in bits and pieces throughout the ledger, exists in the final version only as a great expectancy.[18] But when the moment arrives, right after Carl's shame, Jody doesn't feel the same vengeful urge. Instead he gives up the hunt to wait upon Grandfather. Rebellion and vengeance are thereby replaced by a loving act of service. The full significance of Jody's bestowal of an act of grace upon Grandfather, however, is revealed in Jody's knowledge of death and Grandfather's great dream of westering, a pattern carefully and artistically developed in the work.

If, as Steinbeck so often commented, the *Red Pony* stories were an escape from the pressing reality of his mother's illness, the artistic discipline marking these stories is the more remarkable. The tales contain some of Steinbeck's finest, most carefully controlled descriptive passages to date, especially in the detailed portrayal of setting. The landscape of the Tiflin ranch emerges in crisply detailed portraits, seen by impressionistic snatches through Jody's eyes:

On the fences the shiny blackbirds with red epaulets clicked their dry call. The meadowlarks sang like water, and the wild doves, concealed among the bursting leaves of the oaks, made a sound of restrained grieving. In the fields the rabbits sat sunning themselves, with only their forked ears showing above the grass heads. [pp. 262–63]

Steinbeck is not so much inventing as remembering in such passages; these are his foothills. Such descriptions rivet the landscape in sterling portraits.

The same use of intimate details characterizes Jody and make his youthfulness believable. The boy isn't precious; indeed, his humanity is seen in his relentless mistreatment of the enduring Doubletree Mutt, as fine a character as has limped through any of Steinbeck's stories and a testament to his lifelong affection for dogs. In a sense, Doubletree serves as the convenient displacement for Jody's revolt under his father's rules. But Jody isn't a mean sort; his world is an imaginative, if sometimes lonely one:

Banging his knee against the golden lard bucket he used for school lunch, he contrived a good bass drum, while his tongue fluttered sharply against his teeth to fill in snare drums and occasional trumpets. Some time back the other members of the squad that walked so smartly from the school had turned into the various little canyons and taken the wagon roads to their own home ranches. Now Jody marched seemingly alone, with high-lifted knees and pounding feet; but behind him there was a phantom army with great flags and swords, silent but deadly. [p. 256]

In such portraits, Steinbeck reveals the imaginative quality of Jody that makes him more receptive to the mysteriousness of death and that opposes him to Carl's pragmatic rigidity.

In addition to his precise descriptions of a boy's world and his ability to capture Jody's youthful spirit, Steinbeck admits us to Jody's world through the eyes of others. News of Gabilan's arrival infects the schoolhouse boys with wonder, and Jody suddenly appears huge and marvelous before their eyes:

Before today Jody had been a boy, dressed in overalls and a blue shirt—quieter than most, even suspected of being a little cowardly. And now he was different. Out of a thousand centuries they drew the ancient admiration of the footman for the horseman. They knew instinctively that a man on a horse is spiritually as well as physically bigger than a man on foot. They knew that Jody had been miraculously lifted out of equality with them, and had been placed over them. [pp. 211–12]

While the boys traipse home in awestruck wonder, it is Jody who is left with the work of currying and brushing Gabilan. His wonder is vested in the pony itself.

The care of horses leads also to the care of Grandfather. On the one hand, this care of Gabilan and then Nellie results from Carl's dictates. Carl, who believes it is good discipline to give presents with reservations, adjures Jody to care for Gabilan: "If I ever hear of you not feeding him or leaving his stall dirty, I'll sell him off in a minute" (p. 209). When he decides to breed Nellie, once again Carl admonishes Jody: "You'll have to take care of her, too, till she throws the colt" (p. 260). But Carl's "care" is the rigid code of discipline unaffected by the emotions of the heart. Precisely those stirrings of the heart lead Jody to care for Grandfather after Carl shames him.

Jody is also touched by a sense of the mystical dream that places him closer to Grandfather's vision of westering than Carl. Carl's line of imagination seldom stretches beyond his own land, possibly as far as a sale in Salinas. He is the harsh, pragmatic man, incapable of dreaming. While less successful as a farmer, he is a bit like Raymond Banks, incapable of an imaginative world, and therefore impatient with Grandfather's great vision of westering. But from the outset, Jody has a keen sense of the transcendent vision.

Three great visionary dreams appear in the sequence of the tales, united by the mystical lure of the mountains and threading together the boy Jody, the dying Gitano, and the aged Grandfather. Each of them senses, in his own way, the power in life that transcends pragmatic reality, even mortality. One line of maturation in Jody is in the deepening sensitivity toward and appreciation for that mystical sense. In "The Gift" Jody has fears for the welfare of his colt, the kind of childish nightmares that persist even into the waking vision. But these fears are described by Steinbeck as "a strong and a mysterious journey, to Jody—an extension of a dream" (p. 214). At this point he has no personal experience of life and death, simply feeling its dialectic as a raw possibility, a gray threat. At the end of the story, with Gabilan ill, Jody's sleep is disrupted as "the breathy groans of the pony sounded in his dreams" (p. 232). It is after the death of Gabilan, at the beginning of "The Great Mountains," that Jody first senses the mystical transcendence of vision, rather than merely dreaming. Lying on his back on a hill, Jody seems lifted toward the mountains. He squints his eyes, varying perspective. In a passage reminiscent of Gertie in "Fingers of Cloud," Steinbeck describes the experience:

By closing one eye and destroying perspective he brought them down within reach so that he could put up his fingers and stroke them. He helped the gentle wind push them down the sky; it seemed to him that they went faster for his help. One fat white cloud he helped clear to the mountain rims and pressed it firmly over, out of sight. Jody wondered what it was seeing, then. He sat up the better to look at the great mountains where they went piling back, growing darker and more savage until they finished with one jagged ridge, high up against the west. Curious secret mountains; he thought of the little he knew about them. [p. 240]

The vision sets up the dialectic of the great mountains in the story, this geographical antithesis between the bright, mystical Gabilans and the darker, foreboding Santa Lucia range. Jody feels the mystic pull of the life-holding Gabilans: "They were jolly mountains, with hill ranches in their creases, and with pine trees growing on the crests" (p. 242). He fears the western Santa Lucia range with its strange, dark pull upon his spirit: "In the evening . . . the mountains were a purple-like despair, then Jody was afraid of them; then they were so impersonal and aloof that their very imperturbability was a threat" (p. 242). The paired ranges operate metaphorically here, as they would often in Steinbeck's work. In *East of Eden*, he recollects his own experience of the mountains in words that echo *The Red Pony:*

I remember that the Gabilan Mountains to the east of the valley were light gay mountains full of sun and loveliness and a kind of invitation, so that you wanted to climb into the lap of a beloved mother. They were beckoning mountains with a brown grass love. The Santa Lucias stood up against the sky to the west and kept the valley from the open sea, and they were dark and brooding—unfriendly and dangerous. I always found in myself a dread of west and a love of east.[19]

Jody finds himself juxtaposed between, puzzled by, and finding his way through the contrary pulls of light and dark, life and death.

Having experienced the terror of death in Gabilan, Jody is tutored in the meaning of death and mystical transcendence by old Gitano: "Gitano was mysterious like the mountains. There were ranges back as far as you could see, but behind the last range piled up against the sky there was a great unknown country. And Gitano was an old man, until you got to the dull dark eyes. And in behind them was some unknown thing" (p. 252). When Jody had asked Carl what lay beyond the mountains, Carl answered in pragmatic terms: more mountains, cliffs, and brush and rocks and dryness, at last the ocean. But "Jody knew something was there, something very wonderful because it wasn't known, something secret and mysterious. He could feel within himself that this was so" (p. 241). That sense of the mysterious, the unknown, is unlocked by old Gitano. But when Jody presses Gitano for answers, Gitano simply refuses to tell him. The discovery of mystical transcendence, of a power that lies beyond human understanding, is finally one that each person makes individually.

The questing mind and the deep sensitivity to the transcendent dream admit Jody more fully than any other family member to Grandfather's vision of westering. To the others his tales are just old stories, repeated too often in the fashion of the elderly who have outlived their time and vaguely irritating because they divert attention from pragmatic realities. Grandfather has had his place in the sun, but the sun is declining on the wall of the Tiflin kitchen. Does it matter to Carl how he got this farm, when all of his concern is for its present demands? Does the dream of new possibilities have any influence over actions at this place, actions ruled by responsibilities rather than possibilities? For Carl the answer is adamantly no. But Jody's mind is of a different cast. He has sensed the vision of the transcendent power of a larger dream in old Gitano. Furthermore, he has witnessed the death of his beloved colt, but also the birth of a new colt from the death of Nellie. Intuitively, he has arrived at a deep sensitivity to new life arising from the passing of the old, but also the congruence of the old and new. This hunger for life is raw in him and is nurtured by Grandfather's vision of westering.

The westering concept has been the subject of considerable debate by Steinbeck scholars. Seen by some simply as an old man's maudlin and rambling recollection, it appears to be a flaw in the pattern of the tales. Seen by others as an adumbration of Steinbeck's phalanx theory—which it most certainly is—some have failed to see its close tie to the maturation of Jody and his growing vision of life and death.[20] Grandfather doesn't simply lament the loss of leadership; he laments the loss of the vision that he calls "westering." Life has been reduced to the routine; the dream has disappeared. But Jody has experienced the dream. The legacy of westering now lives in him. The passing of the dream from old hands to new is signified by Jody's serving Grandfather the lemonade. Jody relinquishes the mouse hunt, something he has looked forward to for days and something entirely self-serving, in order to cheer up Grandfather. His selfless compassion marks him, in Grandfather's own terms, as the leader of the people who served others before himself. Robert Morsberger observes, "'Westering' may be dead in subdivisions" in today's world,[21] but Steinbeck demonstrates in *The Red Pony* that the dream does indeed live on, that it may be handed from one generation to the next. Jody's maturation in the stories is, finally, the inheritance of the great vision.

Jody's maturation into knowledge of life and death and his appropriation of Grandfather's great dream of westering do not absolve all conflict, however. It would be more precise to say that he now holds life and death in tension, rather than to say that he sees a transcendent vision of a life force that abnegates death. The latter might be said about Joseph Wayne of *To a God Unknown*, who even while dying feels the rejuvenative surge of rain upon him. The tension develops, possibly, not out of Steinbeck's mystical attraction evidenced in Joseph Wayne, but out of his practical experience of the illness of his mother.

That tension is supplied in several ways in the stories. Billy Buck, whom Jody reveres above all men, finding in him a wisdom born of experience that transcends his father's sternness, is at once a life-bringer and executioner. He must smash Nellie's skull before bringing forth the colt, an action that also tears Billy apart for, as he says, "I'm half horse myself, you see." At the end of "The Promise," Billy Buck bears the blood from Nellie like a wound on his own face. It is that wound that Jody remembers, and the look of despair on Billy's face.

The tension is also supplied in the juxtaposed symbols of the cypress tree and the watering pipe. Frequently Jody wanders between these two places, always feeling a cold dread of the cypress tree and a warm sympathy for the watering place. The two places develop symbolically throughout the stories in direct intensity and proportion to Jody's own understanding of the life-death tension.

In "The Gift" the two are matter-of-factly introduced as physical places on the farm. While drinking from the trough by the spring, Jody can glance downhill and see the cypress:

He leaned over and drank close to the green mossy wood where the water tasted best. Then he turned and looked back on the ranch, on the low, whitewashed house girded with red geraniums, and on the long bunkhouse by the cypress tree where Billy Buck lived alone. Jody could see the great black kettle under the cypress tree. That was where the pigs were scalded. [p. 204]

The cypress, traditional symbol of death and a feature of cemeteries, is immediately associated with death and loss. Having looked upon it, Jody feels "an uncertainty in the air, a feeling of change and of loss and of the gain of new and unfamiliar things" (p. 205). As if in response to the tremulous sense of fear, two black buzzards glide past.

The tension between cypress and watering place is emphasized when Gabilan becomes ill and Jody begins to sense the symbolism of the juxtaposition: "He looked down at the house and at the old bunkhouse and at the dark cypress tree. The place was familiar, but curiously changed. It wasn't itself any more, but a frame for things that were happening" (p. 235). Weighty and thick, the cypress hunkers like a perpetual shadow on the landscape of the story. The pellucid waters of the spring charge along a line of greenery to the watering trough where the animals nourish themselves. The pigs snuffle at the trough; behind them hangs the singletree and the black tub for slaughter.

In "The Great Mountains," where Jody's sense of life and death broadens from the experience of Gabilan to human experiences in old Gitano, the cypress-watering place symbolism intensifies. Having just killed the thrush, Jody washes himself at the trough. It cleanses and rejuvenates, but the cypress stands unyieldingly before him.

In "The Promise" the symbolism is made overt, paralleling Jody's own growth in understanding the tensions of life and death:

The water whined softly into the trough all the year round. This place had grown to be a center-point for Jody. When he had

been punished the cool green grass and the singing water
soothed him. When he had been mean the biting acid of mean-
ness left him at the brush line. When he sat in the grass and listened to the purling stream, the barriers set up in his mind by
the stern day went down to ruin. (pp. 268–69)

The trough is the "center-point," but the cypress is the
counter-point:

> On the other hand, the black cypress tree by the bunkhouse
> was as repulsive as the water-tub was dear; for to this tree all the
> pigs came, sooner or later, to be slaughtered. Pig killing was fas-
> cinating, with the screaming and the blood, but it made Jody's
> heart beat so fast that it hurt him. After the pigs were scalded in
> the big iron tripod kettle and their skins were scraped and white,
> Jody had to go to the water-tub to sit in the grass until his heart
> grew quiet. The water-tub and the black cypress were opposites
> and enemies. [p. 269]

Immediately Jody associates the opposition with Nellie and
the unborn colt, Black Demon. The trilling water nurtures
his dream for the colt, but he cannot escape the presence of
the cypress. As Jody walks into the barn when Nellie is
due, he walks through a blackness in which only the cypress stands out, a darker blackness against the night.

Neither the tree nor the trough appears in "The Leader
of the People." The symbolism is manifested in life itself
with the appearance of Grandfather. This time, Billy Buck
states the tension as Jody prepares to attack the mice in the
haystack:

> Jody changed his course and moved toward the house. He
> leaned his flail against the steps. "That's to drive the mice out,"
> he said. "I'll bet they're fat. I'll bet they don't know what's going
> to happen to them today."
> "No, nor you either," Billy remarked philosophically. "Nor
> me, nor anyone."
> Jody was staggered by this thought. He knew it was true. His
> imagination twitched away from the mouse hunt. (pp. 299–300)

Here the tension is stated overtly: Death and life hang in a delicate balance. This too has been Jody's discovery in the course of his maturation.

Lev Shestov, writing on the conflict between reason and revelation in his major work *Athens and Jerusalem*, argues that our present age is trapped in the cold hands of pragmatic necessity. His essential question might serve as a coda for *The Red Pony*:

Is it given men to judge the truths, to decide the fate of the truths? On the contrary, it is the truths which judge men and decide their fate and not men who rule over the truths. Men, the great as well as the small, are born and die, appear and disappear—but the truth remains.[22]

Jody senses the truth in a way that Carl Tiflin will never approach. From the "little boy Jody," checked constantly by his father's discipline, dignity, and occasional cruelty, he has matured not necessarily to adult wisdom but to a sense of fullness of life that holds living and dying, reality and the dream, in balance. The passage has required loss and desolation, but it has produced the tempered steel of actions of the heart.

Against a backdrop of enervating personal turmoil, *The Red Pony* represents an artistic triumph for Steinbeck. The carefully paced theme of maturity through the desolation of loss, and the heightened sense of a transcendent vision that rises above the narrowness of pragmatic reality, carry the weight of a deeply meaningful work. The artistic craftsmanship, the carefully plotted patterns of description, symbolism, and imagery, carry the energy of an intriguing and moving story. It is an enduring work, a classic by virtue of its profound simplicity, unswervingly faithful in capturing the childhood point of view, disciplined in its narration.

Moreover, in the development of his fictional artistry, the sequence of stories represents a liberation for Steinbeck. In them he moves to the heart of his artistic talent. It is a historical irony that he completed *The Pastures of*

Heaven and *The Red Pony* while simultaneously revising *To a God Unknown,* for these separate works represent the dialectic of his fictional career: stories of personal experience and a recollected past versus a story of philosophical breadth and open-ended speculation. Finding now some scant degree of commercial success with the former—as much as the whimsical wrath of the Great Depression would allow—Steinbeck felt a degree of benediction upon the kind of story he wanted to tell, the stories of *his* heart. A path opened for him in *The Red Pony* that would be well traveled in future years. Even in such a work as *In Dubious Battle,* to be undertaken in the year following and in which Steinbeck grapples with the concept of mob action, he located that concept surely and deliberately in the places and people he knew firsthand.

5

Foothills Around the Long Valley

THE THREE STORIES discussed in this chapter are brought together not for any intrinsic unity they share but for their peculiarities in relation to the other stories in *The Long Valley*. "Saint Katy the Virgin" was drafted long before Steinbeck set to work on the stories included in *The Long Valley*, but it was published with them as part of the collection. "How Edith McGillcuddy Met R. L. Stevenson" was written shortly before the main body of work for *The Long Valley*, in between stories for *The Red Pony*, but was not published until 1941. "The Murder," seems to have been conceived as part of the *Pastures of Heaven* sequence, but was written after that collection was put together for publication. Each of the stories, nonetheless, figured significantly in Steinbeck's growth as an artist.

When one examines Steinbeck's short stories in order of their composition, inevitable oddities appear. It is far neater to consider the stories in order of publication. Traditionally, this proves a safe and legitimate critical approach. In Steinbeck's case, however, that traditional pattern has led to misconceptions of the work and often a neglect of the stories altogether. Nowhere is this more apparent than in *The Long Valley*.

The Long Valley was published not as a cohesive volume but as a collection of random work representing the multifaceted interests and accomplishments of the author. In "Steinbeck as a Short Story Writer," Brian M. Barbour is one of few to pay attention exclusively to Steinbeck's short stories. Although he evidences little familiarity with the chronology and conditions of Steinbeck's short-story writing, he routinely castigates the author for crimes that can be solved in part by an understanding of that chronology. Unevenness marks the literary quality of the stories, to be sure. Barbour's claim, however, that *The Long Valley* reveals confusion of purpose [1] is largely due to his misreading the volume as an attempt to provide a narratively unified work. His claim that "Steinbeck never reached artistic maturity in the short story" [2] is simply mistaken. A clearer bibliographical understanding would have resolved a number of his contentions. For example, Barbour berates Steinbeck for using the British spelling of *color* in "The Murder," which he links to a generally "pretentious" descriptiveness. [3] The fault lies with the Viking Press, which used the text of the October 1934 publication in *Lovat Dickson's Magazine* rather than the April 1934 publication in the *North American Review*. [4]

The publication of *The Long Valley* in 1938 was at Pascal Covici's instigation. By this time, *In Dubious Battle* and *Of Mice and Men* had cemented Steinbeck's place in contemporary letters. In mid-1936 Covici published, through Pynson Printers, the 370-copy edition of *Nothing So Monstrous*, and in late 1936 he published a Christmas edition of 199 signed and numbered copies of *Saint Katy the Virgin*. [5] Covici followed that in 1937 with a 699-copy Christmas edition of *The Red Pony*. Each of these editions sold out rapidly. Since the firm of Covici-Friede was deeply in debt in 1938 and Steinbeck had demonstrated an audience appeal for his short stories, the decision to publish a volume of short stories was a natural one strictly from a business perspective. At the time Covici-Friede's heaviest debt was to the printing and binding firm, J. J. Little and Ives, Inc. When the owner, Col. Arthur W. Little, met with Covici to discuss payment, Covici had on hand a rough proof of the *Long Valley* stories, a collation, apparently, of badly worn old typescripts. Covici's publishing partner, Donald Friede, recollects Little's examination of the rough proofs, which Covici was depending on:

It was at this point that the Colonel had exploded. He produced the manuscript we had sent to Little & Ives to be set up (in type), and shook it under Covici's nose. "Look at it!" he said, pointing to the sheaf of bedraggled papers he held in his hand. "Look at those filthy pages! It is obvious that this book has been turned down by every publisher in the country. And you dare to tell me that it will sell more than ten thousand copies!" In vain Covici tried to interrupt him, to explain that when it had been decided to publish this collection, Steinbeck had not bothered to have the manuscript retyped but had merely collected, from all the magazines that had published these stories, the original manuscripts from which they had been set.[6]

Thus ended Covici-Friede. But Covici took the manuscript to the Viking Press with him, whereupon it underwent two printings in 1938, reached the best-seller lists, and sold over 30,000 copies.

"SAINT KATY THE VIRGIN"

Even if one views the stories in the chronology of composition, the odd story in *The Long Valley* still has to be "Saint Katy the Virgin." The inclusion of the story in the volume has bothered critics for some time; it appears so manifestly at odds in tone and theme with the other tales. While there is no direct, thematic unity linking the stories in the volume, the heavy satirical and fabulist form of "Saint Katy" clearly marks the story as unique. By and large, critics have dealt with the story by ignoring it. In one of the few serious considerations, "The Cryptic Raillery of 'Saint Katy the Virgin,'" Sanford E. Marovitz calls it the "odd thirteenth in John Steinbeck's bakers dozen of stories."[7] Marovitz is correct in his assumption that "the story may have been finished long before 1932."[8] Steinbeck sent a copy of it, along with others, to McIntosh and Otis in May 1932, commenting that its composition had been a pleasant afternoon's work.

In fact, the story dates back to Steinbeck's Stanford days, having been originally submitted as a course project. In her study "Steinbeck at Stanford," Susan Riggs writes, "St. Katy the Virgin was written for Professor Edward M. Hulme's class in European thought and culture."[9] And according to Frank Fenton, it was first written as a "bawdy poem inspired by a Hulme lecture on canonization during the Middle Ages."[10]

Even apart from the extraliterary evidence that dates the origins of "Saint Katy the Virgin" to the mid-1920s, the textual evidence would certainly suggest as much. Satire came easily to Steinbeck during the unsettled years at Stanford. In the years following, his laconic wit moved easily into satire, sometimes as a subtle threat, as when he turns a withering eye upon the foibles of the pretentious; sometimes in a stronger leit motif, as in the *Cannery Row* trilogy; but not again as a full-length study in which satire is the predominant mode until he wrote *The Short Reign of Pippin IV*. Beginning with the stories for *The Pastures of Heaven*, his artistic concerns, voice, and settings became those of a recollected past. Although nearly all scholars have discarded the one-time popular notion of Steinbeck as a mimetic realist, recognizing in the face of overwhelming evidence the tremendous influences upon him of his rich and varied reading, stylistic inventiveness, and philosophical-religious concerns, there was a shift from the purely inventive or even fantastic to realism in the late 1920s. "Saint Katy" would simply be the odd work if it were indeed written during the 1930s.

But "Saint Katy" was very much a part of the Stanford style. It bears evidence of a 1925–26 composition in three ways.

First, satire was very much a part of Steinbeck's social and artistic milieu at Stanford, and also of his personal disposition. His dissatisfaction with things as they were, which led to "Adventures in Arcademy," with its attack upon academics, also led to "Saint Katy," with its attack upon conventional religious practices. Steinbeck came to Stanford with a fairly strong religious tradition rooted in the Episcopal denomination and the practices of his parents, particularly those of his mother, Olive Hamilton Steinbeck. Once living apart from his parents, he shrugged off much of his faith and nearly all of the practice. To him, religion seemed radically at odds with the reality of daily living, and the great failure of organized religion lay precisely in its failure to actively engage daily living. While in later years he would become deeply sensitive to religious practices and, while not a believer, would nonetheless be very sensitive to the beliefs of others, during the 1920s he was intolerant of what he perceived to be the hypocritical cant of orthodox religions. In his pamphlet *The Wrath of John Steinbeck*, Robert Bennett relates Steinbeck's ire, at age eighteen, at a church service during which the minister imparted airy platitudes with little relevance to daily living.[11] Steinbeck stalked out. Such was his spirit during the mid-1920s, and much of that spirit is readily apparent in "Saint Katy the Virgin."

Second, Steinbeck used elements of the beast fable form in "Adventures in Arcademy" and did not return to it again. One might well argue that Steinbeck's heavy use of animal imagery in character descriptions is an outgrowth of this practice, but its strictly fabular patterns occur nowhere in his writings outside of these two satirical pieces. And the beast fable is, of course, a marvelous literary trapping for satire. Several critics have observed the Chaucerian aura to the tale, in both the fabliau and the beast fable. Each genre, in the medieval era, served the writer as a means for castigating the clergy and a generally corrupt religious hierarchy. Professor Hulme's course in European history, the likely genesis for the story, no doubt served as a nexus between a traditional form and Steinbeck's ire.

Third, "Saint Katy the Virgin" stands out in *The Long Valley* because of its markedly different tone. While the other stories are objective narrations using variations of a third-person point of view, "Saint Katy" uses a casual familiarity with the reader, marked by repetitions of "you see." In the opening paragraph, Steinbeck advises the reader,

"When you think of the low, nasty kind of laughter it was, you'll see what a bad man this Roark was, and you'll not be surprised that he didn't pay his tithes and got himself talked about for excommunication" (p. 187). The second paragraph begins, "You see the atmosphere the bad pig, Katy, grew up in, and maybe it's no wonder" (p. 188). In other passages we find the same familiarity. The only other story of the 1920s or 1930s that follows this practice is the unpublished "The White Sister of Fourteenth Street," composed in 1926. That story is also punctuated regularly with direct references to the reader. Such matters date the composition of "Saint Katy" in story form to 1925 or 1926, but clearly Steinbeck retained his interest in the story through later years.

As Sanford Marovitz demonstrated, the story cannot be successfully read as a pure allegory. There are too many loose ends. But as a fable, with its more random levels of meaning, it carries well Steinbeck's dismay at the pretentions of religion. Moreover, it is simply a lively and entertaining work.

Katy is a pig of good lineage gone bad. How did she go bad? Surely not by any original sin: "You must see that the badness of Katy wasn't anything she got by inheritance, so she must have picked it up from the man Roark" (p. 188). While naming his pigs, Roark curses Katy, "turn over you little devil," and henceforth she lives up to her designation. Her initial deviltry is not altogether unpiglike, but simply an expression of her baser nature: "She began by stealing most of the milk; what dugs she couldn't suck on, she put her back against" (p. 188). That base nature, in a kind of Thomistic pattern of evil, opens a door to viciousness. One day she eats her litter mates. In fact, her appetite becomes insatiable, a remarkable manifestation of the deadly sin of gluttony. She devours chickens and ducks, even an occasional child, and in the meantime grows sleek and strong. But the wickedness leaves its mark on her features: "You should have seen the face of Katy. From the beginning it was a wicked face. The evil yellow eyes of her would frighten you even if you had a stick to knock her on the nose with. She became the terror of the neighborhood" (p. 189). Katy's wickedness becomes mythic, a truly legendary sinner, and Steinbeck delights in recounting the vastness of her wickedness. She is bred to boar, who "was sterile from that day on," delivers a litter of fine young pigs, cleans them off nicely, and devours them. Katy is the incarnation of evil.

Into this situation two priests, Brother Colin and Brother Paul, intervene. Their appearance is itself something of a miracle because they arrive at the very moment Katy is about to be slaughtered by Roark. Roark is convinced of Katy's irremediable evil. For Colin and Paul, nothing is too evil to escape redemption by the offices of the church. Actually Colin and Paul are variations of the abhorrent medieval summoners, two strong-arm agents of the church out collecting tithes. They even play the good guy-bad guy pairing: "They went tithing together, because what Brother Colin couldn't get by persuasion, Brother Paul dug out with threatenings and descriptions of the fires of Hell" (p. 190). Before they can begin their threats, Roark readily hands over the pig: "They noted the size of Katy and the fat on her, and they stared increduously. Colin could think of nothing but the great hams she had and the bacon she wore about like a top coat" (p. 191).

The tone of the story, a farcical piece in which the priests become the butt of the joke, is adapted from the medieval fabliau. The fabliau became an established art form in the late twelfth century, within the time framework treated by Professor Hulme's European history course at Stanford University. Begun by jongleurs in the alehouses of France, the fabliau was essentially humorous and could take a number of forms, from good-natured farce to vicious satire. Because it appealed to the lower classes, the humor of the fabliau was often directed against the oppressors of that class, chiefly the clergy, who were stereotyped into a role of comfortable corruption.[12]

The fabliau element of "Saint Katy" surfaces in the farcical dealings of the good brothers and Katy. The brothers
are hardly out of Roark's yard when Katy's avaricious appetite turns on them. She is not fussy, this pig. Whatever
she can bite she will chew. Katy chases them up a tree,
from which they hurl imprecations and religious signs. Paul
holds up his crucifix, rather in the fashion of the paisanos
during the grail hunt in *Tortilla Flat*, and screams, "*Apage
Satanas.*" The exorcism has "little effect except to singe a
few dried leaves on the ground"(p. 193). The brothers have
an appropriate theological response. Indeed, they have a
category for everything: "Brother Paul turned discouraged
eyes to Colin. 'Nature of the devil.' he announced sadly,
'but not the Devil's own self, else that pig would have exploded'" (p. 193).

When the exorcism fails, Paul decides to try faith, walking in the way of Daniel and going into the lion's den. But
with caution. Faith can only be tried so far, after all. Paul
hangs by his knees and lowers the crucifix before Katy's
comminatory nose:

Katy stopped—paralyzed. The air, the tree, the earth shuddered in an expectant silence, while goodness fought with sin.
Then, slowly, two great tears squeezed out of the eyes of Katy,
and before you could think, she was stretched prostrate on the
ground, making the sign of the cross with her right hoof and
mooing softly in anguish at the realization of her crimes.
Brother Paul dangled the cross a full minute before he hoisted
himself back on the limb. [p. 194]

Not only is the pig converted, but Roark, watching from
the gate, "was no longer a bad man; his whole life was
changed in a moment" (p. 194).

Spared from certain condemnation, Katy retires to a life
of saintly vicissitude, with one small question mark: "For a
while it was thought that, because of her sex, she should
leave the monastery and enter a nunnery, for the usual
ribald tongues caused the usual scandal in the country"
(p. 196).

Not only is Katy's life thereafter a parade of good deeds, she also reveals a touch for the miraculous: "While hymns of joy and thanksgiving sounded from a hundred pious mouths, Katy rose from her seat, strode to the altar, and with a look of seraphic transport on her face, spun like a top on the tip of her tail for one hour and three-quarters" (p. 196). Multitudes come to the monastery to be blessed by such a pig. She performs healings and becomes a liberal dispenser of grace. For such a life, fifty years after her death she is nominated for canonization. An easy election, it would seem, for so saintly a life, with one exception. Katy was not a virgin. She had, after all, produced a litter in her sinful way, not to mention having eaten them. The act of procreation is the stumbling block. Following a learned discourse by a debauched barber on what constitutes virginity, "The committee went away satisfied. Katy had without doubt been a virgin by intent" (p. 197).

The legend continues. Katy is canonized, and even her reliquary, bones on a satin bed, provides healing.

Like the medieval fabliau, the first intention of the story is a good laugh.[13] The fabliau, after all, flourished in the alehouses, not in the palaces. It was a story for the lowlife, and brought a bit of comic relief to the tedium of a hard day in the fields. So too "Saint Katy the Virgin." But the lowlife also wanted literary retribution; through the vicarious experience of literature they wanted the high and mighty laid low. This "Saint Katy" also accomplishes. Its satire of the clergy, with its rationalized canonization, its readiness to make a saint out of a sow, its grim lust for fame and fortune, is the clenched fist striking in the tale. It is a more subdued kind of satire than "Adventures in Arcademy," but nonetheless a sparkling and effective one.

Surely there is a prejudice against the mechanisms of the organized church in the tale. Warren French has observed that Steinbeck treated the church "not with hostility but condescension."[14] While not applicable to all of Steinbeck's fiction, the remark is appropriate to "Saint Katy the Virgin." Sanford Marovitz links the satire of the church in *Cup of Gold* with that in "Saint Katy"[15] and suggests that Steinbeck's work may have been inspired by the spirit of revivalism that pervaded Monterey and Pacific Grove at the time. Of historical interest to this point is Steinbeck's unfinished short story of Mizpah, appearing at the end of the *Pastures of Heaven* sequence of tales in his notebook, probably drafted in 1931. The Mizpah story deals directly with a revival. Mizpah is collecting pine cones in a forest three miles from Monterey one day when he stumbles across a caravan festooned with religious slogans. He follows it to a house, peers in, and hears a sound he construes as the voice of the devil. As he tries to flee the imagined horror, he hears his mother's voice calling him in: "Mizpah! Is it you? Come in. There's company and cake." While different people talk to Mizpah at the house, suddenly a man's voice is heard shouting, "Suffer little children to come unto me and forbid them not." It is uncertain where Steinbeck was heading with the story, for at that point he heavily inked the word OUT, underlining it three times.

At that point, it was also clear that Steinbeck had wearied of any use of religion as a subject for satire. When it surfaces again in *Tortilla Flat*, it comes as a natural life pattern of the marvelously mystical paisanos, something Steinbeck records as tenderly and endearingly as he does all facets of their chaotic lives. His former wrath was now displaced by a more realistic and sensitive attitude.

"HOW EDITH MCGILLCUDDY MET R. L. STEVENSON"

Despite the rapidity with which he drafted the story in the summer of 1933, "How Edith McGillcuddy Met R. L. Stevenson" posed an unusual artistic problem for Steinbeck, one that rose out of the penumbra of storytelling like a ghoul: the claim that the story actually belonged to another. It is a problem that afflicts many writers, and perhaps in particular those who are rapacious of stories they have heard or absorbed from a personal past, because that past is always shared by others.

In ransacking his own past for the stories of *The Pastures of Heaven*, Steinbeck borrowed freely from the oral histories of the Corral de Tierra related by Beth Ingels, who lived in the Corral de Tierra, and Susan Gregory, who taught Spanish in Monterey. This borrowing is hardly to be compared to plagiarism; rather, it is a kind of mental net-casting, fishing for the kind of tale that one artistic sensibility finds particularly appealing. All authors do this. When their reputations are firm, they are considered the progenitors. But in their earlier works they seem to be particularly susceptible to the charge of borrowing.

Steinbeck was open to a good story wherever he heard it, and in his eagerness in the early thirties, he was not about to pause to make fine discriminations about sources. If a story was noised about, he had a knack for finding it out. He freely, if eclectically, let whatever literary influences charged along his synapses infiltrate his art. Careful examination of *To a God Unknown* reveals a tapestry of a half-dozen patterns woven earlier by others. *Cup of God* was a frank imitation of swashbuckling romances of the time, even if Steinbeck's stamp upon the work, with his distinct patterns of imagery and sharp satirical thrusts, is clear.[16]

Some early charges about his imitative quality are embarrassing—to those who made the charges. F. Scott Fitzgerald, who fawned sycophantically on nearly every contemporary of his, may have been influenced by Hemingway's jealousy of Steinbeck's success into a similar pique.[17] Fitzgerald, who was overseeing a dramatization of "The Diamond as Big as the Ritz" by an amateur group in Pasadena and who was hoping to have a play produced from *Tender Is the Night* in New York, remarked in 1937, "Mice + Men has been praised all out of proportion to its merits."[18] It was fairly typical of Fitzgerald to denigrate the work of competitors who had not publicly supported him. But he overstepped his own thin boundaries of taste when he wrote Edmund Wilson in 1940:

I'd like to put you on to something about Steinbeck. He is a rather cagey cribber. Most of us begin as imitators but it is something else for a man of his years and reputation to steal a whole scene as he did in "Mice and Men." I'm sending you a marked copy of Norris' "McTeague" to show you what I mean. His debt to "The Octupus" [sic] is also enormous and his balls, when he uses them, are usually clipped from Lawrence's "Kangaroo." I've always encouraged young writers—I put Max Perkins on to Caldwell, Callaghan, and God knows how many others but Steinbeck bothers me. I suppose he cribs for the glory of the party.[19]

The comparison to Lawrence is one that Fitzgerald made often,[20] but the charge against Steinbeck for stealing a scene from Norris is more serious. In regard to Frank Norris's *The Octopus*, the relationship has to be judged as one of historic coincidence, nothing more. Norris's panorama of the San Joaquin Valley, with its clashes of workers and ranchers, happens to be a locale similar to those of *In Dubious Battle* and *The Grapes of Wrath*, but any "enormous debt" of Steinbeck to Norris is untenable.[21]

Several passages from *McTeague*, however, may support Fitzgerald's charge. The first occurs in a sequence of dialogues between Maria Macapa and the junk dealer, Zerkow, in chapters 3 through 5. Like Lennie in *Of Mice and Men*, Maria has a dream of great riches. Instead of showing tenderness, however, as George does toward Lennie by nurturing his dream, Zerkow encourages Maria's dream to satisfy his own greed. As he listens to her tale of the golden plates, "He was breathing short, his limbs trembled a little. It was as if some hungry beast of prey had scented a quarry."[22] Zerkow's encouragement of the dream is almost a kind of masochism as he urges Maria on, torturing himself with the vision of wealth: "'Now, just once more, Maria,' he was saying. 'Tell it to us just once more.'" As Maria swings into the familiar litany, Zerkow becomes obsessed by the vision:

"And it rang like bells, didn't it?" prompted Zerkow.
"Sweeter'n church bells, and clearer."
"Ah, sweeter'n bells. Wasn't that punch bowl awful heavy?"

"All you could do to lift it."

"I know. Oh, I know," answered Zerkow, clawing at his lips.
[p. 54]

While one might observe some echoes in the revelation of
the impossible dream and the pacing of the dialogue, it is
clear that Zerkow is utterly bereft of any of the tenderness
George shows toward Lennie.

A second possibility appears in the fight between Marcus
and McTeague in chapter eleven. When Marcus bites
through McTeague's ear, "The brute that in McTeague lay
so close to the surface leaped instantly to life, monstrous,
not to be resisted" (p. 182). McTeague catches Marcus's
wrists in his huge hands—"Gripping his enemy in his enormous hands, hard and knotted and covered with a stiff
fell of yellow hair"—and breaks Marcus's arm. Only when
Heise cries for McTeague to stop, as George cries out
to Lennie when Lennie crushes Curley's hand, does
McTeague relent.[23]

The case of such borrowings is important here for two
reasons: Any author bears the influence and imprint of stories he has heard and read in the making of his own stories,
and the borrowing had rather painful consequences in the
composition of "Edith McGillcuddy."

One of Steinbeck's closest boyhood friends was Max
Wagner. Steinbeck particularly liked to visit the Wagner
kitchen, where Edith Wagner, Max's mother, would spin
stories of her youth in Salinas—a delight to Steinbeck, who
already felt the storytelling impulse in himself. One such
story was of how, as a child, she had traveled to Monterey
by train and there met Robert Louis Stevenson. According
to Jackson Benson, "In late 1933, she had written to [Stein-
beck] to tell him that she liked *To a God Unknown*. Her
letter triggered the memory of the story she had told him
many years before, and he started writing it shortly thereafter."[24] Wagner had herself written a story of the meeting
and submitted it unsuccessfully to *Reader's Digest* for
publication.

Probably with some reluctance, Steinbeck wrote Wagner in February 1934; "I have been doing some short stories about the people of the county. Some of them I think you yourself told me" (*SLL*, p. 94). It may have taken her some time to respond, for not until June 4, 1934, did Steinbeck write again. Apparently this marks the first time that Steinbeck knew that Wagner had drafted a copy of the story:

> Your letter came this morning. I didn't know you had done a version of the story and I sent mine off with a lot of other stuff. I will do whatever you wish about the affair, divide in case of publication or recall the manuscript. Please let me know. . . .
> I'm terribly sorry if I filched one of your stories. I'm a shameless magpie anyway, picking up anything shiny that comes my way—incident, situation or personality. But if I had had any idea, I shouldn't have taken it. I'll do anything you like about it. [*SLL*, p. 95]

Nine days later, he again wrote Wagner:

> I am writing to my agents today, asking them to hold up the story. It is awkward for this reason—they've had the story for at least two weeks and since they are very active, it has undoubtedly gone out. However, it can be stopped. I hope you will let me know how yours comes out, as soon as you hear. If it should happen to have been bought by the time my letter reaches New York, it can be held up. Mine, I mean. . . . Well, I hope nothing untoward happens about this story. In sending it away I enclosed a note saying it had been told me by you. Plagiarism is not one of my sins. I'll write you when I hear any outcome. [*SLL*, p. 96]

This sequence of letters, among other things, has occasioned some uncertainty among scholars about the actual date of composition of the story. Roy S. Simmonds dates it "late in 1932 or early in 1933." In *Beyond the Red Pony*, R. S. Hughes dates it 1934, guided by Steinbeck's listing in the *Long Valley* notebook held by the Steinbeck Research Center at San Jose State University.[26] In the ledger the first forty-two pages are cut out, and on page 43 Steinbeck enters a note: "Record of stories completed summer of 1934," one of which listed is "How Edith McGillcuddy Met R. L. S." Since the actual writing in the notebook begins on page 45, it is possible that Steinbeck's note was written after the composition of the stories in the ledger and that he included the earlier "Edith McGillcuddy" among them since he had begun submitting it during the writing of the other stories. It was surely written earlier. In the beginning of the notebook that would eventually include the draft of *In Dubious Battle*, the story falls directly between a draft of "The Great Mountains" and a two-page start on *Tortilla Flat*. The story is composed on six pages in tight script with very few revisions. While the notebooks are not an absolute guide to dating because Steinbeck wrote in more than one at a time and let works overlap, it is reasonable to conclude that the story was composed in the late summer of 1933 and that the *Long Valley* notebook merely groups the story with others that he was arranging for publication.

During the years that followed, Steinbeck withheld the story. When, a half-dozen years later, Wagner had been unable to publish her version, Steinbeck requested permission from her to publish his story. He sold it to *Harper's Magazine*, where it was published in August 1941, and forwarded the payment, $225, to Wagner. Steinbeck's sensitivity toward her in withholding his story and his magnanimity in forwarding the payment (she was elderly and in very poor health in 1941) are all the more remarkable in that the Edith McGillcuddy story must have had a personal attraction for him, and his rendition of it is uniquely his own.

Like Junius Maltby, Steinbeck was exceedingly fond of Stevenson's work. Robert DeMott comments:

There was a quality in Stevenson's work, JS believed, which allowed direct and uncritical "participation" in its emotional and imaginative dimensions. *Treasure Island*, for example, becomes a reflection of the reader's subjective state, which then "keys into" the story and "makes him part of it." Besides his love for the fiction and adventure tales, JS considered *A Child's Garden of*

Verses (1905) one of his "favorite collections of poetry" . . . and thought Stevenson's short prayers "some of the most moving and true things" he had ever read.[27]

Moreover, the fact that Stevenson had traveled through Salinas on his way to Monterey in 1879 established a personal tie between the two writers. Since Edith McGillcuddy—in the pattern of Edith Wagner—catches the train from Salinas to Monterey on the day when she met Stevenson, Steinbeck began the story with a brief portrait of Salinas, at the time still a crossroads town of 4,000 inhabitants:

Salinas was a dirty little California cow-town in 1879. There was a small and consistent vicious element; there was a large wavering element, likely to join the vicious element on Saturday night to go church repentant on Sunday. And there was a small embattled good element, temperance people, stern people.

Twenty saloons kept the town in ignorance and vice while five churches fought valiantly for devotion, temperance, and decency.[28]

One observes, then, a deep personal attraction in Steinbeck to the story both for his admiration for Stevenson and for its Salinas-Monterey setting.

Important as these periphral matters may have been to the development of Steinbeck's career and his writing of short fiction in the early 1930s, they are only peripheral and should not overshadow the fine artistic achievement of this unpretentious little story.

The narrative of "Edith McGillcuddy" moves with a simple grace in which twelve-year-old Edith is a kind of village counterpart to Jody Tiflin, experiencing for the first time the "badness" that can befall a person. The first two paragraphs, which set the conflict between Salinas's twenty saloons and five churches, are counterparts in a battle for people's souls. The conflict of ignorance and badness versus decency and temperance also runs along social lines. The problem with Edith is that, "Born to the good element, her instincts were bad in the matter of the company she kept"

(p. 252). She is drawn irresistibly to the ungracious side of life.

On one pristine Sunday morning, Edith is sent to Sunday school with a nickel in her pocket for the offering plate. She dresses as neatly as befits her class, shoes polished, dress glistening, hair tightly braided and beribboned. Along the way she meets Susy Nugger, "a little girl of Edith's age but not of her class." Seduced by the offer of an all-day sucker, Edith joins Susy for a "free" funeral, boarding the narrow-gauge train to Monterey that the 'Tonio Alvarez family has reserved free of charge for the mourners of the funeral. Her capitulation to an abandonment of Sunday School for the thrill of a train ride is secured by Susy's logic that since Edith sometimes has to await an answer from God to her prayers, God can wait a week for her nickel. Thereby the great adventure of the train trip is put in motion.

The trip into worldly affairs is accompanied by a commensurate dissolution in Edith's apparel: "Susy and Edith squeezed in and sat on the floor between two rows of benches. Already Edith's face was streaked with red from the sucker; her hair ribbon was a ruin, and in crawling up on the flat car she had torn the knee out of one of her long ribbed stockings" (p. 254). The train arrives in Monterey and the picnickers-mourners get off for the funeral, the train bell tolling instead of church bells. At the funeral, Susy Nugger meets another companion, and Edith is left alone and forlorn in the wanton reaches of Monterey.

Walking by the shore, Edith meets a "ragamuffin" girl named Lizzie, of still a lower class than Susy Nugger:

There came a scrabbling sound from under the boat. Edith got down on her knees and looked underneath. She leaped back quickly, for a dirty little face was peering out at her. The face and a frousy, frizzled head came worming out from under the boat, and a red dress followed, and long, skinny bare legs. It was a plain ragamuffin. Compared to this little girl, Susy was as elevated as Edith was above Susy; for this little specter of dirt and low-classness not only had a dirty face and uncombed hair; what was infinitely worse, she had on no pants under the dress, and she had not wiped her nose for a long time. [p. 255]

Lizzie completes Edith's knowledge of evil, for she tells Edith of the dissolute woman who smokes and her strange male companion who will spring for a nickel for a bucket of huckleberries. Edith and Lizzie traipse through the huckleberry patch, with further disaster to Edith's clothing, and seek out the strange couple, who live at the Frenchman's hotel.

The discovery of evil, imaged by the train ride from Salinas into the worldly kingdom of Monterey, the disarray of Edith's clothing, and her descent into lower social classes, now focuses upon the woman who smokes and her ill companion, Robert Louis Stevenson. The discovery, moreover, has a subtle undercurrent that twelve-year-old Edith would hardly be aware of. Stevenson met Fanny Osborne in France in 1876, where, with Fanny's two children, they lived together. When Fanny ran into financial difficulties, she returned to Oakland to her husband, who eventually installed her in a cottage in Monterey. She was the object of Stevenson's long journey from Edinburgh, the final leg of which was the seventeen-mile trip by narrow-gauge railroad from Salinas to Monterey.

The voyage was an exhausting one, including eleven days of sea travel and another eleven by rail. Stevenson, whose health was already precarious, arrived in Monterey feverish and drained. Moreover, the relationship with Fanny, which had flourished in the village of Grez-sur-Loing and which now seemed irrecoverable, caused Stevenson great anxiety and disappointment. In fact, by October Fanny had returned to Oakland, ostensibly to seek a divorce but knowing also that the relationship with Stevenson was finished.

There is a parallel, then, between Edith's discovery that evil is not as attractive as it appears to be and Stevenson's discovery that the illicit relationship with Fanny Osborne was doomed.

Edith and Lizzie enter the hotel courtyard with their basket of huckleberries, the quantity inflated by a generous portion of leaves (which also echoes the theme of disillusion), and see the infamous couple:

> On one side of the cloth sat a lady in a white dress smoking a cigarette, and on the other side squatted a long-haired young man with a lean, sick face and eyes shining with fever. A smile came on the young man's face, but the lady did not change her expression; she just looked blankly at the two little girls standing in the open gateway. Edith and Lizzie stood self-conscious and clumsy. [p. 257]

Lizzie sells the huckleberries for a nickel and whirls off, leaving Edith with the couple.

The young man observes that she has been taken in, a fact Edith now recognizes as well. She has gained some knowledge of the world, and as she drinks cambric tea with the unnamed couple, she observes, "I should of gone to Sunday school" (p. 258). But she has not. She has had her experience in the world, and when she suddenly hears the piercing scream of her train whistle calling her back to her world, she runs wildly to board it. She must, of course, find some way to explain her disheveled hair, the soiled dress, the scuffed shoes. But there is an affirmation to her voyage in the final line of the story, one she would not understand until years later: "And that was how Edith McGillcuddy met Robert Louis Stevenson."

Focusing as it does upon the young Edith's point of view, the story relies upon implicit meanings rather than overt statements. Yet, that implicitness is the very quality that gives the story a certain power and grace. It is very much a story about the discovery of the dark side of life, a side revealed with beguiling charm. Edith's descent through the class structure, from the ordered Methodist calm of Salinas to Lizzie's squalor, and her realization that she has been duped all along into bad actions quietly parallel the relationship of Stevenson and Osborne, the descent from Grez-sur-Loing to the secret courtyard in Monterey, and their knowledge of a failed relationship. Stevenson's sickness is mirrored in the tatters of Edith's dress and appearance. The one constant in the story is the train, which, even though it has borne this one pilgrim in search of the secular city, remains in the background, finally shrieking out to Edith that it is time to return once more. The train ride is free, and thus, the story has a happy outcome for Edith at least. There is a way back. And even though the way back would prove thornier for Stevenson, there remains that one inviolate Sunday afternoon in the courtyard when a girl's life was touched by a few words of kindness and a cup of cambric tea. Finally, it is as much a story about grace as it is about the knowledge of evil.

"THE MURDER"

The momentum Steinbeck attained while working on *The Pastures of Heaven* carried directly into the stories collected in *The Long Valley*. There are clear differences between the story patterns, however. *The Pastures of Heaven* was seen, from the start, as a unified whole, a quasi-novelistic structure with a thematic if not an organic unity. The stories ultimately collected in *The Long Valley* have no such unity and were originally drafted as individual pieces.

"The Murder" was most likely originally conceived as part of *The Pastures of Heaven*. Written during the late fall of 1933, the story came after the *Pastures* collection was finished but retained its setting. In the original draft of the story, Steinbeck set it in Corral de Tierra, a name he struck and replaced with Valle del Castillo, "One of those valleys in the hills so frequently found in the Santa Lucia Range which cuts off the Salinas Valley from the sea" (*TFN*). In the final, printed version, it becomes Canon del Castillo, "one of those valleys in the Santa Lucia range which lie between its many spurs and ridges" (p. 169). Geographically, however, the story still takes place in the Corral de Tierra, identified by the "Castle" in the story, an actual rock formation in the valley. In fact, the ruined buildings described in the story still stand at its base. Thematically, "The Murder" is also related to *The Pastures of Heaven*. In his original description of the work to Mavis McIntosh, Steinbeck details "two murders, a suicide, many quarrels and a great deal of unhappiness" (*SLL*, p. 43). In fact, in *The Pastures of Heaven* there is only one murder, that of Hilda Van Deventer by her mother. "The Murder" would have supplied the other one. While there is no Munroe to bring the curse in the story, a horseman named George informs Jim Moore of his rustled livestock, which leads Jim to discover Jelka's infidelity.

In *The True Adventures of John Steinbeck, Writer*, Jackson Benson calls "The Murder" a "strange story, a sort of gothic Western."[29] There is little doubt that the story was influenced in part by Steinbeck's extensive reading in detective magazines in order to write a popular story. Although *Steinbeck: A Life in Letters* routinely confuses "The Murder" with the unpublished "Murder at High Moon by Peter Pym," the two were written nearly three years apart. Nonetheless, they bear faint similarities in their mutual use of techniques employed in the popular mystery stories.[30]

The artistic background of "The Murder," then, brings together diverse strands: the disaffection of *The Pastures of Heaven*, the trappings of the popular mystery story, and the use of mood with its eerie setting on a secluded ranch in the hovering light of the full moon. The thematic heart of the story, however, resides in the conflict of cultures, focused here on two people, Jim Moore and the "Jugo-Slav girl" he marries, Jelka Sepic. Part of that conflict was suggested already by Steinbeck's attempts to title the story. In his notebook he inserted three titles on a line: Šepić   The Murder   Jelka Šepić. In the initial draft, Steinbeck also gave Jim a quasi-Hispanic name: Tomas Ernest Manuelo More, which would have heightened the cultural conflict. The variations also suggest the author's artistic conflicts.

Will this be a story about cultural differences or the murder itself, which springs from the cultural conflict? That cultural conflict is initiated at the outset. Left with a moderate inheritance, Jim Moore is attracted to the rare beauty of Jelka and marries her within a year. But on the wedding night his father-in-law imparts some unsettling advice:

> "Don't be big fool, now," he said. "Jelka is Slav girl. He's not like American girl. If he is bad, beat him. If he's good too long, beat him too. I beat his mama. Papa beat my mama. Slav girl! He's not like a man that don't beat hell out of him."
> "I wouldn't beat Jelka," Jim said.
> The father giggled and nudged him again with his elbow. "Don't be big fool," he warned. "Sometime you see." [p. 171]

The "otherness" of Jelka is emphasized during the early days of the marriage. She is quiet, never initiating conversation. Yet, she waits on Jim with an almost abject servility. He begins to think of her not so much as a wife as one of his domesticated animals: "She was so much like an animal that sometimes Jim patted her head and neck under the same impulse that made him stroke a horse" (p. 172).

Despite their marriage union, their different ethnic backgrounds separate them: "Early in the marriage he told her things that happened on the farm, but she smiled at him as a foreigner does who wishes to be agreeable even though he doesn't understand" (p. 172). Realizing the abyss between them—"He realized before long that he could not get in touch with her in any way"—Jim becomes increasingly disaffected by the marriage and, longing for the noisy company he had known before marrying Jelka, he begins consorting with tavern women at the Three Star. When they ask about his wife, Jim retorts that for her, "Home is the barn."

The tension in the story, then, focuses upon Jim's complete inability to accept Jelka on her terms, allowing the wall of their cultural backgrounds to solidify between them.

Occasionally he defers to her personal needs, sending her off to visit her family, for example, but it is always with a condescending bitterness:

"A fine time you'll have," Jim said to her. "You'll gabble your crazy language like ducks for a whole afternoon. You'll giggle with that big grown cousin of yours with the embarrassed face. If I could find any fault with you, I'd call you a damn foreigner." [p. 174]

In fact, the fault lies in her relationship with "that big grown cousin."

In the evening of a particularly hot and long day of harvesting oats, Jim feels the urge to visit Monterey. He invites Jelka along, but she is content to wait the rising of the full moon while she knits at the ranch. Upon leaving, Jim once again gives his patronizing gesture: "He went to her and patted her sleek head" (p. 176), precisely as he would one of his horses. He rides toward Monterey, hoping he can get "blond May at the Three Star" before someone else does.

On the way Jim meets a neighbor who tells him that one of his calves has been found rustled and slaughtered. After finding the calf, Jim rides to his own ranch to check his herd and discovers a strange horse in his barn. While he has been pursuing May at the Three Star, Jelka has been busy assuaging her loneliness at the ranch. Jim creeps into the house and discovers Jelka in bed with "her grown, embarrassed cousin." After leaving to sit by the water trough a few moments, Jim returns to the bedroom and shoots the cousin through the head. When he faces Jelka, however, Jim turns in panic and runs outside. He can still hear Jelka, who "whimpered like a puppy."

The next day the deputy sheriff and coroner arrive to get the body. The deputy informs Jim that the "technical" charge of murder will be dismissed and advises him to "go kind of light on your wife." Taking a "nine-foot, loaded bull whip" after they depart, Jim finds Jelka in the barn and administers the cruel beating that her father had advised on their marriage night: "And as he climbed the ladder to

the hayloft, he heard the high, puppy whimpering start"
(p. 183). Oddly enough, that is the restorative act to their
marriage. Jim carries Jelka to the water trough and sets her
"tenderly on the ground." Jelka offers to make him breakfast, and when Jim offers to help her remove her blood-
caked shirt she responds, "'No, I'll do it myself.' Her voice
had a peculiar resonance in it. Her dark eyes dwelt warmly
on him for a moment, and then she turned and limped into
the house" (p. 184). They agree to build a new house further down the valley, and we are left with a portrait of rec-
onciliation: "Her eyes smiled. She sat down on a chair beside him, and Jim put out his hand and stroked her hair and
the back of her neck" (p. 184).

Despite its success— "The Murder" was published in the
North American Review in April 1934 and awarded the O.
Henry Memorial Award for that year—this is an odd and
atypical story of Steinbeck's with unusual artistic weaknesses. There are marvelous passages of descriptive energy
in the story, beginning with the evocative description of
setting and the detailed movement of the rising, blood-red
moon. The actual shooting scene is powerfully rendered.
Steinbeck carefully revised that passage to supply more
stylistic energy to it. The original reads, "The back of the
skull was broken out by the hollow pointed bullet and the
pillow and wall were splashed" (*TFN*), which he changed
to, "A small, black, bloodless hole was in the man's forehead. But behind, the hollow-point took brain and bone
and splashed them on the pillow" (p. 181). The complex
plot motif of cultural differences finally overcome by a ritual beating was not so unusual either, given Steinbeck's interest in ethnic groups and his use of a beating in the earlier
"Fingers of Cloud" story. The problems lie in other areas.

The motivation for Jim's actions, for example, are only
weakly supplied. While we might understand Jim's acceptance of his father-in-law's dictum to beat his wife, strange
as it may sound to him at first, the narrative accounting for
that action seems forced. The sudden reversal toward marital renewal by virtue of a beating is too sudden. Robert

Davis sees a psychological renewal in the beating that allows "Jim's becoming a satisfactory husband and complete human being," but that is a bit of extraliterary speculation not sustained by the story.[31] R. S. Hughes observes, "The solution is as absurdly simple as it is unpalatable."[32]

This discussion has focused upon the theme of cultural conflict in the story, but it is most difficult to say precisely what it is really about. Warren French argues, "Its point appears to be that people should be treated according to their own traditions even if we find them incomprehensible."[33] But then one must surely ask, what of Jim's tradition, against which wife-beating is a violation? Too many such contrarieties riddle the story. In "'The Murder'—Realism or Ritual?," Katharine M. Morsberger and Robert E. Morsberger approach the cultural conflict from a different direction, probing for underlying causes. Emphasizing the profuse animal imagery used throughout the story, the Morsbergers conclude that the story is ultimately a discovery of the animal within human personality:

> In the killing and flogging, Jim is not even so much angry as going through the motion of a pre-ordained ritual. There is no cathartic fury, no confrontation, only compulsion. Following the insect imagery in the horse trough, he kills the sleeping man as he would a spider or some other repulsive intruder in his home and bed. Even when he beats his wife it is an unemotional, automatic act, after which he handles her tenderly and speaks to her with concern. He has recognized Jelka's animal nature but is still uneasy with his own.[34]

The Morsbergers conclude that the story is "a testament that mysteriously primitive passions and past are still with us."[35]

Although the Morsbergers do not refer to them, their analysis receives considerable support from subsequent stories written in 1934 in which Steinbeck would follow precisely this pattern of self-revelation through animal imagery. Finally, however, these variations in construing the central theme are not simply examples of cordial critical disagreement; they emanate from the essential confusion of the story itself. Steinbeck admitted that he wanted ambiguity in the story. To George Albee he wrote, "I think you got out of the murder story about what I wanted you to. You got no character. I didn't want any there. You got color and a dream like movement. I am writing it more as a dream than as anything else, so if you got this vague and curiously moving feeling out of it that is all I ask" (*SLL*, p. 91). The key may lie in his comment about not having character, for that is the missing link. Here we may have an instance wherein ambiguity, often an aesthetic merit in literature that contributes to the richness of a work, degenerates to confusion and obscurantism, always aesthetic defects.

The discontinuity of plot is paralleled by structural flaws. One cannot be easily persuaded by Louis Owens's argument that the story bears an "impressive structural coherence" based largely upon Steinbeck's use of the castle in the opening scene.[36] The castle is, of course, illusory, a symbol that Roy Simmonds argues is "inadequately employed" and simply discarded.[37] Owens's argument is that the illusory nature of the castle "casts an ironical light over the entire story. The castle established the perspective through which we are to view events in the story; it informs the story and hovers over it as it does the abandoned farmhouse. Rather than being 'simply discarded,' the image of the castle is a highly effective device integral to the structural coherence of 'The Murder.'"[38] In point of fact, the castle is never again mentioned in the story after the first paragraph. Since the story was originally drafted in connection with *The Pastures of Heaven*, it functioned as a setting for that common locale. Taken separately from this collection, however, Steinbeck would have had to make a great deal more use of the castle in the story proper in order to have it serve either as a structural or thematic device.

Most serious of the flaws, however, is the artistically incomplete portrait of Jelka. She is often depicted as a whining puppy or a head of livestock, with the suggestion that she submissively awaits a beating. But she has little redemptive character of her own. She remains at the end what she is at the beginning, a fairly lifeless caricature. Steinbeck supplies no compelling motivation for her tryst with her cousin. Why not a neighbor? Or the cattle rustlers? Is it simply to affirm her inseparable tie to her ethnic heritage? And what about the cattle rustlers, after all? That whole part of the story is dismissed. Such questions insist upon answers arising from the plot itself. Here, too many odds and ends get thrown together in an eclectic fashion.

Despite its winning the O. Henry Award, presumably on the basis of its descriptive energy and its use of a popular story pattern, close examination of the story raises too many questions to consider it an artistic success. That success would await the stories written in the spring and summer of 1934, those that form the heart of *The Long Valley*.

6

The Long Valley

THE MAIN BODY of stories in *The Long Valley* was written during an intense six months in 1934. They were designed not for a collection but for individual sale to periodicals. The earlier sales of the *Red Pony* stories created a hunger in Steinbeck. Although he was to avow in later years that he had no concerns about being a popular writer and that he would not write simply to appease an editor, during the first half of 1934 he desperately wanted some popular notice, and the sheer variety of his stories was, in part, an effort to appeal to editorial tastes. It is true, nonetheless, that he was telling *his* stories, and telling them in his own way. This half year also marked a coming of age for Steinbeck as a literary stylist, as he fashioned patterns of imagery, narrative points of view, and thematic patterns that would mark his writing for years to come.

Several of the stories evidence great struggle. The revisions on "The Chrysanthemums" and "Flight" were as extensive as any he made on a work. "The Vigilante" was a complete stylistic and thematic overhaul of the aborted first effort, "Case History." With some stories, such as "The White Quail," he knew what he wanted to do but could not kindle the creative fires to do it. And other stories, such as "The Raid," which occurred to him in a sudden flash of insight—"I know, I'll tell the story of the raid in Watsonville"—spun out easily.

Two works were forsaken altogether. Having just finished "Addenda to Flight," which was incorporated with revisions into the conclusion of the published version, Steinbeck entered a note titled "Interregnum":

The nice little time between stories. So far I've kept one ahead of the number set and I have one extra written making 6 in four weeks. I don't want any vacation. I'm enjoying working hard. One third of the time is gone and I have nearly 200 pages of mss done and out. . . . It is kind of exciting. The hard thing will be if nothing turns out. If everything should flop we'll have a bad period to overcome. [*LVN*]

His next story was to be "The Cow": "On the surface it is to be a rather funny story but underneath it is to have a hardness of reality and of symbol. It is a story I shall enjoy writing" [*LVN*]. The enjoyment did not last. After approximately 1 1/4 pages of writing, he cried out, "And right there halt! This is wrong. . . . Too much emphasis on the beginning. I must start with the cow. She's the important person in this story and to hell with Chicago. It doesn't belong. Must start all over again." A third effort lasted a mere half page: "Wrong again all wrong. What the hell's the matter with me" (*LVN*).

A second deserted effort is "Western Art Colony," the story of John Roman, who writes juvenile stories. Steinbeck misspells *juvenile* as *Juvenal*, but the misspelling may be deliberate, for the little bit of the story that appears marks it as a satire of the artist who prostitutes his skills to popular demands. Roman makes $200 a month selling stories to "St. Nicholas, the American Boy, and a syndicate of Sunday School Magazines." The first two were popular magazines of the time, which, incidentally, attracted some top-flight writers of the time. But Steinbeck also saw a large gap between his effort to write "serious" fiction and the financial ease of those who wrote for a popular audience. If anything, however, the aborted effort indicates that he was finished with pure satire as a literary mode until *The Short Reign of Pippin IV*, written twenty-two years later.

The stories he did complete during this period are telling examples of Steinbeck's concerns and artistic development.

Common themes grow out of his own experience: the repression of the artist and a deepening concern for any oppressed people, the effects of mob psychology, the experience of violence. Each casts the isolated individual into some form of conflict.

THE ARTIST IN CONFLICT

"The Chrysanthemums": Repression and Desire

During his period of intense artistic activity during the first half of 1934, Steinbeck fought almost daily against an overwhelming sense of failure. There were days when the words flowed as if some divine muse guided them; there were others during which his ledger entries consisted of little more than despondent notes lamenting his lack of success. It is not surprising, in view of this symbiosis of exhilarating effort and exhausted despair, that one theme to surface regularly in the stories is society's failure to recognize the artistic gift and its consequent repression of the creative genius. Steinbeck explored that theme in three of his stories from *The Long Valley:* "The Chrysanthemums," "The White Quail," and "The Harness."

"The Chrysanthemums" stimulated an unusual interest for Steinbeck. It was, as he noted in a ledger entry, the story of a woman that he could not get out of his mind. Perhaps this closeness to it led to the difficulties he endured in composing the story, for none other in *The Long Valley* seemed to give him quite so much trouble artistically. The labor was worth it, marking the story as one of Steinbeck's short masterpieces. Stylistically and thematically, "The Chrysanthemums" is a superb piece of compelling craftsmanship.

Perhaps the first reference to "The Chrysanthemums" occurs in an undated ledger held by the Steinbeck Research Center of San Jose State University. The notebook consists of only a few random notes, fragments of clippings, and some work of Carol Steinbeck. No unified work appears. One entry has work on a play that Steinbeck never finished called "The Wizard." He returned to it under the title "The Wizard of Maine" in 1944–45, completing about fifteen thousand words on thirty folio leaves.[1] In that notebook, however, one brief note appears in reference to "The Chrysanthemums," probably jotted some time before he began composing the story in January 1934. The note is remarkable for its revelation of an author's discovery of his own story:

My book, all empty. Maybe sometime you will be full. But not now. I am as empty as you are. I wish I could get the lady and the chrysanthemums chrysanthems [sic] out of my mind. If she goes much further and I haven't the least idea what she's about. I'm afraid she's going to get me and she isn't much of a story anyways. But she is interesting and if she did see them along the road— what the hell. She'd feel pretty terrible if she had built up a structure.

All other drafts of "The Chrysanthemums" appear in the *Tortilla Flat* notebook, held by the Harry Ransom Research Center of the University of Texas, Austin. The very early starts on the story give further indication of Steinbeck's process of artistic discovery. The first draft depicts Elisa in the kitchen:

On a shelf over the kitchen sink, a little oblong mirror with fluted edges stood. In front of it lay four big hair pins, bent out of shape, shiny where the enamel was broken off at the U. Elisa, washing the noon day dishes, paused now and then to look in the mirror. Her face was now bloated now cadaverous as its reflection moved on the uneven glass. Her hands came out of the dish water and rested palms down on the spongy wooden sink board. Each finger drained soapy water. She leaned forward, peered in the mirror and then she picked up one of the hair pins, deftly captured a loose strand of light brown hair and pinned it in back of her ear. In the living room, her husband coughed to make his presence felt. Elisa regarded her fingers puckered and unhealthily white from the hot water and strong soap.

At this point, Steinbeck's ink ran out. He switched to purple ink and the switch itself, in a not unusual pattern in his ledgers, stimulated him to a reflection on his writing:

This is to be a good story. Two personalities meet, cross, flare, die and hate each other. Purple, if it were a little bit stronger, would be a good color for the story. It is coming stronger and stronger. I have a definite feeling of change today, Wednesday the 31st of January. I feel that some change has taken place. Good or bad, I don't know. It will be interesting to see. I make the record for checking back. I think either tonight or tomorrow I will receive word of that change.

In the note Steinbeck dates the story-writing as Wednesday, January 31, thus placing the composition in 1934.

A day following, Steinbeck's mind was still absorbed with personal thoughts. He switched back to black ink, his preferred color, and determined to continue the story.

Can the weather account for all of this gathering storm in my mind. What is there about the story which makes it almost impossible for me to write it. There is a section of great ecstacy in it. It is a good story as I see it. I'm having a terrible time writing it. And I should get it done for I suspect I shall get a beastly reception for TF [*Tortilla Flat*] and much as I fight against it, I shall be upset by that reception.

Following some personal reflections, Steinbeck concludes the note:

Now the story of the Chrysanthemums is to go on and may the Lord have mercy on it. A story of great delicacy, one difficult to produce. I must do this one well or not at all. I'm getting the feel back. Curious how my spirit was undermined a few days ago. Almost came crashing down too. I shouldn't like to start all over at the very beginning.

Evidently Steinbeck did not start all over. The next entry begins with a portrait of Henry Allen, following upon the earlier paragraph of Elisa washing dishes. Its importance lies in the insight it gives us to Henry's character:

Henry was in the living room waiting for her, she knew. He wanted to tell her something. Strange ceremonious man he was. He couldn't come right out with it when he entered the house for lunch. No, he must keep silence, what he considered a poker face, he must arrange his scene, the living room, after she had finished washing the dishes—a little ceremony. Henry was always that way. And whatever his secret was, he thought it would be a surprise to Elisa. She would fool him as she had so often before. He thought she could read his mind. How many times had she not told him what he was thinking and amazed him.

Steinbeck suggests a potential conflict between Henry and Elisa; he being ritualistic and dependable, she intuitive and quick. The following paragraph accentuates the conflict, focusing now upon Elisa's native intelligence and Henry's rather dull, methodical pattern of living:

Eliza [sic] took a towel from the rack and dried the dishes slowly. She would wear down his patience, and then start him wrong. It amused her to do this and it gave her a nice secret sense of power with which to combat the fact that she, Elisa, valedictorian of her class in Salinas High School, winner of two statewide essay contests, was the wife of a fairly successful farmer.

. . . The essay contests had placed her very high, and sometimes this marriage with a farmer seemed to place her rather low.

Elisa goes into the sitting room to berate Henry for not wiping his feet, but then Henry shares his secret with her: "'Why the Ferry Seed People want me to put in sweet peas in that 20 acres out by the county road[,] ten of mixed and five of pink and five of blue. They say the land's perfect for sweet peas.'" Elisa thinks that the field of sweet peas, an idea later picked up in "The Harnass," will be beautiful; Henry thinks only of the profit. To celebrate the decision, Henry invites her out: "'I thought we should have a little celebration tonight, go into town for dinner and then to a picture show.' He grinned. 'Or how would you like to go to the fights[?]' 'Oh no,' she said. 'I don't think I'd like fights.'"

Elisa then decides to reset the chrysanthemums before going out.

But here Steinbeck broke off. In midsentence he switches from the narrative to his unease in writing it: "She heard Henry hammering metal in the tractor shed and she went to the back porch where she kept her gardening things— This was the day's work. There's no sureness of touch in me today. I don't seem to be able to get at this story. I should not be writing this story this way at all. It should be a hard finish story."

Several days passed before Steinbeck returned to the story, starting this time with the memorable opening lines retained in the published version, but focusing now upon Henry's labor in the field versus Elisa's work in the garden.

The versions from this point on have been ably analyzed by William Osborne in "The Texts of Steinbeck's 'The Chrysanthemums'" and Roy S. Simmonds's superb textual analysis in "The Original Manuscripts of Steinbeck's 'The Chrysanthemums,'"[2] the last particularly important for the sexual implications of the story arising from the scene where Elisa kneels before the Tinker. Simmonds observes, "A textual study of the original manuscript of the final version of the story makes it patently obvious that Steinbeck was obliged to tone down some of the sexual implications in the work to mollify the editors of *Harper's Magazine*."[3] The several starts on the story, however, also signify Steinbeck's efforts to relate his theme of repression to Elisa's femininity and native genius. Whether with Henry, who wishes she would use her gifts more profitably in service to the farm, or the Tinker, who frankly abuses her gifts, the pivotal center of the tale is the complex character of Elisa Allen.

Compulsively orderly and neat, Elisa has regimented her bursting creativity into rituals. While Steinbeck deleted the passage recounting her scholastic achievements, he retains her fierce eagerness in a more subtle imagery pattern allied with her gardening. She exudes energy. Her work with the scissors is rapacious, "over-eager, over-powerful." Her "terrier fingers" probe the flower stems with sureness and skill. Yet, for all her energy, her life is very much like the valley itself on this cloudy December day, "a closed pot."

In the story Elisa receives two contrary pulls from outside forces upon her energy. One emanates from the Tinker, who stands as her personal and physical opposite. Languid and disheveled, the Tinker poses a host of polarities to Elisa. While her body looks "blocked and heavy in her gardening costume," the Tinker slouches like a lean rail in a spindly fence. Her powerful force is frequently depicted in masculine terms—"handsome," "strong"—while the Tinker is effeminately deferential. Her energy is opposed by the Tinker's sad, melancholy disposition. Her eyes are "clear as water"; the Tinker's are "dark and full of brooding." She works with living things; he with inanimate objects. Her dog is a lively ranch shepherd; the Tinker's "a lean and rangy mongrel dog." She sports a yellow print dress; he a black suit worn to threads. Elisa's plants stand in soldierly rows of exuberant health; his horse and donkey "drooped like unwatered flowers."

The elaborate but artistically well-hidden list of juxtapositions function ironically, for this disheveled panhandler is also a master con man who manages to probe to the heart of Elisa's need in a way that her husband can never approach. He carries with him, beside the reek of long days on the road, the unqualified freedom to follow that road where he wills, his only aim "to follow nice weather." Freedom is the dream he brings.

Despite her keen awareness from the very start that the Tinker is a shyster, Elisa bows to the manipulation as she senses it opens on freedom. Her flowers have been her life, her children, her talent. Her gift is "planting hands," the chrysanthemums her offspring. When the Tinker acknowledges her gift, admitting its dangerous reality, Elisa reveals more of herself—physically and psychologically. She removes her hat and shakes out her long hair, removing layers of repressed desires from her soul. The unmasking comes to a climax, artistic as well as sexual, when she kneels before him to hand him one of her flowers. They are her progeny, her true and secret self. The sexual overtones of the passage are clear. Elisa exclaims, "'I've never lived as you do, but I know what you mean. When the night is dark—why, the stars are sharp-pointed, and there's quiet. Why, you rise up and up! Every pointed star gets driven into your body. It's like that. Hot and sharp and—lovely'" (p. 12).

And suddenly, like the dissipation of a sexual climax, it is over. The Tinker mends her pots, now once more just a slouch of a man rather than the revealer of her inmost heart. His retort cuts her to the quick: "It ain't the right kind of life for a woman." As she pays him, Elisa insists, "How do you know? How can you tell?" And he leaves, with the plant she knows full well is as doomed as her momentary dream. She whispers, "There's a bright direction. There's a glowing there." A bright direction opens, briefly, but it is a "gray afternoon" as she bathes to prepare for her evening out with Henry.

If the Tinker, almost inadvertently, opens a dream for Elisa and then quickly retreats, Henry is the second contrary tug upon Elisa's life. Having little sense of her gifts or her longing for full expression of them, Henry has also closed Elisa into a pot of routine expectations. From the start he is depicted as one who values the pragmatic more than the artistic, suggesting to Elisa that her gift could be put to better use in his orchard. When he tweaks her with the offhand compliment, "You look so nice!" he is hardly prepared for her response: "Nice? You think I look nice? What do you mean by 'nice'?" (p. 16). He will take her out for one more routine evening and return her to her routine at the ranch.

Steinbeck's creation of Elisa Allen is a remarkably insightful portrait with enduring relevance. She represents at once the repression of womanhood and of the artistic gift. Torn in one direction by the mechanisms of a slovenly Tinker who nonetheless opens a dream of recognition for her, and from the other by the routines of a pragmatic husband who fails to understand her, Elisa is left with little but her chrysanthemums. And the littleness of that is signified by her cherished progeny, this nurtured part of herself, that lies wilting by the roadside, tossed out by the Tinker so that he could keep the pot. It is no wonder that we are left with the portrait of her "crying weakly—like an old woman." It is all that others have permitted her to be.

It is possible, as Roy S. Simmonds has suggested, to consider Elisa as a headstrong woman blinded by her own femininity. In this view, the Tinker's abuses of her "symbolically re-established the position of male dominance she imagined she had wrested from him, in exactly the same way as over the years she had deprived, emasculated, her husband."[4] Read in this way, as Elisa's yearning for dominance, the garden signifies her surrogate kingdom, one in which she wields absolute authority in all matters of life and death. She is the sovereign queen. Simmonds argues,

Elisa's need for this sense of dominance over the male is not confined solely to her feelings towards her husband. She experiences this need to assert her superiority over all men, contriving always to keep them at arm's length. Her flower garden is surrounded by a protective wire fence ostensibly to keep out animals, but the fence also serves to exclude her husband and the tinker. It is not until the tinker has verbally seduced her with his assumed interest in her chrysanthemums and is admitted to her side of the fence that Elisa finds her defenses in danger of collapsing to the extent that she almost allows herself to succumb to male dominance. Almost, but not quite. . . . Her shame is the shame of a woman who realizes that she has momentarily lowered her defenses and all but offered herself to the male dominance she so greatly despises.[5]

Support for such a revisionist view may be engineered from the fact that Elisa and Henry have no offspring and that Elisa has displaced both sexuality and femininity to her flowers. Some support may also be extrapolated from Steinbeck's personal relationship with Carol. The gardening costume Elisa wears, for example, is similar to one Carol wore frequently. She too could look "strong," "blocky," and "handsome." And more than once in his letters Steinbeck refers to the fact that Carol had great pride and that he sometimes could not feel close to her.

Such a reading of the story seems at odds with Steinbeck's strong rebellion against any repressive power in civilization's power bloc and his strong sensitivity toward any repressed individual. This is a theme that wends through the stories of *The Pastures of Heaven* and continues here in *The Long Valley*. Moreover, this revisionist view leaves begging this important question: What exactly would the "bright direction" that the Tinker opens for Elisa represent? Her "closed pot" of a valley does not seem, metaphorically, to be the action of her own mind, a kind of self-imposed willfulness. Rather, like the oppressive gray clouds on this December day, it is imposed upon her from without. Finally, with such a view, one wonders why Elisa would be weeping like an old woman at the conclusion. That final portrait is one of undeserved subjugation, not willful dominance.

"The Chrysanthemums" more likely should be understood as a unique and vital variation in Steinbeck's theme of social repression of the artistic gift. The personal disillusionment that Steinbeck felt at this point in his artistic career—the frequent rejections, the sense of a loss of self worth, the overwhelming loneliness—is also the guiding motif in shaping Elisa's character. The theme of the self-repressive female character more neatly fits Mary Teller of "The White Quail" than it does Elisa Allen, who typifies the individual whose gifts are ignored or repressed by the society about her.

"The White Quail": Little Foxes in the Vineyard

R. S. Hughes observes that the principal strength of "The White Quail" is "neither in its plot nor its characters. Its distinctive quality can more accurately be called 'lyric.'"[6]

The first part of his claim is certainly accurate; "The White Quail" possesses little strength of character or plot. The grapplings of critics with the story are more often exercises of their own ingenuity than revelations of the story's artistry. The very lack of carefully shaped character and plot, however, emphasizes the psychological theme of the story. If this portrait of narcissism gone mad is to have any validity at all, it has to be as a polarity to Elisa Allen of "The Chrysanthemums." Surely Mary Teller possesses an artistic gift, but like Henri, the mad artist of *Cannery Row* who deliberately constructs a private mythos that prevents anyone, or any life, from intruding upon it, Mary's gift becomes an obsession. Arthur Simpson is not far off the mark when he argues that Mary's obsession excludes life itself:

The story . . . portrays the humanly destructive effects of an absolute commitment to what M. H. Abrams would term an expressive aesthetic. Through symbol and plot, "The White Quail" demonstrates in the character of Mary Teller both the nature and the personal and social effects of a subordination of life to an art which takes its sole value and reason for being as a unique expression of the artist's private vision.[7]

While Simpson sees this subordination as a potentially sacrificial act for the artist, however, it may be better understood as a sacrifice of life itself for art's sake.

"The White Quail" moves in two synchronously paced directions: Mary Teller's obsession with her garden, with its lush foliation, is paralleled by the sexual aridity of the marriage. From the start, her marriage to Harry is subordinated to her garden. When Harry proposes, she consults herself: "'Would the garden like such a man?' For the garden was herself, and after all she had to marry someone she liked" (p. 22). It is important that at this stage the garden is only an idea. Her marriage to Harry is simply a means of making the concept a reality. From the start she dwells in a kind of Platonic Ideal, but unlike Plato's good philosopher, she is unable to translate the Ideal into the reality.

The garden Mary constructs is an artifice, severed by a

neat line of fuchsia standing like phalluses against the surrounding wilds. The fuchsias are manifestly male and serve
as her surreal lover in her dichotomous world: "She pointed
to a fuchsia tree. 'I didn't know whether he would succeed,'
she said, just as though the plant were a person. 'He ate a
lot of plant food before he decided to come around'" (p. 25).[8]
Similarly, like the male defender of the hearth, the fuchsias
protect her from the violations of the real world. Looking at
the dark thicket on the hill behind the garden, sealed off by
the erect row of fuchsias, Mary murmurs, "That's the enemy. . . . That's the world that wants to get in, all rough
and tangled and unkempt. But it can't get in because the
fuchsias won't let it. That's what the fuchsias are there for,
and they know it" (p. 26).

Mary's schizophrenic world, her displacement of reality
into the artifice of her garden, is further evidenced by her
uncanny ability to stand outside herself to see herself. While
going out into the garden to fetch her scissors one night, it
seems to her that she is transported out of body to see herself still sitting in the house. Her vision serves only to separate her further from her husband:

She saw him looking over his paper with an intent, puzzled, almost pained look in his eyes. He tried so hard to understand
when she told him things. He wanted to understand, and he
never quite succeeded. If she told him about this vision tonight,
he would ask questions. He would turn the thing over and over,
trying to understand it, until finally he ruined it. He didn't want
to spoil the things she told him, but he just couldn't help it. He
needed too much light on the things that light shriveled. [p. 28]

Mary believes that her extraworldly vision is "the curse of
imagination," but this passage clearly makes a threat of
Harry's realistic thinking. She does not tell him because
she is afraid of the light that his analysis might bring.

If her imagination is a curse to Mary, it is a curse she herself has willed, nurtured, and clung to. She has willfully
separated herself in a world of artifice while her relationship with Harry shrivels into sterility. From the start of

their courtship she is oblivious to Harry's sexual yearning. When he professes, "You're so pretty. You make me kind of—hungry," Mary is startled. "A little expression of annoyance crossed her face. But nevertheless she let him kiss her again, and then sent him home" (p. 23). When she retires to her room, she mechanically writes her name over and over, only occasionally interrupting the flow with the name "Mrs. Harry E. Teller." Her obsession continues with her perpetually locked bedroom door, which Harry discreetly tries to open each night, and each night finds shut upon his yearning. Harry represents, for her, the intrusion of the wild hungerings of nature that can violate the pristine order of her garden.

Like some of the Romantic poets of the preceding century, Mary Teller deifies the imagination, often at the expense of reality. Speaking of Blake and Coleridge in *The Romantic Imagination*, C. M. Bowra observes,

They reject [Locke's] conception of the universe, and replace it by their own systems, which deserve the name of "idealist" because mind is their central point and governing factor. But because they are poets, they insist that the most vital activity of the mind is the imagination. Since for them it is the very source of spiritual energy, they cannot but believe that it is divine, and that, when they exercise it, they in some way partake of the activity of God.[9]

In much the same way, Mary Teller has become her own divinity, and her garden has become a sacred manifestation of that divine mind. Bowra states, "For Blake the imagination is nothing less than God as He operates in the human soul. It follows that any act of creation formed by the imagination is divine and that in the imagination man's spiritual nature is fully and finally realized."[10] Having made one's own kindgom by the divine power of the imagination, the huge danger, for both the Romantics and Mary Teller, is the expurgation from that garden of all reality. Reality represents the defilement of Eden, the serpent from the wilds.

"The White Quail" thereby takes its place very much in

the lineage of a number of literary gardens. From Spenser to the modern age, the garden represents an unspoiled order, but also an artificial order severed from life. The garden, after the Genesis fall, is disordered, and humans must make the best of their way in it. In Milton's *Paradise Lost,* Michael admonishes Eve,

> Lament not, Eve, but patiently resign
> What justly thou hast lost; nor set thy heart,
> Thus over-fond, on that which is not thine;
> Thy going is not lonely, with thee goes
> Thy husband, him to follow thou art bound;
> Where he abides, think there thy native soil.
> [XI,11.287–92]

The words might well have been directed to Mary Teller, for her clinging to the artifice of her garden divorces her from the companionship of her husband. Her "native soil" is forsaken for the ethereal soil of the romantic garden.

In the same way, Steinbeck found that an artwork which divorces itself from life, which finds life threatening and abhorrent, is despicable. Mary Teller's garden is a bit like Andrea del Sarto's paintings in Robert Browning's poem; yet, Mary lacks del Sarto's understanding: "All is silver-grey/ Placid and perfect with my art: the worse!" While del Sarto laments the fact, Mary clings to it as an ultimate reality. In his analysis of Browning's poetry, Roma King observes, "Art significantly is not an analogy for or a symbol of the Infinite. Neither is it a platform from which man leaps from this world into another. On the contrary, art fixes firmly on this world, circumscribing man's activities, indeed, but at the same time imbuing his finite efforts with a boundless significance."[11] Mary Teller's garden is the opposite of the one King describes, or that del Sarto wishes he could reach, for it is a sterile world of imaginary symbols eternally separated from life. Of this garden Stanley Renner comments, "Steinbeck has deftly symbolized the romantic ideal that lies at the heart of it all, a spiritualized, sexless, and thus, in several senses, pointless love."[12]

As with any garden in the literary tradition, Mary's also
has its malign intruder, bent upon destroying the pristine
symbol of holiness in the garden. In this case it is the cat
that stalks the white quail, the odd bird, the very symbol
and manifestation of Mary's otherworldliness. If the garden, as Mary says, is "herself," then the white quail is her
deepest psychological and sexual being. Mary's sexual fri-
gidity finds a sudden ecstatic release when she first sees the
white quail. In one of the most overtly sexual passages in
Steinbeck's work, she experiences a surreal sexual climax
in her identification with and her spiritual penetration of
the bird:

> A shiver of pleasure, a bursting of pleasure swelled in Mary's
> breast. She held her breath. The dainty little white hen quail
> went to the other side of the pool, away from the ordinary quail.
> She paused and looked around, and then dipped her beak in the
> water.
> "Why," Mary cried to herself, "she's like me!" A powerful ec-
> stasy quivered in her body. "She's like the essence of me, an es-
> sence boiled down to utter purity. She must be the queen of the
> quail. She makes every lovely thing that ever happened to me
> one thing." [p. 33]

The white quail, moreover, is also threatened by a creature
of the wilds, the gray cat. While the quail glistens in the
pristine white feathers that separate it from the wilds, the
cat is gray, an admixture of light and darkness that marks it
as a thing of the wilds.

Mary recognizes the threat. She hysterically beseeches
Harry, "You don't understand. That white quail was *me*, the
secret me that no one can ever get at, the me that's way
inside. . . . Can't you see, dear? The cat was after me. It
was going to kill me. That's why I want to poison it" (p. 35).
While he refuses to poison the cat, Harry agrees to frighten
it away with his air gun the next morning. In a sudden
eruption of his rage and sexual frustration, however, he
turns the air gun on the white quail itself: "The white quail
tipped her head and looked toward him. The air gun spat

with a vicious whisper. The quail flew off into the brush. But the white quail fell over and shuddered a moment, and lay still on the lawn" (p. 36). He takes the body and hides it far up the tangled slope behind the garden. Having killed the white quail, Harry is undeniably linked with the gray cat that Mary so loathes. His final reflection evokes a cringe of sudden pain. "'What a skunk I am,' Harry said to himself. 'What a dirty skunk, to kill a thing she loved so much.' He dropped his head and looked at the floor. 'I'm lonely,' he said. 'Oh, Lord, I'm so lonely!'" (p. 37). As a number of critics have observed, that loneliness was also Steinbeck's. He felt lonely as a writer, but also as a husband. A note dated August 1934 in the *Long Valley* notebook captures the mood:

Always the problem, who shall survive? . . . Still we have no money. I've sent off story after story and so far with no result. Both of us are beginning to worry. I thought there might be a loss of one out of four but the loss seems to be all out of all. . . . We've lived twenty years of pain in a year. . . . There's nothing in me but greyish darkness in which vague figures move about. . . . I am at a low ebb.

Another note is more to the point, however. After starting "The White Quail" Steinbeck paused and jotted these notes in the ledger:

Now the day has changed. The story still seems valid but method more difficult. However, it will be tried. There are so many piercing things. Being alone only helps some. Memory and apprehension keep working right on. Too many factors. They have to be brushed aside and the brushing process causes pain. . . . Some people have a light fabric into which tragedy is easily woven while others are helped by a canvass [sic] so hard that no needle can penetrate into the threads. [*LVN*]

Mary Teller has woven her canvas at an enormous cost—the exclusion of human intercourse and life itself. She is a bit like Nathaniel Hawthorne's Father Hooper, who clings to his black veil at the expense of life and love. Hawthorne's observation of Father Hooper may also be applied to Mary Teller: "All through life that piece of crape had hung between him and the world; it had separated him from cheerful brotherhood and woman's love, and kept him in that saddest of all prisons, his own heart." Mary's world is one of a make-believe kingdom, one that shuts all kinds of doors— the line of fuchsias a door against the wilds of life on the hillside, the locked door of her bedroom a closure upon her husband.

In her obsession, Mary Teller is also not unlike Cathy Ames of *East of Eden*. While Mary divorces herself from reality by artifice, Cathy does so by violent aberration. But both are, to use Steinbeck's term for Cathy, "moral monsters," those in whom some cog got out of alignment, leaving a twisted and depraved moral sensibility. While Mary retreats to her garden, Cathy retreats to an ever-narrowing sequence of rooms, winding up finally in the small lean-to affixed to her bedroom in which "the gray walls seemed to suck up the light and destroy it." In Book 1 of *Paradise Lost*, Satan says, "The mind is its own place, and in itself / Can make a heav'n of hell, a hell of heav'n." As a prison of her own mind, despite its effulgence and order, Mary Teller's garden is one such hell, divorcing her from life.

"The Harness": The Weight of Freedom

Elisa Allen's artistic gift, repressed by the pragmatic concerns of her husband and the Tinker, surfaces in her world of chrysanthemums. Mary Teller's artistic gift consumes her, in turn repressing her own ability to enter life fully. In no story, however, is the repression of an individual more acute than in "The Harness" and its protagonist, Peter Randall.

Readers may have been a bit too quick to read biographical details into these stories. Thus Elisa Allen and Mary Teller become two sides of Carol Steinbeck, the aggressive nurturer and consumed individual. While bits and pieces of Steinbeck's life, and particularly his mood, enter nearly all his stories, such readings can too easily detract from the artistry of the works. In the same manner, Peter Randall is often read as a portrait of Steinbeck's father. Jackson Benson reports that according to Carol, "the central character in 'The Harness' was patterned after a real person who lived near King City, a man who went against everyone's advice and succeeded." But Benson goes on to observe, "There may also be a tenuous connection with Steinbeck's perception of his father, particularly of his condition after Mrs. Steinbeck's death. [13] It is true that Mr. Steinbeck was a devastated person following the death of his wife. Always a rigid and stern man, he seemed severed from life after 1933. Steinbeck himself wrote,

Two things I really want and I can't have either of them and they are both negative. I want to forget my mother lying for a year with a frightful question in her eyes and I want to forget and lose the pain in my heart that is my father. In one year he has become a fumbling, repetitious, senile old man, unhappy almost to the point of tears. [*SLL*, p. 93]

Typically, Steinbeck responded to these desires by burying himself in his work.

It is true, of course, that events in an author's life color his conception of reality and provide experiences transmuted by art into his characters. This may be particularly true for an author as heavily dependent upon personal experience and a recollected past as John Steinbeck. Yet, "The Chrysanthemums," "The White Quail," and "The Harness" may be better understood in terms of the other overwhelming personal crisis in his life, the sense that his work would go unappreciated by society and the sense of being repressed by that society's pressures to conform. What makes "The Harness" intriguing ground for biographical criticism is the fact that the pressure originates in Peter Randall's family. If Elisa Allen's artistic gift surfaces in her garden, if Mary Teller's is consumed by her garden, the tragedy of Peter Randall is that his gift never has a chance to surface at all, for "people knew there was a force in him, but force held caged" (p. 109).

In this case, the bars of that cage are cast by the iron tyranny of Randall's wife, Emma. Physically she is the antithesis to Peter. He is tall and broad, with eyes "blue and grave almost to the point of sorrowfulness." Emma is a shriveled shell of a woman, aged beyond her years, "but her dark eyes were feverish with a determination to live." Psychologically the two are also antithetical, for while Peter's dream is to slouch around and farm according to his whims, Emma holds the farm, as well as Peter's posture, in a harness of rigid order. Peter casts off his harness but once a year on his annual pilgrimage to San Francisco, ostensibly on a business trip but in reality to satisfy the unencumbered desires of his flesh. The trips are restorative to him. Upon returning, he dons his harness once again and engages in farm chores with renewed energy.

From an exterior view there is much to admire in the Randall marriage. The farm is successful; Peter attains a position of leadership in the county; and, because there are no children to nick and mar them, household items are inordinately neat. But Steinbeck's aim as a writer is not to show exterior things; rather, it is a grueling probing of what lies underneath. And what lies under the surface of this apparently smooth household is a seething current of discontent.

As Emma lies dying, three patterns of imagery coalesce. A light, frail woman, she is imaged as a bird: "The good neighbors took cakes to the Randall farm, and they tiptoed into the sickroom, where the little skinny bird of a woman lay in a tremendous walnut bed" (p. 112). Also like a bird, Emma's spirit continues to hover over the household after her death. When Ed Chappell commiserates with Peter after Emma's death and Peter relates the true story of his business trips, Ed goes to the fireplace: "Lots of sparks flew up the chimney like little shining birds." It is as if the birdlike Emma were still there, castigating Peter.

Furthermore, as she lies dying, Emma insists that the curtains remain drawn because the light "worries" her eyes. In Steinbeck's fiction, the repressive and malevolent characters are typically afraid of the light. Cathy Ames is one

such person, withdrawing to a gray, windowless lean-to.
Throughout her illness Emma's curtains remain drawn.
When he is found on his last foray in San Francisco, Peter
indicates to Ed Chappell that Emma's hold upon him has
not diminished. He vows, "When I get back you know what
I'm going to do? I'm going to put in electric lights. Emma
always wanted electric lights" (p. 127). He still lives under
Emma's rules and wishes, and he will return once again to a
frenetic outburst of repairs to set the farm in her order.

Third, Emma's feverish, beady eyes continue to watch
Peter after her death. In her prolonged dying, her eyes are
still very much alive: "The doctor's suggestion that a nurse
be employed met only beady, fierce refusal in the eyes of
the patient; and, ill as she was, her demands were respected" (p. 113). And then, "It was two months before the
dark, sharp bird eyes veiled, and the sharp mind retired
into unconsciousness" (p. 113). After Emma's death, Peter's
own eyes undergo change. At first, his eyes were "grave almost to the point of sorrowfulness," but after Emma's death
"his eyes had begun to shine" (p. 117). But when he gam-
bles on the sweet peas, "There were lines of worry about
his eyes" (p. 124). When Ed Chappel finds him drunk in
San Francisco, "his eyes were glassy." And, then, as he tells
Ed, "She didn't die dead. . . . She won't let me do things.
She's worried me all year about those peas," his "eyes were
wondering" (p. 127).

Like Pat Humbert in *The Pastures of Heaven*, Peter Randall is unable to shrug off the impositions of others. The lit-
eral harness that Emma fitted him into is replaced by a psychological one. He is still under Emma's rule. Freedom is a
sweet thing Peter tasted but could not digest.

While not a particularly complex or artistic story, "The
Harness" voices well Steinbeck's dismay at the repression
of the human psyche. In each of these stories the protagonists are childless, a reflection of the sterility of their lives.
Although Emma's character may not be sufficiently developed to warrant Joseph Fontenrose's observation that
"Emma, puritanical and pleasure-hating, is one form of

Steinbeck's *femme fatale*, a frigid variety of the Virgin Whore,"[14] he is certainly correct that Emma has dominated Peter like a vengeful god, holding him in abject servility. Surely this sense of being an outcast and subjugated by forces beyond his control was also Steinbeck's in 1934. Personal notes in the ledgers are riddled with a lament of failure, a consistent excoriation of his own soul. In a revealing letter to George Albee, he wrote, "When they [McIntosh and Otis] get tired of my consistent financial failures, they will just have to kick me out. I'm a bum, you see, and according to my sister, a fake, and my family is ashamed of me, and it doesn't seem to make any difference at all. If I had the drive of ridicule I might make something of myself" (*SLL*, p. 94).

This keen sense of repression of creative or personal desires was to have a far more dramatic effect artistically, however. It set the stage, I believe, for his sensitivity to the downtrodden and oppressed in his major novels. Already Steinbeck's attention was turning to real-life events in his valley, and he was about to engage his first major novelistic breakthrough with *In Dubious Battle*. While he presented *Tortilla Flat* with warmth and charm, his outrage was kindled by the gratuitous violence of the power holders depicted in *In Dubious Battle*. That flame never fully diminished. It led to his days of tramping the muddy fields while covering the story of the migrants for the *San Francisco News* and eventually to *The Grapes of Wrath*. Then the fires of outrage burned brightly, but carefully controlled by his artistic craftsmanship. In 1938, Steinbeck wrote Elizabeth Otis,

I'm sorry but I simply can't make money on these people. . . . The suffering is too great for me to cash in on it. I hope this doesn't sound either quixotic or martyrish to you. . . .

It is the most heartbreaking thing in the world. . . . I break myself every time I go out because the argument that one person's effort can't really do anything doesn't seem to apply when you come on a bunch of starving children and you have a little money. I can't rationalize it for myself anyway. So don't get me a job for a slick. I want to put a tag of shame on the greedy bastards who are responsible for this but I can best do it through newspapers. [*SLL*, p. 161–62]

The sense of personal outrage also gave Steinbeck a tough-minded sureness of purpose in his art. If in early years he longed for a "sureness of touch," he felt it in his writing about the repression of the creative individual or of any human life impulse. To Pascal Covici, Steinbeck wrote in 1939, "This book [*The Grapes of Wrath*] wasn't written for delicate ladies. If they read it at all they're messing in something not their business. I've never changed a word to fit the prejudices of a group and I never will. . . . I've never wanted to be a popular writer—you know that" (*SLL*, p. 175). That I take to be the larger personal significance of this triad of stories on repression of creative and personal desires. Steinbeck was discovering and nurturing his own creative and personal desires, and he would allow them to form and guide his writing for years to come.

THE TELEOLOGICAL POINT OF VIEW

"Flight": What Is Man That Thou Art Mindful of Him?

Steinbeck's interest in marine biology was inflamed to a passion in the early 1930s. The sea, with its endless surgings and its proliferation of life, would remain a powerful influence upon his life and art throughout his career. We can acknowledge the homing quiet and clashing of dubious battles in his valleys; we can celebrate the high, sunsplashed reaches of his mountains; but we must return over and over to the timeless swell of life and death in the sea as a metaphorical pattern as well as a geographical place in his work.

The sea represents, at once, life and death. For Steinbeck it is the mother: the bringer of life in swarming generation. It is also, beneath its unruly and deceptive surface, a place of primeval violence. That uneasy juxtaposition is captured superbly in *Cannery Row*. In chapter six, Doc surveys the sea, from quiet tidal pools to the deep reaches. His vision moves from the serene grace of the shallows to the primeval undertows. There a chaotic world of ferocity reigns, a feral world. For Steinbeck, probing into the sea is a probing into the origins of life itself, a descent into the mythic subconsciousness of human nature. From *The Log from the Sea of Cortez* to *The Winter of Our Discontent*, the sea functions powerfully in Steinbeck's prose.[15]

The sea also functions metaphorically in "Flight"—by its absence. In one of his notebooks of the early 1930s, during one of his frequent breaks from writing stories to pen personal reflections, Steinbeck turned his attention to the sea. "Man is so little removed from the water," he observes. "When he is near to the sea near the shore where the full life is, he feels terror and nostalgia." There we find our evolutionary predecessors, our lost memory: "Come down to the tide pool, when the sea is out and let us look into our old houses, let us avoid our old enemies" (*TFN*).

Having paused to look into the tidal pools, Steinbeck recounts the course of humanity:

We came up out of the water to the barren dry, the desert dry. It's so hard to get used to the land. It is a deep cry. Oh man who in climbing up has become lower. What good thing but comes out of the depths. What nobility except from pain, what strength except out of anger, what change except from discomfort. We are a cross race so filled with anger that if we do not use it all in fighting for a warm full body, we fight among ourselves. Animals fight nature for the privilege of living but man having robbed nature of some of its authority must fight man for the same right.

It is precisely that movement into the dry reaches, where we fight like animals "for the privilege of living," that marks the thematic pattern of "Flight." The story is a fictionalization of the idea Steinbeck expressed in this notebook entry;

Pepe is very much modern man in search of his manhood and finding the animal within. But, as Steinbeck discovered in telling the story, Pepe also discovers something more, a human spirit that is inviolable and undefeatable, possessing an enduring power that lies below and rises above the animal in man.

The change in the title of the story from "Manhunt" to "Flight" is in itself significant. The story changes from a simple narration of a posse's manhunt to an exploration of one individual's flight into unknown regions—a spiritual odyssey into the high, arid regions far from the nurturing sea. Like the change in title, the story itself changed dramatically in the writing. As it first developed, far more attention was given to the knifing itself. After buying the necessary things in Monterey, Pepe stops at a church to light a candle for his father and then visits the house of Mrs. Rodriguez and her two daughters. After affirming that Pepe has grown to be a man, Mrs. Rodriguez tells him that the surly Carlos is drunk in the kitchen. Pepe, avowing that he is a man, says he will send the troublesome Carlos away. He enters the kitchen to confront him.

The passage that follows, from the *Long Valley* notebook, amplifies the scene. In a fashion he adopted to conserve ink and paper during this penurious time, Steinbeck did not pause in his writing to observe minor paragraph breaks:

"Awaken!" said Pepe. He shook a pan. A big black face arose from the table, and sullen sleepy eyes looked at him. "Who are you?" "I am Pepe Torres. Mrs. Rodriguez wants you to go away now." Behind him, Mrs. Rodriguez said helplessly[,] "This is the son of Jose Torres. You know him[,] Carlos." The sullen eyes looked at her and then back at Pepe. "I know Jose Torres. He was a thief." The sentence was uttered as an insult, was meant to be insulting. Pepe stepped back. "I am a man." He looked inquiringly at Mrs. Rodriguez. She shook her head. Pepe's stomach was sad and then ice got into his stomach and then the ice grew up to his beard. His hand went into his pocket and came out and hung listlessly in front of him. He was surprised at the sound of his voice. "Thou art a liar and a pig." Carlos stood up. "Dirty naked Indian. You say that to me?" Then Pepe's hand flashed. The blade seemed to bloom from the black knife in midflight. It thudded into the man's chest to the handle. Carlos['] mouth was open in amazement. His two black hands came up and found the knife and half pulled it out. And then he coughed, fell forward on the table and drove it in again. Pepe looked slowly around at the woman. His sweet girlish mouth was quizzical[,] "I am a man," he said. "I will go now."

While Steinbeck conveyed the entire scene indirectly in the final version, having Pepe report what happened in several quick sentences, the excised portion shows that the act of killing is allied with Pepe's manhood, and death itself is attended by blackness, both of the knife and of Carlos.

The opening line of the next paragraph in the first draft, inked out in a heavy line, indicates one direction the story might have taken: "They found him in the church sitting in a pew and looking at the lights on the altar. He had said many [undecipherable word] Ave Marias." After the crossed-out line, Steinbeck wrote, "Pepe's movements were swift but unhurried." He heads back to his house, covering the same route through Point Lobos that he had taken earlier. From here the final version follows with a few exceptions. In the first draft, Pepe shoots one of the trackers; in the final version he does not. Most of the revisions were the ones Steinbeck typically made, changing passive verbs to active constructions and sharpening details. The materials included in the two-page notebook entry, "Addenda to Flight," written several days after the first draft, are incorporated into the conclusion of the final version.

With its riveting power as a story, its feral imagery that stalks nearly every paragraph, and its mystical ambiguity, "Flight" has both enchanted and puzzled critics. It has occasioned some of the very best literary criticism of Steinbeck's work as scholars match their wits against a compelling drama. For its sheer, evocative power, few of Steinbeck's short stories match it.

Artistically, the tale is a tour de force, with layer upon

layer of craftsmanship revealed in close reading. The ostensible plot and conflict—Pepe's quest for manhood against intractable odds of humanity and nature—appear simple enough. Since his father's death from a rattlesnake bite, Pepe inherits the place of manhood in the family. The one legacy from his father is the black-handled knife, with which Pepe demonstrates a fluid grace. But Mama Torres is reluctant to allow Pepe the place of manhood, berating him incessantly as a "peanut," "lazy coyote," or "big sheep." Nonetheless, she "thought him fine and brave, but she never told him so."

As Pepe leaves for Monterey to buy some medicine, his parting words are, "I will be careful. I am a man." The trip is allied with his manhood, and indeed he will acquire the adult knowledge of death on the trip. When a drunken man at Mrs. Rodriguez's house calls him a name—in the first draft he called Jose Torres a thief—Pepe's sense of manly honor will not permit it. The knife, says Pepe, "went almost by itself."

Many readers have focused exclusively upon that action and the subsequent flight to the exclusion of suggestive imagery patterns undergirding the tale. Thus, Dan Vogel sees the tale as "the ordeal of transformation from innocence to experience, from purity to defilement.[16] In a brief note on the story, William M. Jones suggests,

The details of Pepe's flight show how Pepe gradually conquered the family pride that caused his original sin and how through suffering he expiated that sin. Not only does he subdue the proud flesh . . . but in so doing he regained a place in nature that his family, scratching away to get what they could out of the world, had failed to find. This progress seems to be Steinbeck's explanation of the maturing process.[17]

Walter K. Gordon argues, "What is important in 'Flight' is not the crime itself but Pepe's mental and physical response to it, how he deports himself when the circumstances are propitious for a boy to become a man," an effort at which, in Gordon's view, Pepe ultimately fails.[18] Like Steinbeck's

note in the *Tortilla Flat* notebook, detailing humanity's
trek from the sea to the arid heights, however, the story
bears a yet more supple richness and probing of what it
means to be human than these views suggest.
In Flannery O'Connor's "The Life You Save May Be Your
Own," Mr. Shiftlet, spellbound by his own empty phrases,
asks Mrs. Lucynell Crater, "What is a man?" The answer
comes some time later: "a moral intelligence." The same
question puzzled John Steinbeck. Is humanity the product
of evolutionary eons, the offspring of the dark sea's surging?
The Log from the Sea of Cortez suggests as much:

There is tied up to the most primitive and powerful racial or collective instinct a rhythm sense or "memory" which affects everything and which in the past was probably more potent than it
is now. It would at least be more plausible to attribute these
profound effects to devastating and instinct-searing tidal influences during the formative times of the early race history of
organisms. [19]

Or, in Steinbeck's view, is humanity also a moral intelligence? His answer unfolded steadily throughout his literary career. In *The Grapes of Wrath*, he speculates,

For man, unlike any other thing organic or inorganic in the universe, grows beyond his work, walks up the stairs of his concepts,
emerges ahead of his accomplishments. This you may say of
man—when theories change and crash, when schools, philoso-
phies, when narrow dark alleys of thought, national, religious,
economic, grow and disintegrate, man reaches, stumbles forward, painfully, mistakenly sometimes. Having stepped forward,
he may slip back, but only half a step, never the full step back. [20]

And in a letter to John O'Hara written a decade later, he
asserted,

The great change in the last 2,000 years was the Christian idea
that the individual soul was very precious. Unless we can preserve and foster the principle of the preciousness of the individual mind, the world of men will either disintegrate into a scream-

ing chaos or will go into a grey slavery. And that fostering and
preservation seem to me our greatest job. [*SLL*, pp. 359–60]

Steinbeck's own answer to the question is that humanity is
unique by virtue of mind and spirit.
   In the hot, sun-blasted world of "Flight," however, when
a lazy boy asserts his manhood with a knife, when civilization's code of conduct is violated and the posse mounts,
man is very much reduced to an animal. One recalls Steinbeck's reflection in his notebook: "Oh man who in climbing
up has become lower." Pepe's flight into the mountains is
also a devolution, paced by a divestment of civilized tools
and in incrementally intensifying animal imagery. He loses
gun and knife, saddle, horse, and food. John Ditsky notes
the pattern of loss:

Beyond the simple deterioration of his possessions—as when his
clothing tears away or his flesh is ripped—leading to a contem-
plation of man's naked state like that in *King Lear*, there is the
importance of the fact that the objects just named are Pepe's from
his father; they are, as the knife is in fact described, "his inheritance." Pepe's attempt to sustain the manhood he has claimed in a
single violent act—by means of the tools which were his father's
badge of manhood and his estate—fails; he is finally stripped
down to what he brings with him *within* himself: his own gifts,
his own courage.[21]

Stripped of civilized tools, Pepe's movements are increasingly described in verbs that suggest a primordial or serpentine creature. Pepe "crawled," "wormed," "wriggled,"
"darted," "flashed," "slid," "writhed," and "squirmed" in
the final stages. Furthermore, his paralyzing thirst strips
him of the one thing that separates humanity from animals—speech: "His tongue tried to make words, but only a
thick hissing came from between his lips" (p. 64). Even his
tongue becomes infected with blackness—"Between his
lips the tip of his black tongue showed"—and the only
sound of which he is capable is a "thick hiss."
   As several critics have mentioned, a third pattern is

woven into the loss of civilized tools and the heavy use of animal imagery—the increasing images of darkness. From his early fascination with the lights on the altar and the sun-swept cliffs of his home, Pepe's world is subsumed by blackness, culminating in the Dark Watchers. He leaves for his flight on a morning when "Moonlight and daylight fought with each other, and the two warring qualities made it difficult to see" (p. 50). Louis Owens observes,

> The theme of death is woven on a thread of blackness through the story. It is Pepe's black knife which initiates the cycle of death. When Pepe flees he wears his dead father's black coat and black hat. It is the two "black ones," Rosy and Emilio, who prophesy Pepe's death. The line of gangrene running the length of Pepe's arm is black, foreshadowing his death, and it is the "dark watchers" who finally symbolize death itself. From the beginning of the story, Pepe grows increasingly dark, until in the end he will be black like the watchers.[22]

The climactic final portrait is thick with darkness, and even as a new morning breaks the sky, the eagle, which has been present from the start, is replaced by predatory black vultures.

Yet that progression is incomplete. Too many readers confine their attention to that stripping and figurative pattern. At his moment of most profound abnegation, wandering a black wasteland, stripped of civilized tools, an animal contending with animals, Pepe reclaims a uniquely human attribute, the power at once to defy and to submit to his own death. It is the conscious decision of a human, not an animal, and it is accompanied by spiritual awareness: "Pepe bowed his head quickly. He tried to speak rapid words but only a thick hiss came from his lips. He drew a shaky cross on his breast with his left hand" (p. 66). When the first bullet misses him, Pepe hauls his broken body straighter still to receive the death blow.

John Antico is one of the few scholars to pay attention to that scene and the story's religious dimension. He observes, "It is only by standing up on two feet and *facing death* that the sub-human Pepe can give birth to Man. An animal does not face death; death happens to it. A man is aware of what he is facing, and it is this awareness that makes him a man."[23] Yet, Antico wonders what exactly enables Pepe to get up and face death. What is this quality of manhood that he has discovered? It is not a miracle in response to his sign of the cross. Rather, it arises from an indomitable power within Pepe himself:

Indeed it was a long struggle for Man to emerge, and what prompts this sub-human to get up from all fours and stand on two feet is the inexpressible quality within him which later developed into what we call religion. To attempt to name or define this quality would, however, falsify it. It is not God or religion as civilized man knows them, but that inner quality which eventually leads to religion and the concept of God.[24]

Many have read the story as a supreme document of literary naturalism—as indeed it is. Stripped of all civilized customs and tools, man engages in an animalistic struggle for survival. In the naturalist tradition, "Flight" ranks with London's "To Light a Fire" and Crane's *Maggie: A Girl of the Streets* as among the best of a kind. But the story is not only that. It is a discovery of what separates humankind from the animals.

In the article "Cutting Loose," Michael Ratcliffe provides a narrative account of an interview with Steinbeck in 1962 on the occasion of his receiving the Nobel Prize. Steinbeck reflected on the Nobel speech he had made, pointing out, "A story is a parable; putting in terms of human action the morals—and immorals—that society needs at the time. Everyone leaves the bullfight a little braver because one man stood up to a bull. Isaiah wrote to meet the needs of his people, to inspire them. It is a meeting of needs."[25] Ratcliffe asked what kinds of needs, and Steinbeck responded, "Needs of beauty, courage, reform—sometimes just pure pride." It may well be that Pepe's response in "Flight" is pure, indomitable pride. His standing to receive the fatal bullet is the asseveration his speechless

tongue can no longer make: I am a man! But it is signaled
by religious signs, and that too is a pattern of the story.
Antico correctly notes, however, that

One hesitates to mention the numerous triads with all their Biblical overtones throughout the story, for then one is tempted to
find or seek out strict Biblical parallels or a rigid sort of symbolism or religious allegory which twists the significance of these
details all out of proportion. Steinbeck's method is not symbolism
or allegory; he merely *suggests* religion and Biblical overtones;
he actually seems to blur the edges of his analogies so that one
feels a religious atmosphere but not a strict and limited Christian
reference.[26]

Antico's caution is well observed. The religious references
do not suggest that the story is a parable, a modern crucifix-
ion of a saintly man. Rather, the imagery supports the central premise—that Pepe, finally, is not an animal but a man
discovering, albeit tragically, that indomitable, spiritual
consciousness of himself as human that separates him from
the animals.

   While Steinbeck changed the title of his story from
"Manhunt" to "Flight" to draw attention from the civilization that pursues to the individual that flees, there is an applicable irony in the first title. Pepe also hunts his manhood, and in his act of knowing acceptance, he finds it.
While the story bears all the trappings of a naturalistic document, or to use the terminology Steinbeck was becoming
fond of, a nonteleological telling, the flight of Pepe does arrive at a goal. The distinction may be made clearer by con-
sidering as a contrast one of Steinbeck's thoroughly nonteleological stories of the period, "The Snake."

"The Snake": From Observation to Art

Although Steinbeck would not fully develop his ideas about
nonteleological versus teleological thinking until 1940, when
he and Ed Ricketts made their memorable journey on the
Western Flyer and produced *The Sea of Cortez*, the germ

of the idea was in his mind long before. The working title of *Of Mice and Men*, for example, was "Something That Happened," an indication of the nonteleological artist's effort to capture an event in story form with great immediacy and for its own self-contained significance. Despite several critical efforts to apply the nonteleological pattern to Steinbeck's work, it is clear that he employed symbolism and suggestive patterns of imagery too freely to ever be considered a purely nonteleological author.[27] Yet, if a case were to be made for him as such, no better work could be used than "The Snake."

Essentially, a nonteleological view, as elucidated in *The Sea of Cortez*, meets a life experience on its own terms and refuses to impose questions of why or how upon that experience. Such an attitude, Steinbeck insisted, allows an individual to live more fully, to "live into" an experience rather than separating himself from it by the objective distancing of rational scrutiny. A teleological attitude toward life, on the other hand, sees life not as an experience but as a progress, a chain of causes and events, that insists upon interpretation through examination of the why and how. The teleological view projects human designs, needs, and goals upon the event. The nonteleological view sets aside the individual's assumptions to fully experience the event. Put into artistic terms, nonteleological writing seeks to capture the event without dogmatic or didactic intrusions by the author.[28]

Fascinated as he was by marine biology and scientific method in the early 1930s, it is not surprising that Steinbeck utilized some of the same objectivity of that study and method in his fiction. He does so most strikingly in "The Snake." Related in spare, taut prose, the story is documentary in style and nonteleological in its premise of observing an event. It presents a frightening scene, but suspends any judgment upon it. When he sent the story to Elizabeth Otis, she returned it as "outrageous" (*SLL*, p. 114). He did in fact publish the story in the *Monterey Beacon* in exchange for riding privileges at a stable.

The story is the first in which Steinbeck's champion of nonteleology, Ed Ricketts, overtly appears as a character, although the Dr. Phillips of the Helen Van Deventer story may be an earlier type. And the story first occurred in Rickett's laboratory as an actual event. In his 1951 essay "About Ed Ricketts" in *The Log from the Sea of Cortez*, Steinbeck recollects the event that triggered the story. His introductory comment to it indicates the nonteleological position he wished to take as an artist:

A thing happened one night which I later used as a short story. I wrote it just as it happened. I don't know what it means and do not even answer the letters asking what its philosophic intent is. It just happened. Very briefly, this is the incident. A woman came in one night wanting to buy a rattlesnake. It happened that we had one and knew it was a male because it had recently copulated with another snake in the cage. The woman paid for the snake and then insisted that it be fed. She paid for a white rat to be given it. Ed put the rat in the cage. The snake struck and killed it and then unhinged its jaws preparatory to swallowing it. The frightening thing was that the woman, who had watched the process closely, moved her jaws and stretched her mouth just as the snake was doing.[29]

Webster Street, in an interview recollecting John Steinbeck, offers a slightly different view of the incident from his eyewitness point of view:

This girl happened to be there and took a fancy to Ed, and Ed invited her to the lab. And she was a kind of sexy-looking dame and so while she was there, he said that he had to feed the snake. He had a big cage, quite a big cage full of white rats—and he went in there and selected one and put it in with the rattlesnake. The mouse [sic] ran all around, and this girl was just fascinated by the damned thing. And then, pretty soon, the little mouse stopped and the rattlesnake struck.[30]

Street goes on to describe the feeding habit of the snake, and the fascination of the girl who watched awestruck for "perhaps half an hour." By calling the girl a "sexy-looking

dame," actually one of the entertainers from the Blue Bell
Cafe, Street makes apparent the subliminal sexual side of
the story. He concludes, "John made a story out of it and
gave it a lot of implications that probably were there." [31]
But did Steinbeck consciously aim at such implications,
and if so, how did he do this artistically? In his own recollection in "About Ed Ricketts," he is evasive: "What happened or why I have no idea. Whether the woman was
driven by a sexual, a religious, a zoophilic, or a gustatory
impulse we never could figure. When I wrote the story just
as it happened there were curious reactions. One librarian
wrote that it was not only a bad story but the worst story
she had ever read." [32] Such questions obviously beg the nonteleological premises of the story, calling them into serious
question, for it is indeed suggestive of much more than
simply observable event. Even Steinbeck's effort, through
Dr. Phillips, to suspend any judgment at the end is thwarted
by a stylistic pattern he has set for telling the story. The
spare, documentary nature of the story—providing an observable event without comment—is nonetheless colored
by the narrative point of view through Dr. Phillips and by
Steinbeck's suggestive patterns of imagery.

Selection of narrative point of view, particularly important here and in the sketch "Breakfast," became a telling
hallmark of Steinbeck's style. Were this to be a completely
nonteleological story, the narrator would have had to remain entirely objective. By admitting the reader to Dr.
Phillips's mind, Steinbeck also allies the reader with a particular sensibility by which to observe the events. The nature of the character through whom we see the events,
then, is of utmost importance to the story.

The shock Dr. Phillips feels while watching the woman is
intensified by the practicality of his science. Nothing unusual strikes the reader about the character of Dr. Phillips:
"He was a slight young man with the mild, preoccupied
eyes of one who looks through a microscope a great deal.
He wore a short blond beard" (p. 70). The only thing that
might attract a reader's notice is the fact that he is young,

an adjective used twice in the opening descriptions and
thereby suggesting a certain vulnerability. While he is not
the hardened scientist, inured to whatever the world has to
offer, he is still very much the scientist. He moves about
his equipment and animals with smooth efficiency. There is
a natural interplay of life and death, necessitated by the science he adroitly serves:

A bottle of milk stood on a glass shelf between a small mounted
octopus and a jelly fish. Dr. Phillips lifted down the milk and
walked to the cat cage, but before he filled the containers he
reached in the cage and gently picked out a big rangy alley tabby.
He stroked her for a moment and then dropped her in a small
black painted box, closed the lid and bolted it and then turned on
a petcock which admitted gas into the killing chamber. While the
short soft struggle went on in the black box he filled the saucers
with milk. [p. 71]

The same professional objectivity that marks Dr. Phillips
here would also typify the later type of Ed Ricketts in the
character of Doc from the *Cannery Row* trilogy.

Furthermore, a certain deferential politeness marks his
character. Were he more assertive or demanding, the scene
might never have occurred. When the woman enters, Dr.
Phillips responds, "'I'm very busy just now,' he said half-
heartedly. 'I have to do things at times.' But he stood away
from the door. The tall woman slipped in" (p. 72). Only
when she seems to make a sport out of his science does he
bristle: "His tone had become acid. He hated people who
made sport of natural processes. He was not a sportsman
but a biologist. He could kill a thousand animals for knowledge, but not an insect for pleasure. He'd been over this in
his mind before" (p. 77). From the start, however, we see
Dr. Phillips as particularly susceptible to revulsion, for the
woman will make of his science a sport that he never dared
imagine. And we see that through his eyes: our own attitude
changes from deference, to hatred, to revulsion with his.

Accompanying the changes in Dr. Phillips's attitude is a
subtle interplay of color and animal imagery that supports

the psychic transformation of the woman from human to animal. From the start, the color black is associated with death. The cat is gassed in "a small black painted box." When the woman enters, just two paragraphs later, her appearance is heavily colored by black: "A tall, lean woman stood in the doorway. She was dressed in a severe dark suit—her straight black hair, growing low on a flat forehead, was mussed as though the wind had been blowing it. Her black eyes glittered in the strong light" (p. 71). Most unnerving, to Dr. Phillips, are her eyes: "Her black eyes were on him, but they did not seem to see him. He realized why—the irises were as dark as the pupils, there was no color line between the two" (p. 73).

With that description of her eyes, reflecting the "dusky" eyes of the snake from the third paragraph of the story, the woman becomes closely allied with the snake in imagery. Dr. Phillips observes her as analytically as he would a laboratory specimen: "Her hands rested side by side on her lap. She was completely at rest. Her eyes were bright but the rest of her was almost in a state of suspended animation. He thought, 'Low metabolic rate, almost as low as a frog's, from the looks'" (p. 73). As she continues to watch him, her eyes undergo further change, now almost identical to the snake's eyes: "He looked around at her again. Her dark eyes seemed veiled with dust" (p. 74). Her facial features also become increasingly serpentine: "He noticed how short her chin was between lower lip and point. She seemed to awaken slowly, to come up out of some deep pool of consciousness. Her head raised and her dark dusty eyes moved about the room and then came back to him" (p. 74). When she asks to see the rattlesnake, she moves her head as her body remains limp.

When the woman purchases the snake, then insists upon feeding it, Dr. Phillips feels his outrage growing. Something in his practice of and attitude toward science is being violated. Here the story becomes decidedly teleological; Steinbeck, by having selected his narrative point of view, also has us experience the act as somehow morally reprehensible.

As the snake kills and devours the rat, the woman watches spellbound. If previously she had awakened slowly, "to come up out of some deep pool of consciousness," now she seems to slide back into that primeval pool of consciousness identified with the snake. Dr. Phillips tries to ignore her by going about his tasks, but he cannot. The woman's body crouches and stiffens in rhythm with the snake's body. She weaves as it does. But when the snake strikes, Dr. Phillips forces himself to turn away: "Dr. Phillips put his will against his head to keep it from turning toward the woman. He thought, 'If she's opening her mouth, I'll be sick. I'll be afraid.' He succeeded in keeping his eyes away" (p. 81). When the snake finishes, the woman leaves: "Her eyes came out of their dusty dream for a moment" (p. 82).

At the last moment, the story seems to switch back to a nonteleological mode. Dr. Phillips refers to "psychological sex symbols," but nothing there seems adequate to explain this experience. He says, "If I knew—no, I can't pray to anything," thereby rejecting any divine recourse. And the woman never returns. There was simply this one event, presented as it happened, with no explanations offered. Nonetheless, by virtue of the sympathy of point of view, by admitting us to Dr. Phillips's mind so that we experience his revulsion, Steinbeck has already passed judgment upon it.

Indeed, there do seem to be those animals among humankind that no amount of psychology, theology, or science will ever be able to explain. Steinbeck will use such characters occasionally in his work to come, and the teleological patterns of this story supply a response to them. The key to understanding them lies in a comment by Dr. Phillips as the snake moves in for the kill of the unsuspecting rat: "'It's the most beautiful thing in the world,' the young man said. His veins were throbbing. 'It's the most terrible thing in the world'" (p. 79). Precisely. Everything depends upon the point of view. For the snake the captive rat is the most beautiful thing in the world; for the rat it is the most terrible. From a strictly scientific point of view, this delicate interplay of life and death is a thing of rare beauty. But life is not always as neat as science.

"Breakfast": The Warm Feeling of Sunken Memory

Commonly considered a fragment, and lacking any specific plot, the short sketch "Breakfast," like "The Snake," provides an interesting experiment in point of view. This sketch also seems outwardly to present a nonteleological rendition of an event but is colored by the narrator's attitude toward that event.

The composition of the story is indeterminate, but can very likely be dated from the summer of 1934. As we will consider more closely in the discussion of "The Raid," Steinbeck had begun meeting with a farm-labor leader named Cicil McKiddy in early 1934. As his interest in the labor movement grew during 1934, Steinbeck found his artistic attention drawn toward the story of strikers that is central to "The Raid" and *In Dubious Battle*. During the summer of 1934, he began walking out into the fields to talk to the laborers and to absorb the sounds, sights, and smells that nurture an artist's creativity by firsthand experience. It is likely that the short sketch derives from one such actual morning of observed experience, a sudden impression captured by the imagination and rendered in words as realistically, as photographically, as possible. Despite its brevity, it is a moving portrait.

A laborer, the narrator, wanders through the camp at dawn, acutely aware of the interplay of light. The story has two foci: the light washing over the camp and the preparation for breakfast in one tent. The sketch opens in the "very early" morning, with the light faintly coloring the "black-blue eastern mountains." Colors shift as the sun rises—from black-blue, to gray, to lavender-gray. In one tent "a flash of orange fire" seeps through a rusty stove. The light of the rising sun meets the light in the tent and they coalesce. There a woman prepares breakfast, cradling her infant while cooking bacon and baking biscuits. Two men emerge, wearing newly purchased dungarees because they have had twelve days of work, and invite the narrator to breakfast with them. As they eat, the colors continue their shift into morning, turning now to a "reddish gleam." By the time they finish eating, "The two men faced the east and their faces were lighted by the dawn, and I looked up for a moment and saw the image of the mountain and the light coming over it reflected in the older man's eyes" (p. 88). The two laborers walk away into air "blazing with the light at the eastern skyline."

The pattern of color change with the rising light of the sun is accompanied by temperature changes. The air "was cold, not painfully so, but cold enough so that I rubbed my hands and shoved them deep into my pockets, and I hunched my shoulders up and scuffled my feet on the ground" (p. 85). Coming to the tent stove, the narrator recalls, "I came near to the stove and stretched my hands out to it and shivered all over when the warmth struck me" (p. 86). The men sip the "hot bitter coffee." The light of the sun is so clean that it makes the air seem colder, but the small group finds a circle of warmth around the shared meal.

The warmth also becomes a part of the narrator's perception and tells the reader how to view the scene. This is not a miserably wretched crew afflicted with cold. Indeed, the warm generosity is the thing of beauty that made the scene worth recollecting. The narrator tells us at the outset that this is a pleasurable recollection: "This thing fills me with pleasure. I don't know why, I can see it in the smallest detail. I find myself recalling it again and again, each time bringing more detail out of sunken memory, remembering brings the curious warm pleasure" (p. 85).

By virtue of the narrator's attitude toward the event, we have a theme, if little plot. Clearly, this ready sharing of a few moments together and a bit of food creates a warmth of human kinship. It captures in a few pages, and points ahead to, the majestic theme of "the fambly" of man elucidated over hundreds of pages in *The Grapes of Wrath*. The girl who serves breakfast, her infant tucked in her arm, is also a type of Rose of Sharon.

While the sketch was written during preparation for *In Dubious Battle*, it in fact appeared in revised form in chapter 22 of *The Grapes of Wrath*.[33] Although the revision is necessarily quite extensive in order to adapt the sketch to a larger plot, the adaptation is revealing of the narratively implied theme of "Breakfast." By evoking a "sunken memory" in the sketch, the narrator also evokes his attitude toward the event and directs the reader in how to perceive the significance of that event.

While "Flight," "The Snake," and "Breakfast" are quite different thematically, their variations in use of narrative point of view demonstrate Steinbeck's growing skill and sureness as a craftsman. These three stories are as significant for the development of his artistic craft as "The Chrysanthemums," "The White Quail," and "The Harness" are for his thematic craft.

THE CASE HISTORY OF "THE VIGILANTE": A TALE OF TWO TELLINGS

Even a dispassionately factual account of the lynchings in San Jose, California, on November 16, 1933, cannot dispel a chill of horror. Lynching has often served as the terrible, swift sword of American justice. Just how often is difficult to ascertain. Since no accurate records were kept prior to 1889, one can only speculate on the extent of lynching prior to that date. Highly inaccurate records kept since 1889 tally 7,731 deaths by lynching. It has not been a phenomenon isolated to the old West or the deep South. The prosecution of witchcraft in Salem tallied nineteen hangings between June 10 and September 22, 1692. It is reasonably certain that the lynchings of John Maurice Holmes and Thomas Harold Thurmond in San Jose were the twenty-fourth and twenty-fifth of 1933 in the United States.

What is peculiar about the San Jose lynchings is the public arena for the action. Historically, lynchings have been

associated with a handful of dusky figures known as vigilan-
tes, operating under cover of darkness in remote places.
Estimates of the crowd observing the deaths of Holmes
and Thurmond in a central city park range from five to ten
thousand, depending upon which newspapers one reads.
The size of the crowd is only one factor; the spirit of revenge permeated an entire region, from the drunken rabble-
rouser to the staid gentry. The Santa Clara Valley screamed
vengeance, and San Jose acted on the cry. The animal spirit
that possessed so many and such different people gave the
incident national notoriety. It also inflamed the creative
mind of John Steinbeck.

The facts of the case may be stated briefly. Brooke Hart,
son of wealthy San Jose merchant Alex Hart, was kidnapped
shortly after 6:00 P.M. on November 9, 1933. The family received a ransom demand for $40,000 by telephone at ap-
proximately 9:00 P.M. However, Brooke had already been
slain by then. The abductors had tied young Hart's arms
with wire, clubbed him over the head with a brick, and
dropped his body, weighted by two twenty-two-pound con-
crete blocks, from the San Mateo Bridge into San Francisco
Bay. In later testimony, Thurmond stated that shots were
fired at the body in the water.

On November 16 Thurmond was traced by a phone call
and arrested. He immediately implicated Holmes, and the
two men were incarcerated in the San Jose City Jail. Facing
the bitter mood of San Jose citizens, the two were removed
to San Francisco for a time and later returned to San Jose
when authorities believed the public mood had cooled.

When arrested, Thurmond made a full confession, spar-
ing none of the gruesome details. Charles Dullea, captain
of inspectors on the San Jose Police Department, said,
"Well, son, you are in a hell of a jam." Replied the sobbing
Thurmond, "I'll say I am."

Over the next few days, public hostility grew, fueled by
outrage over the insensible cruelty of the murder, but also
by increasingly volatile newspaper reporting that pounced
upon every detail. It did not help that Governor James J.

Rolph, Jr., issued statements that could only be construed as incendiary. When the first suggestions of potential mob violence were received, Rolph replied, "Let the sheriff handle the matter. He can appoint as many deputies as he wants; he has the power. I am not going to call the guard to protect kidnappers who wilfully killed a fine boy like that. Let the law take its course."[34] The invitation to vigilante retribution was clear.

The invitation was accepted. On the evening of November 26, the crowd outside the San Jose jail grew more threatening by the hour. At 9:00 P.M., the crowd made its first move on the jail. Fifteen police officers linked arms to hold them back. A growl sounded in the mob. A hundred men lunged forward. The police shouted orders, fired tear gas. An eerie chant—"Brooke Hart, Brooke Hart"—rose from the fringes of the crowd. Momentarily swayed by the tear gas, the phalanx of the mob reformed. Seizing an iron pipe from the post office construction, they battered down the door and breached the jail. Thurmond was on the third floor, Holmes on the second. The leaders trampled Sheriff William Emig out of the way. Undersheriff Howard Moore, fearing they would seize the wrong man, shouted directions to their cells. The crowd surged into Thurmond's cell first, and in one of the strangest actions in lynching history, six members of the mob knelt and prayed for the soul of the man whom they were about to lynch.[35]

No one prayed for Holmes.

They dragged the two men down First Street, across to St. James Park. Again the eerie confusion. They had forgotten ropes. It took fifteen additional minutes to find the necessary tools of the grisly trade. Then the act was completed amid cheers and screams from men, women, and children. The bodies hung high above the crowd for everyone to see. Some of the crowd wanted to burn the bodies. They had already stripped Thurmond's pants from him. Someone set fire to his rubber coat, which flamed momentarily. Lit matches and twigs were held to his bare feet.

And Governor Rolph? He was quoted the next day as

praising "those fine patriotic San Jose citizens, who know
how to handle such a situation."

Such are the raw facts of the case. They gained national
attention largely through the reporting of Royce Brier for
the San Francisco *Chronicle,* for which he won the 1934
Pulitzer Prize for Journalism. The case riveted the attention not only of California, but also of the nation. It also
seized the attention of John Steinbeck, who used the materials as the basis for his story "The Vigilante." But, in fact,
there were two tellings of "The Vigilante," quite different
from each other in method and content. To examine the
reasons for the artistic changes between the early version,
titled "Case History," and "The Vigilante" one has to place
Steinbeck in his personal and artistic relationship to this
dramatic historical event.

For much of 1933, Steinbeck had been tending his
mother, working at his writing in the adjoining room, but
always within earshot of her incessant needs. The situation
had been exacerbated by his father's growing confusion and
inability to help, and the situation prevailed for months. It
was one of the most demanding periods on Steinbeck's
health and stamina. On page 80 of the *Long Valley* notebook, he wrote of the terrible loneliness of this period:
"The bottom of my stomach is dropping out under accumulated loneliness—not loneliness that might be mended
with company either." And then he added, "Only work
cures the gnawing."

He did work, under the most impossible circumstances,
constantly interrupted by his mother's needs, during the
ensuing months. But when the dramatic news of the San
Jose kidnapping hit the Salinas *Index-Journal* on Friday,
November 10, 1933, it must have seized Steinbeck's attention, as it did nearly everyone's from the region. From the
start, the reporting in the *Index-Journal* worked the story
for every spark of inflammatory excitement. One sees the
penchant for rumor and hearsay already in the November
10 edition. Under a rather straightforward rendition of the

facts of the case, a story was added about a deputy sheriff's belief that Charles "Pretty Boy" Floyd had directed the kidnapping. Someone thought he might have seen Floyd in California. The deputy thought he might be right. From the start, rumor played as heavily as news in the *Index-Journal*.[36]

The rumors swung into full gear by the next edition. A certain San Jose private detective, identified as S. Narducci, had "private information" that the Spreckels and Bisceglia families, then living in the San Francisco area, had been targeted for kidnappings. And there were the allied stories, such as that of Oscar Rouef of Santa Clara that appeared in the Saturday, November 11, *Index-Journal:* "Flying into a rage as he discussed the alleged Brooke Harte [sic] kidnapping with his parents, Oscar Rouef, 28, a radio technician, today shot and killed his father, Jacob Rouef, and then committed suicide with the same shotgun."

The story was left to such rumors and related items during the next week, until Thurmond (which the *Index-Journal* spelled "Thurman" or "Thurmon" until the end) and Holmes were arrested. The headlines grew increasingly bolder, the statements more sensational, the adjectives angrier. The subhead from the lead story on Thursday, November 16, reads:

"Snatchers" Truss Up Scion of Wealthy Family With Wire, Slug and Drown Him; Savage Killing Is Bared By Prisoners; Angry Lynching Mobs Form Near Jail

The Friday, November 17, issue trumpeted, "Fiendish Killer Weeps in Jail" and ran a photo of Thurmond under the heading, "Fiend Talks to Sheriff."

With increasing talk of lynching and mob action, the *Index-Journal* was also running front-page news of a local murder story involving Thad Lake. His trial had just concluded, and the Wednesday, November 15, issue reports that seven members of the jury voted on a first ballot for hanging him. Suddenly, stories of hangings and lynchings appear in tandem with the Brooke Hart stories. Such tacit incitement approached a crisis with the headlines of the Thursday, November 23, issue: "Rolph Will Not Call Troops To Protect Hart Murderers."

Here is the psychology of the unfolding scene. Thurmond and Holmes are publicly denounced as fiends. Accompanying stories on lynching and gallows justice appear. Then Governor Rolph issues a scarcely veiled invitation to mob retribution. Seldom has a story developed to so inevitable an end.

On Monday, November 27, the day after the lynching, the *Index-Journal* headline reads: "Victims Writhe As Frenzied Mob Strips and Hangs Them." The startling subhead reads: "'Well Done' Says Governor Rolph." There is more to that subhead than meets the eye. After the first assault by the mob was aborted by tear gas, Sheriff Emig contacted Rolph and pleaded for state forces to be sent to San Jose. Governor Rolph refused, saying later, "No convicted kidnapper will ever be turned free or pardoned while I'm governor." The Governor's whole-hearted endorsement of the mob action appears as startling as the mob action itself.

The lead story reported the lynching of Holmes this way:

A boy shinned up a nearby elm tree. The mob dragged the nude Holmes beneath it. The youth reached the first branch. "I can't put a rope here. It'll slip off," he shouted. He climbed higher and someone tossed him the rope.

"San Francisco police are on the way—we'd better hurry," one of the lynchers yelled.

"President Roosevelt has just wired Sunnyvale navy base to rush aid," another cried. "There are 10 trucks of marines on the way."

"Don't wait—hang them," came another voice.

Someone made a hangman's noose. "We're all ready," he shouted.

A man slipped the noose over Holmes' neck. "Heave to, boys," he yelled.

The rope was pulled taut and Holmes was lifted by his neck to his feet.

"How do you like it?" a score of voices chorused.

The rope was slackened and Holmes dropped. A second time it was drawn taut. Then he was dropped again.

"Torture him. Cut him up. Tear him apart. Make him suffer like Brooke Hart did," came new cries.

Fists rained blows on the helpless man. Fingernails tore into his flesh.

"Better hurry before it's too late," someone shouted.

"All right, let him have the finishing yank," said a man.

Slowly, deliberately, a dozen pairs of hands heaved. Holmes dangled 25 feet from the ground. His hands went up in a frantic effort to jerk the rope from his neck. He died a few minutes later.

The insensible cruelty, the mad and malicious violence of it all—these were not the actions of individual people. They were the actions of a collective psychology, at once sub-human and suprahuman. This singular animal, composed of individual units but ruling those units inexorably to the satisfaction of the one animal called the mob, attracted Steinbeck's intense interest.

As one might expect, there was an aftermath to Governor Rolph's irresponsible comments and lack of action. The Tuesday edition of the *Index-Journal* bears the headline, "Governor Blamed for Inciting Noose Death of Kidnap Pair; Huge Damage Claim Foreseen" and carries a United Press report highly critical of the governor. Here, too late, decent citizens stepped in to criticize the mob animal that ruled so briefly but so terribly. The Los Angeles *Daily News*, far removed from the events geographically, was particularly recriminatory: "It is possible that this man, who has made a mockery of justice . . . has lost his mind."

The incendiary story certainly fueled Steinbeck's concept of mob psychology. The phalanx idea had been in his mind for some time, but particularly so during his mother's illness. The June 21, 1933, letter to Carlton Sheffield,

quoted in chapter four, comprises one of the earliest statements of Steinbeck's theory of the phalanx. Of particular
importance to the later case of the lynching is a comment
such as this: "When acting as a group, men do not partake
of their ordinary natures at all. The group can change its
nature" (*SLL*, p. 75). Similar comments appear in other
letters of the period, most notably to George Albee (*SLL*,
pp. 79–81).

The concern appears in his journals also. On page 49 of
the *Long Valley* notebook, in which "The Vigilante" was
drafted, Steinbeck wrote,

We have been prone to consider life as being broken up first into
phyla, classes, orders and each of those larger groups being broken up into individual, the crab, the dog, the man. We know that
the unit of all these is the same. We know that the appearance of
the kinds are different, their forms, their habits, their habitats.
We have overlooked the unit and the relationship this may establish between all forms of life. Man remembers his progress up the
phyla well enough to duplicate it. Man, in his cells, probably remembers other things—the great tides, the warm damp muck
that shrouded the world from the sun; the voraciousness of enemies long extinct.

The theory of the phalanx, particularly the primeval sense
of surging together into one force that is described in the
above quotation, gave Steinbeck a way of accounting for
mob action. But how to render his theory in fiction? That
was the harder question. Perhaps he provided his fullest
answer in *In Dubious Battle*, but not until he had struggled
through the two tellings of "The Vigilante," for the difference is nothing less than that between treatise and story.

It was not unusual for Steinbeck to outline and reflect
upon his stories in accompanying notes. The careful journals kept during the writing of *The Grapes of Wrath* and
East of Eden are testament to his care as an artist. With the
short stories, however, the pattern occurs more rarely and
often signals some difficulty. Although he had some false

starts on short stories, most notably "The Cow" and "Western Art Colony" from this period, his usual technique was to write straight through. The technique forms a pattern. The stories begin with a quick, impressionistic paragraph of setting, move to character, and then develop the plot.

Shortly before drafting "Case History," Steinbeck entered an odd note in his ledger: "One story which occurred to me last night is so delicate and different that I don't feel justified in taking regular work time to do it. If I do it, it will be at night on my own time. There is too much work to get out. This is not a time for experiments on company time." There would be something intensely personal in this story for him, very much a working out of his own theory in fiction. Struggling mightily with finances, heavily dependent upon his parents and Carol's part-time secretarial work, Steinbeck had been writing short stories with the clear goal of making money. Sales would provide him with some measure of financial independence but would also validate his own sense of artistic worth. A telling note in his ledger, dated June 14, 1934, describes the sense of personal crisis. Steinbeck reflects on the possibility of writing a quick novel to provide the leisure and money to write carefully the things he really wanted to write. He states, "I must lay enough money aside so that the careful work can be done. And I must go on with these short stories for that purpose. There that's down. That must be followed" (*LVN*).

His unease over "Case History" arises from two sides, then. This would be an intensely personal rendering, full of his own thoughts and theory, and it very likely would not satisfy gnawing financial demands by a ready sale. Yet, he could not put the story out of his mind.

The first mention of the plot details of "Case History" occurs in a synopsis note:

John Ramsey—hated the war and misses it. Came home to the quiet, the lack of design, for the war was a huge design. Wanders lost on his farm looking for a phalanx to join and finds none. Is nervous and very lost. Finally finds the movement in a lynching.

War shock not so much war as the ceasing of war drive. Hunger for the group. Change of drive. What does it matter. The mob is not a wasteful thing but an efficient thing. [*LVN*]

The basic plot and conflict were clear in Steinbeck's mind. The mob experience of war—the many individual units with a leader at its head—would be replaced by the mob experience of the lynching. The draft begins with some promise as Steinbeck develops the tensions of John Ramsy, now spelled without the *e*. But already in the introductory paragraph, one senses the loose ends, the fact that too much is being packed into one character too quickly:

When John Ramsy came home from the war, he was robust and his eyes were sparkling. His cashiership had been held open for him in the Monterey and Farmer's National. His wife said over and over, "Why, the war's been good for him. It has brought him out." He settled into his job with enthusiasm and energy. A tall blonde man John Ramsy, with dark eyes and lashes that made him seem always either brooding or burning up inside. Having too much nervous energy to be drained into ordinary work, his feet moved constantly. When he sat down, he crossed and recrossed his legs. His long fingers worked out intricate patterns with paperclips, with rubber bands, with pencils or matches. He was welcomed back in Salinas society—a captain of infantry with several decorations and citations. And for a time he plunged into the life of the small town with apparent enjoyment. [*LVN*]

In the nervous fidgeting of the main character, Steinbeck begins to suggest that all is not well with John Ramsy. And here is where the artistic difficulties start. By stressing Ramsy's return from the war in good health and with sparkling eye, Steinbeck sets the stage for his character's being fully alive only in a mob movement. The difference between wartime heroism and the murky shadows of a mob lynching, however, is huge, and confronts the writer with nearly insuperable problems in transition. Here lay the artistic hurdle.

Steinbeck's solution drove him into deeper difficulty simply in terms of the story. Rather suddenly, Ramsy lapses into a morose mood. The reason? Shell shock from the war. Ramsy is hospitalized for a time, but one night he is found "dead drunk in a negro house of prostitution." Thereafter, Ramsy leaves his wife for a while to live by himself. In terms of storytelling and plot development, Steinbeck himself must have been aware that he was forcing the action through a sequence of contrived coincidences.

Another follows. Will McKay, who edits a small-town newspaper, enters the story. McKay has just written the prize story of his career: "The kidnapping and murder of a child filled Salinas with excitement. Will reported the finding of the body and he described the angry movement of the people." The character may have provided Steinbeck a much-needed clue about how to retell the story. On the night of the lynching, McKay is the observer. The focus shifts suddenly:

Then a suspect was caught and put in jail. The crowds stood about the county jail all day but when the night came they broke into determined action. Will McKay in his role of reporter stood on the fringe of the mob, making an occasional note. The street lights had been smashed for blocks around dropping the neighborhood into blackness. The thumping indicated that they were going after the jail door with a ram. [*LVN*]

Will McKay provides the reader more distance from and objectivity toward the action than did the changing character of John Ramsy. Even though he is a participant in the action recounted in "The Vigilante," the protagonist, Mike, appears after the actual lynching. In effect, "The Vigilante" starts at approximately this point in "Case History."

"Case History" also relates the action of the lynching more directly, as John Ramsy spearheads the mob. The prisoner is taken away screaming, and, despite Will McKay's efforts to break John away, the lynching is completed.

Afterward, Will McKay and Ramsy depart to talk over the night's actions. The discussion that ensues allows Stein-

beck to fully explore his phalanx theory, but the story of
the lynching ends here. Several pages of discussion follow.
McKay initiates it by asking, "But why did you help lynch
that poor devil tonight?" John responds in words lifted directly from Steinbeck's notes on the phalanx:

> I was hungry for the group and besides—I wanted to verify cer-
> tain thoughts I've had. I've come to think of a new individual, the
> human group. And because that group is made up of individual
> men who are no longer individual but controlled units all going in
> one direction, I've been thinking of the group under the name of
> Phalanx. It's rather like the Macedonian Phalanx. The unit men
> have lost their emphasis except as cells in the whole. [*LVN*]

Will tries to raise the moral implications of the argument:
"'I want to argue with you because this seems wrong.' He
grinned—'It seems sinful.'" But, in Ramsy's mind—as in
Steinbeck's—the phalanx transcends moral suasion. It is
simply a mass movement with a primeval will of its own:
"Of course it's sinful to the individual man. The phalanx has
no interest in the individual when his function differs with
the direction of the phalanx." McKay protests, "Why didn't
I help hang the poor devil?" Ramsy responds, "Because
you tried to stay out. You kept physical space between
you and the mob. If you'd yelled one curse or thrown one
brick, you'd have been caught too." The comment may have
greater implications than Steinbeck himself was aware of.
In ethical terms, the fact that McKay did choose to stay out
provides evidence that the movement of the phalanx can be
denied by the individual. In narrative terms, however, it
also suggests that the story can be told differently, with
greater dispassion and objectivity. While Mike of "The
Vigilante" is a participant in the lynching, Steinbeck provides the objectivity by opening the story in the aftermath
of the lynching.

By this point in the "Case History" narrative, however,
the plot itself has been lost and theory has taken over. The
telling becomes rote, the characters simply mouthpieces to
articulate Steinbeck's ideas. The dialogue runs out of en-

ergy for the simple reason that it has no plot to sustain it. Like Steinbeck's "L'Affaire Lettuceberg," the discarded precursor to *The Grapes of Wrath,* the work is a treatise with characters as accidents for the articulation of theory, rather than as the substance of the story itself.

A good short story changes thought into a kind of knowledge; it objectifies thought, through character and plot, to a lesson derived by experience, a lesson the audience participates in rather than listens to. Weary of his own sermon, Steinbeck simply stepped out of the pulpit that "Case History" had become. For some time he left it that way—an undirected and unresolved telling.

A further clue to the treatise-like exposition of the phalanx theory in "Case History" appears in a 1934 letter to George Albee. In a portion of the letter that was edited out from *Steinbeck: A Life in Letters* (pp. 92–94), Steinbeck stated, "Just now I am writing my phalanx theory into an essay, Socratic in method, light and informative because I want to make some record of it."[37] While "Case History" is hardly "light and informative," the Socratic method is very much in evidence as Will McKay draws Ramsy's thoughts out through a series of strategic questions. The phalanx theory itself—how a human organism emerges, coalesces, and reaches a climactic action—is particularly well suited to a Socratic method of exploration. It fails, however, to meet the dramatic needs of a short story.

The drama of the story itself, apart from Steinbeck's philosophical accoutrements, maintained its pull on his mind. In the interval before "The Vigilante," Steinbeck wrote "The White Quail," the two-page addendum to "Flight," "Johnny Bear," and the failed short story "The Cow." Then in August 1934 he returned to the story of the lynching, now called "The Vigilante." No longer a case history incarnating an idea, the focus now turns upon a character in an event.

In "Case History" Steinbeck's aim was to show the effect of a mob action on one of the units of that mob, John Ramsy. That effect is realized in "The Vigilante" by several artistic shifts.

Now the story immediately follows the lynching. The focus is intensely narrowed to the point of view of the main character, Mike. The lengthy and complicated introduction to the character John Ramsy, the virtually unmanageable accounting for his psychological transition and consequent actions, are all stripped away as we meet Mike wandering away from the park in the aftermath of the lynching. The thing has happened; that is the fact of the story. This sense of immediacy is enhanced by the carefully controlled pace of the prose. The introductory paragraph begins with a sharply charged rhetorical pace, then subsides gently, like a great emotional wave crashing and ebbing:

The great surge of emotion, the milling and shouting of the people, fell gradually to silence in the town park. A crowd of people still stood under the elm trees, vaguely lighted by a blue street light two blocks away. A tired quiet settled on the people; some members of the mob began to sneak away into the darkness. The park lawn was cut to pieces by the feet of the crowd. [p. 131]

The actual event is still not identified. We simply have a huge emotion washing away.

Another shift that narrows the story to a manageable artistic entity involves replacing the complicated "confessor figure" of Will McKay with the barkeeper, Welch. He is a common figure, speaking as the voice of the common people rather than as a philosophical foil. Welch is a prop, an ear for Mike to speak his feelings into, rather than an active force.

Surprisingly, with the intensely narrowed focus, Steinbeck is far more faithful to the actual events of the San Jose lynching than in "Case History." Essential differences between history and fiction are immediately evident. In "The Vigilante" one man is hanged, rather than two. Steinbeck identifies the hanged man as black rather than white. Since historically three out of four victims of lynching have been black, the changes universalize the story somewhat. However, the lynched man is referred to as a "fiend," using precisely the term from the newspaper headlines that so inflamed public sentiment.

Other than those artistic decisions to broaden the base of the story for a larger audience, "The Vigilante" is remarkably faithful to the details of the San Jose lynching. It almost seems that Steinbeck reread the accounts to verify authentic data, in the same way that he returned to Salinas to study his hometown newspaper when preparing to write *East of Eden*. For example, while the setting of "Case History" is ambiguous, the geography of "The Vigilante" is specifically that of San Jose. In San Jose, the site of the lynching was St. James Park, located between First and Third streets. Mike walks two blocks from the park to Welch's bar. When they walk home, Welch tells Mike that he lives on South Eighth Street, which, as Mike observes, is two blocks past his own house on South Sixth Street.

The parallels between the historical fact and fictional accounting accumulate in many minor details. When Mike leaves the park, several people are trying to burn the body of the lynched man: "In the center of the mob someone had lighted a twisted newspaper and was holding it up. Mike could see how the flame curled about the feet of the grey naked body hanging from the elm tree." The front-page story of the November 28 *Index-Journal* reports "Someone made a torch of newspapers and burned the bottoms of Thurmond's feet. Slowly the flames licked up around him and singed his hair."

Mike makes several comments that echo historical accounts of the lynching. As he leaves the park, an unnamed man comments, "It's a good job. . . . This'll save the county a lot of money and no sneaky lawyers getting in" (p. 132). Mike affirms the sentiment. In fact, at the time of the lynching a legal maneuver was underway by Holmes's attorneys, Vincent Hilliman and Nathan Loughlan, to establish that his confession had been forced. Similarly, Mike tells Welch, "Of course everybody knew it was going to happen" (p. 135). Royce Brier had suggested several days before the hanging that a vigilante group was being formed.[38]

In his recounting of the event to Welch, Mike says, "The Sheriff came out and made a speech," as Sheriff Emig did in fact, urging the men to go home. In Mike's account, "A guy with a twenty-two rifle went along the street and shot out the street lights." In the confusion of the actual event, it is uncertain whether the street lights were shot out or knocked out by thrown rocks, but after the first tear gas attack by the police, someone knocked out the lights, whereupon the mob descended on the jail again.

When the mob broke into the San Jose jail, there was some question of where Thurmond and Holmes were lodged. Thurmond was on the third floor, Holmes on the second. Directions were shouted out. In "The Vigilante," Steinbeck reports, "Well, the sheriff started yelling, 'Get the right man, boys, for Christ's sake get the right man. He's in the fourth cell down.'" Thurmond was seized first. He was crouched among the plumbing pipes above the toilet. Someone grabbed him by the leg; he fell, hitting his head on the toilet. In Steinbeck's account: "Well, we got to the nigger's cell. He just stood stiff with his eyes closed like he was dead drunk. One of the guys slugged him down and he got up, and then somebody else socked him and he went over and hit his head on the cement floor" (pp. 135–36). Whether from being struck or from fear, Thurmond was virtually unconscious throughout the lynching. Holmes insisted until his lynching that he was not Holmes, finally admitting his identity when he was beaten in the park prior to lynching. In his conflation of Thurmond and Holmes into the "nigger fiend," Steinbeck used the less brutal scene of the unconscious prisoner. Mike says several times that the prisoner was dead before he was hanged.

One of the key episodes in "The Vigilante," a rather macabre one, involves the souvenir piece of denim from the hanged man's trousers. A page 3 story in the November 27 *Index-Journal* reports, "One man got one of Thurmond's shoes and triumphantly waved it aloft. Another got a piece of his trousers. Still others broke branches from the two death elms." To this day, posters made from photographs of the hanged bodies are sold in San Jose. In "The Vigilante" the souvenir plays an important thematic role. Mike takes out "the piece of torn blue denim." The bartender becomes avaricious for a piece of the souvenir, offering a dollar for the whole thing, then two dollars for half of it. He ups the ante: "Here! Give me your glass! Have a beer on me. I'll pin it up on the wall with a little card under it. The fellas that come in will like to look at it" (p. 136). Mike complies. The bartender too, although not directly involved in the lynching, is affected by the mob spirit. Rather than through lengthy discourse of a John Ramsy, Steinbeck has made his point, sharply and effectively. There is this mysterious part of human nature inevitably drawn to the mob action. No one is free from it.

As Mike walks the deserted streets with Welch toward their homes, the bartender presses Mike for his feelings: "I never been to a lynching. How'd it make you feel—afterwards?" He wants to participate; he is compelled to share the feeling by those instincts that fuel the mob. At first Mike wants to avoid a response:

Mike shied away from the contact. "It don't make you feel nothing." He put down his head and increased his pace. The little bartender had nearly to trot to keep up. The street lights were fewer. It was darker and safer. Mike burst out, "Makes you feel kind of cut off and tired, but kind of satisfied, too. Like you done a good job—but tired and kind of sleepy." [pp. 138–39]

The comment brings him to the front door of his house. It also provides a transition that helps explain the conclusion to this story, which has puzzled many readers. Mike returns to his home, where "his thin, petulant wife was sitting by the open gas oven warming herself." The scene parallels that of Mike before the flames of the burning newspapers in the park. The story opens and ends with flames, with a darkness falling in between. His wife immediately accuses him of having been with another woman: "You think I can't tell by the look on your face that you been with a woman?"

In the closing paragraph, Mike responds to her question: "He walked through the kitchen and went into the bathroom. A little mirror hung on the wall. Mike took off his cap and looked at his face. 'By God, she was right,' he thought. 'That's exactly how I do feel'" (p. 139). The mob action has been very much like a sexual one for Mike. Some mysterious urge in him has responded to the promptings of others, has erupted in a violent climax, has left him drained and empty, but curiously satisfied.

"The Vigilante" is an important work in the development of Steinbeck's artistry. Steinbeck recognized that he had to subordinate exposition of a private theory to the structure of a short story—a character acting out the idea in the time and place of the plot. That idea may be suggested, or implied by the character and action, rather than overtly stated. Furthermore, in the actions of that character, in the spare and intensely focused accounting, Steinbeck has packed the story with a suggestiveness, as opposed to overt statement, that powerfully intrigues the reader. Finally, the difference between "Case History" and "The Vigilante" is the difference between writing for himself or writing for an audience, the difference between philosophical exposition and art.

"THE RAID": RED BADGE OF COURAGE

The outrage of the agricultural workers in the lush valleys of central California had fomented for several years before Steinbeck's attention was drawn to them. In the space of a half-dozen years, dating from the late 1920s, wages had dropped dramatically, as much as seventy percent for picking cotton.[39] The depressed wages, combined with increasing migration to California from the dustbowl states, created tensions as volatile as any in the modern labor movement. Bands of people wandered, workless and homeless, across the valleys. Unusually heavy rains brought with them a plague of illnesses. California hospitals could not handle the crush of the infirm, the infected, the dying.[40] Despair and anger were the two wretched twins born to family after family. A people in need is also a people in need of direction, and the labor leaders descended on the valleys to direct the movement. Having worked the fields during his Stanford days, and having known migrant laborers all of his life, Steinbeck was well aware of the seething unrest. But his attention was riveted in 1934 by acquaintance with several labor and strike leaders. Although the leaders obviously shared Marxist goals, their efforts to help the helpless, the hungry, and impoverished, to nurture unity and compassion where there were discord and maltreatment, were huge. Principles were often set aside for humanity. This revelation— of human need, oppressive forces, and the power of compassion—steadily drew Steinbeck's interest.

The critical consensus toward Steinbeck's three major novels of the latter 1930s—*In Dubious Battle, Of Mice and Men*, and *The Grapes of Wrath*—is that they are the indictments of a social reformer. It is certainly true that they are akin to some degree in that all emerge from the migrant labor situation in California. It is also true that they have continued to exacerbate the social conscience of readers. The indictment is there. The tyrannical financial ploys of the landowners in *In Dubious Battle* and *The Grapes of Wrath* robbed a people of their welfare, dignity, and health. The whimsical power of a nervous pretty boy in *Of Mice and Men* kills both a gentle dream and a gentle giant. Steinbeck charges these people and finds them guilty of trafficking in human lives to line their own pockets.

Perhaps that clear alliance against the moneyed oppressor led to the charges against Steinbeck of his being a communist sympathizer. Such charges were frequent, but when Mary McCarthy suggested in *The Nation* that Steinbeck might have written *In Dubious Battle* better had he been a better communist, they could no longer be escaped.[41] Most injurious to Steinbeck, perhaps, are McCarthy's charges that his failure is one of artistic craft. She allows that he is an adequate storyteller but an incompetent philosopher,

providing "infantile verbalizations" that are simply unfortunate. Jackson Benson characterizes McCarthy, as he does
the editor with Covici-Friede who originally rejected *In
Dubious Battle*, as having "the cocksure certainty of the
parlor theoretician who never got his hands dirty."[42]

The kind of cerebral castigation that McCarthy represented in New York was as far removed from Steinbeck's
gritty storytelling as was his geographical location in California, where he was in fact getting his hands dirty. Nonetheless, the communist-Marxist brand had been burned on, re-
inforced by the censorious reaction to *The Grapes of Wrath*,
and Steinbeck had a hard time shedding that brand.[43] While
for McCarthy Steinbeck was an insufficient artist because
he was an insufficient Marxist, for others he was a despicable artist because he was a despicable communist.

Steinbeck was not unaffected by the turmoil and made it
clear in numerous letters where his sensitivities lay. To
Elizabeth Otis in 1935, when the young editor had rejected
In Dubious Battle at Covici-Friede, an action hastily cor-
rected by Pat Covici, Steinbeck wrote,

Let's get to this rejection now. I had a letter, unfortunately destroyed, in which they said they didn't want to print the book and
they gave three pages of reasons for not wanting to print it. Between you and me I suspect a strong communist bias in that
office, since the reasons given against the book are all those I
have heard from communists of the intellectual bent. . . . My information for this book came mostly from Irish and Italian communists whose training was in the field, not in the drawing room.
They don't believe in ideologies and ideal tactics. They do what
they can under the circumstances. [*SLL*, pp. 109–10]

Steinbeck's sympathies did not ally with the ideology, but
with the people who worked in the fields for the cause of
humanity. He also wrote, "That is the trouble with the
damned people of both sides. They postulate either an
ideal communist or a thoroughly damnable communist and
neither side is willing to suspect that the communist is a

human, subject to the weaknesses of humans and to the greatnesses of humans" (*SLL*, p. 108). In early 1934, the labor revolt escalated, and Steinbeck became increasingly a part of it. Even Salinas was affected: "There are riots in Salinas and killings in the streets of that dear little town where I was born. I shouldn't wonder if the thing had begun. I don't mean any general revolt but an active beginning aimed toward it, the smouldering" (*SLL*, p. 132). But as Steinbeck was drawn into it, his interest focused on the people. His conscience was raked by the terror of suffering, and he responded to the anguish. *Of Mice and Men* captures the love and compassion of migrant to migrant, as well as their huge loneliness as a people divested of honor by the system. That system, or what he elsewhere calls "civilization" to mean any powerful group that holds others in subjection, becomes increasingly the target of Steinbeck's wrath. It was a target now, as it had been in the past, for the outcry against oppressive forces.

That outcry unfolds steadily throughout the letters also. Other than the ledger notes, they are our most reliable resource to knowing the mind of the artist. That resource is indisputable on this score: compassion, not ideology, is the motivating factor for his work on the migrants, and it also serves as the common theme of those works. While beginning work on *The Grapes of Wrath*, Steinbeck noted,

I must go over into the interior valleys. There are about five thousand families starving to death over there, not just hungry but actually starving. The government is trying to feed them and get medical attention to them with the fascist group of utilities and banks and huge growers sabotaging the thing all along the line and yelling for a balanced budget. In one tent there are twenty people quarantined for smallpox and two of the women are to have babies in that tent this week. I've tied into the thing from the first and must get down there and see it and see if I can't do something to help knock these murderers on the heads. [*SLL*, p. 158]

And while he openly admitted to Elizabeth Otis that he wanted "to put a tag of shame on the greedy bastards who are responsible for this," he did it not by raw vitriol and indictment, but by allying the reader's sensibility with the oppressed themselves, so that we see our humanity in them and their dream, and need, in us.[44]

The significance of this for his short stories in *The Long Valley* that deal directly or indirectly with the labor movement or mob psychology cannot be overlooked. While "The Raid" has plenty in it to fuel the most imaginative speculations of critics, such as Peter Lisca's examination of Christian elements and the "conversion" of a person to the cause,[45] the more fundamental theme is the human compassion of the laborers and the leaders. Their cause is not Marxism, first of all, but human need.

While it is indeed true that Mac of *In Dubious Battle* subordinates humanity to his grand design, always on the lookout for a way to "use" someone in the cause, his is not the authoritative voice in that novel either. The narrative and thematic focus rests upon Jim, as it does upon Root in "The Raid." Jim has every reason to hate the system, as does Root. Jim relates,

My whole family has been ruined by this system. My old man, my father, was slugged so much in labor trouble that he went punch-drunk. He got an idea that he'd like to dynamite a slaughter-house where he used to work. Well, he caught a charge of buckshot in the chest from a riot gun.[46]

Root "tried to keep the bitterness out of his voice" when speaking of his father: "Sure, he works on the road. He's a brakeman. He kicked me out when he found out what I was doing. He was scared he'd lose his job. He couldn't see. I talked to him, but he just couldn't see. He kicked me right out" (pp. 92–93). Both lose their families and find a surrogate family in the larger cause. The personal hatred each feels, however, does not affect his view of humanity. Root stops himself short in his personal history: "Root's voice was lonely. Suddenly he realized how he had weakened and how he sounded homesick. 'That's the trouble with them,' he went on harshly. 'They can't see beyond their jobs. They can't see what's happening to them. They hang on to their chains'" (p. 93). While no Doc appears in "The Raid" as he does in *In Dubious Battle* to articulate Steinbeck's views, it should be clear that Steinbeck sides against any interested use of humanity and fights for human freedom to find its own way.

The story of "The Raid" takes place under cover of darkness and thick shadows, a metaphor both for the uncertainty of Dick and Root's enterprise and for the dark oppression of the power of the system against which they labor. The story is charged by an acute sense of loneliness. It resides in the texture, the feeling or coloring of the story, with its opening tune of "Come to Me My Melancholy Baby" and its turgid shadows, rather than as an overt theme as in *Of Mice and Men*.

Through the omniscient third-person narrator, we discover that there is also a darkness of indecision and anxiety in Root. We dive into the dark recesses of his psyche as he wonders fearfully, "I wish I knew the ropes better. You been out before, Dick. You know what to expect. But I ain't ever been out" (p. 92). The story thereby focuses upon a trial under fire of a young man, his confrontation with fear, his own test of the value of his beliefs. He will be tried by enduring the ritual of beating. He will confront his fear and find his courage. His beliefs will coalesce by that trial into a statement of forgiveness and the realization that humans are more important than systems.

Root's fear, as the confrontation draws near, is that he will run, that the surge of emotion in the face of the unknown will blot out conviction. In this sense, Root bears striking similarities to Henry Fleming of Stephen Crane's *The Red Badge of Courage*. When Root first expresses his fear, Dick warns him that he has to endure the trial:

"Do you think you'd try to get away, Dick?" Root asked.
"No, by God! It's against orders. If anything happens we got to stick. You're just a kid. I guess you'd run if I let you!"

Root blustered, "You think you're hell on wheels just because you been out a few times. You'd think you was a hundred to hear you talk."

"I'm dry behind the ears, anyway," said Dick.

Root walked with his head down. He said softly, "Dick, are you sure you wouldn't run? Are you sure you could just stand there and take it?" [p. 93]

While Root's fear is very much like Henry Fleming's, Dick is far less tolerant than Jim Conklin, the tall soldier in Crane's novel. Nonetheless he functions in much the same way, as a foil for the younger man's fears. When Henry Fleming questions Jim about battle, he asks, "Think any of the boys'll run?" Jim responds, "Oh, there may be a few of 'em run, but there's them kind in every regiment," 'specially when they first goes under fire."[47]

Snatches of conversation in *The Red Badge of Courage* and "The Raid" are similar enough to bear evidence of a strong, direct influence. During the night before battle in *The Red Badge of Courage,* all is a confusion of darkness: "From off in the darkness came the trampling of feet. The youth could occasionally see dark shadows that moved like monsters. The regiment stood at rest for what seemed a long time. The youth grew impatient. It was unendurable the way these affairs were managed. He wondered how long they were to be kept waiting" (p. 15). Similarly, in "The Raid" Root seems to hear footsteps and voices in the night. As his anxiety grows, he wonders how long they will be kept waiting at the deserted store:

Root leaned back against the wall again. "I wish they'd come. What time is it, Dick?"

"Five after eight."

"Well, what's keeping them? What are they waiting for? Did you tell them eight o'clock?" [p. 96]

When Henry Fleming's regiment starts to form, he says,

"How do you know you won't run when the time comes? . . . "

"Run?" said the loud one; "run?—of course not!" He laughed.

"Well," continued the youth, "lots of good-a'-nough men have thought they was going to do great things before the fight, but when the time come they skedaddled." [p. 19]

And Root, too, when the word of imminent attack comes, once again confronts his own untested courage. Looking at the poster of an unidentified hero of the movement, Dick says to Root, "Listen Kid. . . . I know you're scared. When you're scared, just take a look at him." Root replies, "You suppose he wasn't ever scared?" But when the informer comes, it is he who runs while Root stands by Dick's side.

Both Henry and Root undergo the savage rite of battle, both are stripped of cowardice and hesitation, both achieve a remarkable manhood. Both receive their red badges of courage by head wounds. For Henry Fleming it happens like this: "'Well, then!' bawled the man in a lurid rage. He adroitly and fiercely swung his rifle. It crushed upon the youth's head" (p. 59). For Root, "A piece of two-by-four lashed out and struck him on the side of the head with a fleshy thump" (p. 103). The result for Henry Fleming is a certain hardening of vision, as he forsakes his religious past: "And at last his eyes seemed to be opened to some new ways. He found that he could look back upon the brass and bombast of his earlier gospels and see them truly. He was gleeful when he discovered that he now despised them" (p. 109). Root is told by Dick to "lay off that religious stuff," and Root replies, "There wasn't no religion to it. It was just—I felt like saying that. It was just kind of the way I felt" (p. 105).

In another sense, however, Root's ordeal is not comparable to Henry's. This soldier's war is for another cause, at another time, and in a different spirit. As the raiders are about to storm the empty store, Dick adjures Root, "Take hold, kid! You take hold! And listen to me; if some one busts you, it isn't him that's doing it, it's the System. And it isn't you he's busting. He's taking a crack at the Principle. Can you remember that?" (p. 100). Root brings the fight upon himself, inciting the hesitant raiders with incendiary

words: "'Comrades,' he shouted, 'you're just men like we
are. We're all brothers————'" (p. 103). The first blow
kindles his own fervor: "His breath burst passionately. His
hands were steady now, his voice sure and strong. His eyes
were hot with an ecstasy. 'Can't you see?' he shouted. 'It's
all for you. We're doing it for you. All of it. You don't know
what you're doing'" (p. 103). Thus we witness a transformation from potential coward to a soldier in the cause.

But what cause? The cause of Mac from *In Dubious
Battle*, who will "use" anything and anyone? Has Root become another Jim, picking up the creed of the revivalist
communist? Mac says at one point in *In Dubious Battle*,
"You're getting beyond me, Jim. I'm getting scared of you.
I've seen men like you before. I'm scared of 'em." To which
Jim replies, "I wanted you to use me. You wouldn't because
you got to like me too well. . . . That was wrong. Then I
got hurt. And sitting here waiting, I got to know my power.
I'm stronger than you, Mac. I'm stronger than anything in
the world." [48] Or will it be the cause that Doc Burton takes
up, the long labor of helping humanity? At one point Mac
presses Doc, "It's a funny thing, Doc. You don't believe in
the cause, and you'll probably be the last man to stick.
I don't get you at all." To which Doc replies, "I don't get
myself. . . . I don't believe in the cause, but I believe
in men." [49]

One clue to answering such questions lies in the closing
lines of the story, when Root says, "You remember in the
Bible, Dick, how it says something like 'Forgive them because they don't know what they're doing'?" (p. 105). Dick
retorts with the communist rejoinder: "You lay off that religion stuff, kid. . . . 'Religion is the opium of the people'"
(p. 105). But Root's comment is precisely the same phrase
that Jim Casy will use when he lays down his life for the
cause of humanity, the same that Jesus used when he laid
down his life. It is the same phrase, furthermore, that stimu-
lates Tom Joad to lay down his life in the cause of any oppressed people. After asserting that he now knows that "a

fella ain't no good alone," Tom Joad quotes from Eccle-
siastes, chapter 4: "Two are better than one, because they
have a good reward for their labor. For if they fall, the one
will lif' up his fellow, but woe to him that is alone when he
falleth, for he hath not another to help him up."[50] In "The
Raid," Dick and Root stand side by side, are beaten down
together, and together lift each other up.

To be sure, in 1934 Steinbeck had not fully realized the
vision of the "fambly of man" that he would articulate in
The Grapes of Wrath, but surely Root placed him on that
path. A man has been converted in "The Raid," under the
rough baptism by night fires, from fear to courage and from
bitterness over his own family's maltreatment to a recognition of humanity's oppression.

Although a singularly important step toward Steinbeck's
novelistic career, "The Raid" is a superbly wrought artistic
work in its own right. Steinbeck achieves a notable suspense in the story through three devices. The events occur
in a maze of darkness and shadows. Coming upon the empty
store where the meeting is to be held, Dick asks Root if he
has filled the oil lamps. Root remonstrates that they have
enough oil. They don't. Soon one lamp gutters down. All
the events occur in a weird half light that accentuates both
Root's fear and his untested mettle. Furthermore, the night
resonates with mysterious sounds. The wind rustles eerily
through the deserted streets. A dog barks an uneasy lament. Over and over the anxious Root imagines that he
hears voices or footsteps. The night is alive with a presence
soon to descend upon them. Finally, the selection of the
third-person omniscient point of view places the reader at
the heart of the impending action. We feel Root's fear,
sense his inadequacy, share the shaping of his vision. Steinbeck doesn't permit a disinterested objectivity; he wants to
bring the reader into a shared vision of humanity.

Stylistically and thematically, "The Raid" placed Steinbeck on the threshhold of his major work. While the story
lacks the decisiveness and the depth of exploration of the

future novels, it is an important work for Steinbeck's decision to explore more fully the human condition and human need through the migrants.

"JOHNNY BEAR": THE TASK OF THE ARTIST

It is regrettable that "Johnny Bear" has attracted so little critical attention, for it is one of the richest, most complex, and most powerful stories that Steinbeck wrote. If Steinbeck said of "The Chrysanthemums" that it "is designed to strike without the reader's knowledge" (*SLL*, p. 91), then "Johnny Bear" strikes with the jarring force of whiplash. Steinbeck often spoke of his works' having several layers of meaning. Few of them so successfully weave those layers into one whole tapestry as "Johnny Bear." Yet the story is also a masterpiece of veiled disclosure, so that one is hardly aware of those layers of meaning striking insistently, pointedly, until one steps back a moment to assimilate the whole. The several layers of meaning can be arranged around three narrative focal points: the first-person narrator; the subject, Johnny Bear; and the story of the Hawkins sisters.

"Johnny Bear" is one of only two works in *The Long Valley*, and one of very few of Steinbeck's canon, to be narrated by the first person. It is a fairly dangerous point of view, subject to reader distrust and a narrower focus than a third-person narrator. The eyes of this narrator are remarkably objective, however, and lend credibility and unity to the diffuse string of events.

A crew foreman on a dredging barge assigned the task of draining the black tule swamps north of Salinas, the narrator is from the working class. As such, he is realistic about his own life—the hard labor of dredging, the fearful accidents that occur—and also about life in the small town of Loma. Disliking the mosquito-choked bunkhouse in the swamp, he takes a room in town with Mrs. Ratz, observing with acid humor that the room, a seedy little dump, befits her name.

He is similarly realistic about Loma itself, a weary little
town of 200 people, the prominent buildings of which he
can list in a very brief sentence. Among those is the Buffalo
Bar. Presided over by the dour Fat Carl, who serves only
whiskey, the Buffalo is the town newsroom, social life, and
shelter: "In the course of an evening every male inhabitant
of Loma over fifteen years old came at least once to the
Buffalo Bar, had a drink, talked a while and went home"
(p. 144). Throughout the story the narrator plays a delightful mind game with Fat Carl. The barman insists upon asking "What'll it be?" He has only one whiskey to offer.

As spartan and ugly as the bar is, displaying a wall of
aged posters, decorations, and cards, including a poster of
Sheriff Rittal that "still begged for re-election although Rittal had been dead for seven years," the Buffalo is a nexus
among the narrator and townsmen. The narrator is recognized there, and there also he meets Johnny Bear. The relationship between the narrator and Johnny Bear, however,
has to do with a lot more than plot structure, and has very
much to do with the writer's task.

While Steinbeck alternated between two titles for his
story while drafting it—"Johnny Bear" and "The Sisters"—
it was first published in *Esquire* (Sept. 1937) under the
title, "The Ears of Johnny Bear." The title is applicable, for
Johnny Bear, the eavesdropper, is also very much like the
ears of the artist listening in on the secret murmurings of
life and revealing them to the public.

Physically, Johnny Bear is a freak: "His name described
him better than I can. He looked like a great, stupid, smil-
ing bear. His black matted head bobbed forward and his
long arms hung out as though he should have been on all
fours and was only standing upright as a trick. His legs were
short and bowed, ending with strange, square feet" (p. 146).
Afflicted with a huge thirst for Fat Carl's whiskey, Johnny
Bear reveals an inimitable ability not just to act out but to
replay like a tape recorder conversations he has heard. For
a whiskey, he turns on the tape and *becomes* the person he
plays:

I'm sure I nearly fainted. The blood pounded in my ears. I flushed. It was my voice coming out of the throat of Johnny Bear, my words, my intonation. And then it was the voice of Mae Romero—exact. If I had not seen the crouching man on the floor I would have called to her. [p. 147]

Johnny Bear is the idiot savant, the retarded mentality, like Tularecito, with one great gift. The narrator's friend Alex Hartnell comments, "He can photograph words and voices. . . . He doesn't know the words he's saying, he just says them. He hasn't the brains enough to make anything up, so you know that what he says is what he heard" (p. 149). The narrator, however, asks the hard questions: "But why does he do it? Why is he interested in listening if he doesn't understand?" (p. 149). Alex's response is that Johnny Bear loves whiskey, but there is more to it than that.

When attention turns to the Hawkins sisters, Alex, who has known them best and longest of anyone in Loma through the friendship of their fathers, reveals his fears about Johnny Bear's revelations:

"But Miss Emalin is fighting something terrible and—I don't think she's going to win."
"What do you mean?"
"I don't know what I mean. But I've thought I should shoot Johnny Bear and throw him in the swamp. I've really thought about doing it."

The narrator responds, "It's not his fault. He's just a kind of recording and reproducing device, only you use a glass of whiskey instead of a nickel" (p. 162). Is this also the task of the artist? To be simply a recording and reproducing device, supplying words without fully understanding their meanings or contexts?

That very question was raised by Steinbeck in a letter to George Albee several years earlier. Not unusually, Steinbeck's disposition was affected at the time by the weather, and the gray day stimulated a poignant reflection on his artistic task:

It is a gray day with little dusty spurts of rain. A good day for inwardness. Only I doubt that I have many guts of my own to look inward at. That is one of the great troubles with my objective writing. A constant practice of it leaves one no material for introspection. If my characters are sad or happy I reflect their emotions. I have no personal nor definitive emotions of my own. Indeed, when there is no writing in progress, I feel like an uninhabited body. [*SLL*, p. 48][51]

Taken simply on its own terms, the letter suggests Steinbeck's view of himself simply as a processor of the emotions of others, a recording device very much like Johnny Bear.

The narrator of the story provides the context of meaning for Johnny Bear's tape recording of life. As he walks back to Loma after talking with Alex, he reflects, "I smiled as I walked along at the way a man's thought can rearrange nature to fit his thoughts" (p. 162). In the same way, the artist also rearranges nature to fit his thoughts.

As we have already observed in this study, Steinbeck's storytelling method belies his nonteleological premises. One may also observe a deepening awareness of the artist's task to rearrange observed experience in Steinbeck's letters. It is clear, for example, that the drama of the migrant workers was so compelling to Steinbeck at this time that he believed the simple act of exposing their situation was sufficient. Their story needed no adumbration by didactic exhortations. His task as a writer was to get that story, as cleanly and powerfully as his talent permitted. When he wrote *In Dubious Battle*, he used precisely the same terminology to describe his writing that the narrator uses for Johnny Bear. Steinbeck wrote in January 1935, "The book is brutal. I wanted to be merely a recording consciousness, judging nothing, simply putting down the thing" (*SLL*, p. 98). Even in *In Dubious Battle*, however, that recording is not simply of the surfaces of observable experience; it is also attuned to the psychological rhythms of human experience.

A year and a half earlier, Steinbeck had dismissed objective realism as a literary mode:

I don't think you will like my late work. It leaves realism farther
and farther behind. I never had much ability for nor faith nor belief in realism. It is just a form of fantasy as nearly as I could figure. . . . There are streams in man more profound and dark and
strong than the libido of Freud. Jung's libido is closer but still in-
adequate. [*SLL*, p. 87]

The transition from rejecting mimetic realism to exploring
human experience develops finally into "living into" the
character. In a paradoxical sense, this was the teleological
end of his nonteleological writing: to identify completely
with the character. In 1935 Steinbeck wrote Joseph Jackson,

In the last few books I have felt a curious richness as though my
life had been multiplied through having become identified in a
most real way with people who were not me. I have loved that.
And I am afraid, terribly afraid, that if the bars ever go down, if
I become a trade mark, I shall lose the ability to do that. . . .
Sometimes in my own mind at least I can create something which
is larger and richer than I am. . . . Not being brave I am glad
when I can make a brave person whom I believe in. [*SLL*, p. 119]

Two years later, in November 1937, he expressed the same
idea: "Sometimes in working, the people in my head become much realler [sic] than I am" (*SLL*, pp. 144–45). By
the time he began work on *The Grapes of Wrath*, having
lived with the people and having participated in their experience, Steinbeck wrote, "Actually if there has been one
rigid rule in my books, it is that I as me had no right in
them" (*SLL*, p. 176). Having set himself aside, he entered
fully into the lives of his characters.

This was to be a view Steinbeck held for the rest of his
career. A work grows from the inside out; the experience is
arranged by the artist to suggest rather than declare. When
Steinbeck wrote that *The Grapes of Wrath* had "five layers"
of meaning (*SLL*, p. 178), those layers were the work of a
conscious artistic design, not a tape recording. To Peter
Benchley in 1956, he wrote,

A writer out of loneliness is trying to communicate like a distant star sending signals. He isn't telling or teaching or ordering. Rather he seeks to establish a relationship of meaning, of feeling, of observing. . . . Of course a writer rearranges life, shortens time intervals, sharpens events, and devises beginnings, middles and ends, and this is arbitrary because there are no beginnings nor any ends. [*SLL*, p. 523]

In 1934, however, Steinbeck had only begun to sense this aesthetic attitude, which would later emerge as a creed. "Johnny Bear" is the crucial work in his developing understanding that an artist rearranges observed experience to "establish a relationship of meaning."

Artistically, this rearrangement is accomplished in several subtle and interlocking methods. Observed experience in the story is metaphorically figured by the relentless fog rolling in off the swamps around Loma. Through the fog, the reader, like Johnny Bear, catches only glimpses of the total reality. It is the narrator, however, who orders events to supply a pattern of meaning to those glimpses.

The fog is a consciously and skillfully constructed pattern of imagery, as well as a natural phenomenon. The village of Loma is situated upon a small rise of land almost totally surrounded by swamp. Out of these swamp marshes, fogs roll incessantly across the land. Importantly, the fog is imaged much like Johnny Bear himself. On the night of his first meeting with Johnny Bear, the narrator has been out with Mae Romero "until the nasty fog drove us back into town" (p. 146). Johnny Bear has also been there, he later discovers when Johnny Bear replays his conversation with Mae. From our first meeting with him, then, Johnny Bear is allied with the fog.

Physically, Johnny Bear is pictured as a huge mountain of fog: "He moved forward and for all his bulk and clumsiness, he seemed to creep. He didn't move like a man, but like some prowling night animal" (p. 146). The fog, too, is described as a prowling night animal: "I was about to remark that the night was clear when, looking ahead, I saw the rags of fog creeping around the hill from the swamp side and climbing like slow snakes on the top of Loma" (p. 157). Like the fog, Johnny Bear is nearly omnipresent in Loma. When the narrator wonders, "It's funny somebody hasn't shot him while he was peeking in windows," Alex responds, "lots of people have tried, but you just don't see Johnny Bear, and you don't catch him. You keep your windows closed, and even then you talk in a whisper if you don't want to be repeated" (p. 149).

While Johnny Bear is imaged like the fog, sliding up to and listening at every window, his recording device mind would provide no more coherence for the story than the fog. It is the narrator who arranges the experience into meaning. Metaphorically, the small rise of Loma is somewhat like the narrator himself, rising above the fogs of recorded experience to arrange experience into a meaningful pattern. It is not an accident that the narrator is by profession the crew foreman of a dredger, draining the swamp, beating back the fog. And his further importance is demonstrated in the third focus of the story—the Hawkins sisters.

The unmarried sisters are more than simply a first family to Loma; they are, as Alex says, symbols to the community. The narrator later observes that they represent staid order in a disordered land:

A community would feel kind of—safe, having women like that about. A place like Loma with its fogs, with its great swamp like a hideous sin, needed, really needed, the Hawkins women. A few years there might do things to a man's mind if those women weren't there to balance matters. [p. 156]

They are the aristocrats, the two who by wealth and position and seclusion provide a kind of center for the village. Thus, when sin intrudes upon their household, it is devastating for the townsmen as well.

The narrator carefully arranges the revelation of that sin. Truly, Johnny Bear gives voice to it, but the narrator supplies the meaning. The action has a parallel in the revelation of the cook for the dredging crew. A seemingly mean-

ingless figure in the story, without apparent reason or artistic purpose other than to flesh out the realistic details of the
dredging operation, the cook too has a secret sin. Bit by bit
we receive clues—the nervousness, the twitching limbs.
When the narrator discovers his drug habit, the cook is
fired. But cooks are dispensable; the Hawkins sisters are
symbols, and symbols are not so easily dispensed with.

The mystery in the story is why Amy first attempts suicide and then succeeds in it. What evil could have intruded
upon the staid, orderly life of these ladies? We discover,
through Johnny Bear's recording, that Amy is pregnant.
But by whom? That is the mystery that could infect the
town. The narrator places a series of clues throughout the
story that make it read like a mystery. Still, the revelation
at the ending comes with a shock of recognition.

When Johnny Bear relates the voices of the Doctor
and Emalin at Amy's suicide, suspicion seems to fall upon
Johnny Bear himself. And why not? He slips like a shadow
through the night. It is known that he listens by the Hawkins's window. Alex enters the bar just after Johnny Bear
has related the voices:

"You've heard?" he asked softly.
"Yes."
"I've been afraid," he cried. "I told you a couple of nights ago.
I've been afraid."
I said, "Did you know she was pregnant?"
Alex stiffened. He looked around the room and then back at
me. "Johnny Bear?" he asked. [p. 164]

The way he asks the question suggests two answers: that
Johnny Bear provided the information, or that Johnny Bear
impregnated Amy. The reader does not know at this point.
Alex's outrage may even suggest the latter. He says to
Johnny Bear, "You ought to be ashamed. Miss Amy gave
you food, and she gave you all the clothes you ever had"
(p. 165). But when Johnny Bear begins uttering the dialogue in Chinese, first a high, singsong voice, then "the
other voice, slow, hesitant, repeating the words without

nasal quality," Alex hits him. Johnny captures Alex in a
bear hug and does not relent until Fat Carl beats him unconscious. The clue, revealed in the last sentence of the
story, lies in that second voice. It is Miss Amy's, speaking to
her Chinese lover.

That last revelation only sets in order a list of clues subtly
arranged from the beginning. Once before, Johnny Bear
has provided a recording of the two Chinese voices, but the
men laughed it off as a harmless joke. The narrator had
asked Alex then, "Nothing Johnny Bear said would hurt
them, would it?" Alex responds quickly: "'I don't know. I
don't know what it means. I mean, I kind of know. Oh! Go
on to bed. I didn't bring the Ford. I'm going to walk out
home.' He turned and hurried into that slow squirming
mist" (p. 153). Alex's hope is that the truth, which he has
suspected from the outset, may also remain in the mist.

Tracing the clues, we discover that the Hawkins sisters,
who live next door to Alex, let some Chinese farm the land
on shares.[52] The narrator, moreover, is mindful of the sisters' painful loneliness: "Remembering the tones, I could
see the women who had spoken, the chill-voiced Emalin,
and the loose, misery-broken face of Amy. I wondered
what caused the misery. Was it just the lonely suffering of a
middle-aged woman? It hardly seemed so to me, for there
was too much fear in the voice" (p. 153). When he passes
by the house a second time with Alex Hartnell, the association of the Chinese workers to the house is made again:
"A shadow crossed his face. He waved at a white-washed
square building standing out in the field. 'That's where the
Chink share-croppers live. Good workers. I wish I had
some like them'" (p. 155). A third time the narrator passes
the house. Suddenly the thick fog is stirred by a wind and
breaks clear:

In the starlight I could see those big silver fog balls moving like
elementals across the fields. I thought I heard a soft moaning in
the Hawkins yard behind the hedge, and once when I came sud-

denly out of the fog I saw a dark figure hurrying along in the field, and I knew from the dragging footsteps that it was one of the Chinese field hands walking in sandals. The Chinese eat a great many things that have to be caught at night. [pp. 160–61]

At this point, the moaning of the Chinese and his dragging departure are merely written off as a racial peculiarity. In reality, we find it one more clue in the sequence of events that culminate in Amy's suicide. In a casual reading one is hardly aware of the pattern, and thereby the revelation at the ending that Amy is pregnant by her Chinese lover hits with jarring impact. But that revelation has been carefully prepared throughout.

It is surprising that a story which deals so directly with the task of the artist has elicited so little study by scholars, for surely "Johnny Bear" is a gem. Most of what has appeared in critical studies is stated in the fashion of cursory judgment rather than sustained and compelling argument. Peter Lisca gave the story a passing nod in *The Wide World of John Steinbeck*, observing, "On one level, it is an exploration of the artist's role in society; for, like the artist, Johnny Bear holds the mirror up to mankind and reveals through his mimetic talent the festers of society."[53] The central interest, in Lisca's view, is the conflict of social orders and the perpetuation of "symbols of decorum." About the narrator or Steinbeck's own view of literature, which is quite different from that suggested by Johnny Bear, he offers nothing. But Lisca's study was a very early one, and its interest lies more in the development of the major works. What is surprising is that critical opinion has not varied much from this early view.

Warren French focuses upon "the subnormal character" of Johnny Bear in *John Steinbeck*. Louis Owens suggests the inadequacy of an exclusive focus upon Johnny Bear or the theme or class conflicts by taking to task Brian M. Barbour's denigrating views of the story, and focuses attention, briefly, upon the crucial role of the narrator.[54] R. S. Hughes, while explicating well the imagery of the story, follows closely Lisca's sense of class conflict as a thematic principle in the story.[55]

A welcome change appears in Charlotte Byrd's essay, "The First-Person Narrator in 'Johnny Bear': A Writer's Mind and Conscience." Byrd correctly notes the central role of the narrator, superseding Johnny Bear's role as a "recording device." Her study also focuses attention away from the class conflict, relating it more precisely to the effects of the artist's telling:

By having a member of the community reveal to the narrator the facts behind the drama that Johnny Bear enacts, then showing the narrator weaving all of the information into the story that we read, Steinbeck indicates that the artist is not solely responsible for what he produces, though the price he often pays for exercising his talent is exile from the community. The artist takes reality, applies his imaginative craft to it, and produces a story that reveals a truth or truths about human nature.[56]

"Johnny Bear" functions both as a powerful story in its own right and as an important document in Steinbeck's artistic development. The pairing of the mimetic gift of Johnny Bear and the arranging task of the narrator, however, should not be seen as mutually exclusive polarities. Rather, they are synchronously merged by the mind of the artist—the one who faithfully represents "what is," then arranges it in such a way that the full life is revealed and the reader can also "live into" the event.

7

The Later Short Stories

BECAUSE STEINBECK EXPENDED such intense energy on short stories early in his career, one wonders why there are so few of them in the years that follow. However significant Steinbeck's short stories were for his development as an artist, critical attention has always focused primarily upon his novels to the neglect of those stories. In retrospect, they may seem almost a literary diversion, a passing whimsy exercised with varying degrees of success over a short space of years and sporadically thereafter.

In actuality, of course, the stories were instrumental in his growth as an artist, and that fact by itself may explain the transition. It may also be argued that a number of the short stories, those collected in *The Pastures of Heaven* and those from 1934 inspired by the migrants, were either quasi-novelistic in conception or were anticipations of the novels. The stories may be seen, in this line of reasoning, as shorter manifestations of his essentially novelistic technique, a preparing ground for supposedly more fertile productions.

That response, however, is by itself insufficient. More satisfactory answers may be found, and they essentially respond to the fundamental question of why Steinbeck wrote the short stories in the first place.

One such reason was financial. His first two novels, *Cup of Gold* and *To A God Unknown*—assuming *The Pastures of Heaven* to be a collection of short stories rather than a novel—failed miserably as commercial ventures. Determined to make his way as a literary author, Steinbeck seemed nonetheless to face insuperable financial obstacles.[1] Dependent to some degree upon his parents' stipend and Carol's meager income, money represented both artistic acceptance and independence for Steinbeck, and the sale of short stories seemed the likeliest avenue to a quick financial return. In 1934, Steinbeck entered a telling note in his ledger: "I must lay enough money aside so that the careful work can be done. And I must go on with these short stories for that purpose. There that's down. That must be followed" (*LVN*).

When in later years he discovered large checks in his mail, the idea of the money in itself nearly overwhelmed him. In 1949 he dashed off "His Father," and Elizabeth Otis immediately sold it to *Reader's Digest*. Steinbeck wrote her,

> You know darned well you done good with the little four page story. What a price! It is next best to Air Wick. Very good news.

> In the same mail with your letter, one from Ralph Henderson (Editor of *Reader's Digest*) assuring me that they bought the story because they liked it and not because of my name. Apparently you cut them deeply by asking for money as well as the honor of being published. In the light of this $2,500 for four pages—do you remember when you worked for months and finally got $90 for the longest story in the *Red Pony* series and forty for the shorter ones? I hardly made $1,000 on my first three novels. [*SLL*, pp. 353–54]

But he never forgot the impoverished days. In 1949, he reflected, "I watched the postman with gleaming eyes this morning. Once long ago when a letter with a tiny check meant the difference between dinner and not, there was a long desert time and the postman got so ashamed that he walked on the other side of the street" (*SLL*, p. 372). One way to explain the transition from short stories to novels, then, lies in Steinbeck's growing financial independence, particularly with the startling sales of *Tortilla Flat*. Suddenly he had the financial freedom to consider longer works, to be written without the immediate pressure of financial need. The income introduced other problems, however. To

George Albee, Steinbeck wrote of the crowds that had begun to harass him and the difficulty of finding quiet and leisure to write (*SLL*, p. 117). Nonetheless, it should be clear
that one reason Steinbeck wrote short stories was the prospect of quick remuneration, a reason obviated by the success of *Tortilla Flat* and subsequent novels.

Steinbeck had been writing, and telling, short stories
since his youth. In one sense, the more focused work he
started at Stanford University was a natural outgrowth of
what he had been doing. But a second reason he turned his
attention so intensely to short stories in the early 1930s was
the prospect of recognition. As much as he lamented the
publicity obtained by *Tortilla Flat*, it was something Steinbeck had deeply hungered for.[2] The early years of obscurity
and rejections seemed vindicated by that reception.

Short stories were indeed one way to garner recognition
in the early 1930s. It is difficult for us in our age, when hundreds of little magazines struggle for survival, limping along
on ever-dwindling pensions by universities and benefac-
tors, to understand the immense popularity and prestige of
the literary magazines of the 1930s. Short stories were the
initiation rites into the fraternity of the famous, and popular acceptance assumed one's status as a genuine author.

Although he never experienced the financial rewards of
some of his contemporaries writing short stories in the
1930s, Steinbeck did acquire recognition through them.
Over the space of a year and a half, his stories appeared five
times in the prestigious *North American Review.* "The
Murder" was awarded the O. Henry Prize for 1934. Although he did not win it, he was considered for the Phelan
Award in 1935.

Third, it is undeniable that the short stories were not artistic ends in themselves for Steinbeck, but part of a process of self-discovery. In them Steinbeck was solidifying his
artistic aims, serving a kind of self-imposed apprenticeship.
Those same aims—use of a recollected past, writing from
experience, mastery of imagery patterns and narrative
points of view—were, however, leading him beyond the

short story into the world of the novel even as he mastered them. His deepening attraction to the labor unrest in mid-1934 could no longer find full expression in the short story. He needed a larger canvas to paint the needs and lives of these people. The work on *In Dubious Battle, Of Mice and Men,* and *The Grapes of Wrath* opened entirely new aesthetic arenas, and Steinbeck's athletic mind responded agilely to the challenge. In this respect, the training ground of the short stories served him well for the longer marathon of the novel.

We might also observe the fact that Steinbeck was a streaky writer, one easily consumed by a new project and quite willing to put behind him past efforts. He always seemed to have a new project in mind and dwelt little on projects once completed. Thus, while his interest was consumed by short stories for several years, it is not surprising that he moved to another mode. The next great cycle was, of course, completed by *The Grapes of Wrath,* a work that drained every nervous and creative resource he had. In the journal he kept while working on *The Grapes of Wrath,* Steinbeck referred often to a "blind weariness" that limited his ability to work, or he would comment, "My nerves blew out a fuse and today I feel weak and powerless." In the white heat of writing, Steinbeck did not understand the word *moderation.*

The third great cycle culminated in *East of Eden,* a work begun far earlier than many have imagined. His interest in writing a history of his valley had been in his mind, really, since the early 1930s. In 1933, Steinbeck wrote Albee,

I think I would like to write the story of this whole valley, of all the little towns and all the farms and the ranches in the wilder hills. I can see how I would like to do it so that it would be the valley of the world. But that will have to be sometime in the future. I would take so very long. [*SLL,* p. 73]

The essential trappings of *East of Eden,* the germ of the idea, may be found in that statement: to write a history of the valley, to have it represent a larger world, to spend a long period writing it. In 1944, Steinbeck announced his intentions to begin working on the novel: "Within a year or so I want to get to work on a very large book I've been thinking about for at least two years and a half. Everything else is kind of marking time" (*SLL*, p. 273). When he engaged the work on *East of Eden*, he often spoke of all his other work having been a kind of practice for this masterwork. The same idea appears in a 1946 letter to Carl Wilhelmson: "I'm working on a thing now that is giving me hell—a long novel. I want to take a long time with it. It seems to me that I have been rushing for five or six years, rushing as though I were trying to beat something" (*SLL*, pp. 28–29). In 1948 Steinbeck was ready to do actual research for the novel. He wrote Paul Carswell, editor of the *Salinas-Californian*, for permission to consult his files. In April of 1948 he wrote Ed Ricketts of his growing excitement with the long project, and in 1949 he wrote Pascal Covici for "a Grey's [sic] Anatomy" and "a Pharmacopaea (can't even spell it)" (*SLL*, p. 346)—two of the works that were to be instrumental to the realistic and thematic details of the novel.[3] Because of the combined effects of Ed Ricketts's death and the agonizing divorce from Gwyndolyn, his second wife, however, Steinbeck was unable to continue. Not until revitalized by his marriage to Elaine, his third wife, was he able to engage the work systematically, but the long progress of preparation, research, and writing demonstrate his complete absorption by a new project.

The fourth great cycle in Steinbeck's career centered upon his translation of *Morte D'Arthur*. In this case also, the project worked steadily, slowly, into every fiber of his nature until it became a consuming interest. Steinbeck announced his intentions in a November 1956 letter:

> I am taking on something I have always wanted to do. That is the reduction of Thomas Malory's Morte d'Arthur to simple readable prose without adding or taking away anything, simply to put it into modern spelling and to translate the obsolete words to

modern ones and to straighten out some of the more involved sentences. . . .

It was the very first book I knew and I have done considerable research over the years as my work will show. . . . I don't know any book save only the Bible and perhaps Shakespeare which has had more effect on our morals, our ethics and our mores than this same Malory. [*SLL*, p. 540]

In one sense, *Travels with Charley in Search of America* and *The Winter of Our Discontent* grew out of this central interest. Both are studies of the moral character of the present age, and Steinbeck often spoke of a wish to bring the moral rigor of the Arthurian court to bear upon this age.

In another sense, however, it can be argued that Steinbeck never left off writing short stories. The six sections of *Of Mice and Men*, so successfully adapted to the stage, may be seen as six interlocking short stories. Each has an independent wholeness and unity. Similarly, many of the intercalary chapters of *The Grapes of Wrath* and *Sweet Thursday* may be seen as independent short stories, and in fact, one outtake from *Cannery Row*, "The Time the Wolves Ate the Vice-Principal," was published independently as a short story.[4]

The story may have been well excised from the novel, for even though the novel is surely one of the darkest in Steinbeck's canon, "The Time the Wolves Ate the Vice-Principal" possesses a unmitigatedly violent and shocking tone. *Cannery Row* is a novelistic probing of the dark, subconscious urges in humanity, based upon the metaphorical alliance with the sea and its violent subsurface world. In the story, a pack of wolves appears in Salinas—not in Monterey where the rest of the novel is set. They rampage through the town, devouring what they can seize, including an old Airedale. They locate Mr. Hartley and rip him to shreds on a woman's front porch, not even disturbing her sleep. Here is a mob violence, enacted grimly and terribly while some local citizens merely sleep through it.

While this study will not consider those outtakes or

interchapters, designed as they were for the most part in connection with a larger novel, they do demonstrate a continuation of Steinbeck's ready facility for the short story. This continued use of the short story in a larger context may be most dramatically seen, however, in Steinbeck's World War II journalism collected in *Once There Was a War.* Constructed as a series of vignettes rather than as straight journalism, the collection captures the lives of characters in sharp, independent sketches much like his short stories. Steinbeck's intention was to give the feeling, the texture, of the war zone through stories. After recounting a sequence of little stories on the London bombings, he writes, "In all of the little stories it is the ordinary, the commonplace thing or incident against the background of the bombing that leaves the indelible picture."[5] So too his task in this journalism: to give the stories that leave an indelible imprint.

In 1943 Steinbeck was hired by the *New York Herald Tribune* as a war correspondent, but prior to accreditation he had to be cleared by the War and State departments. The process was delayed considerably by charges of Steinbeck's sympathy to Marxist causes. Jackson Benson recounts the investigation at some length in *The True Adventures of John Steinbeck, Writer,* but one example, released under the Freedom of Information Act long after Steinbeck's death, may indicate the difficulties Steinbeck confronted:

In some ways the investigation was almost funny. As John's widow commented after seeing the report, "If John were only here to see this. He would especially like the witness who reported that the 'subject' was usually badly dressed and the agent who said he was a.k.a. Dr. Beckstein." But other aspects may have been ludicrous, though not very funny. Of the eight people interviewed, two didn't know him at all and two had had barely any contact with him. In fact the only really damaging personal report came from one of those who had never met him, the man who purchased the Los Gatos ranch. This gentleman read Steinbeck's second-class mail and found it "apparently communistic" and "very radical." On the basis of the conditions in the house when he bought it, the gentleman reported Steinbeck to be "very impulsive, eccentric, and unreliable socially."[6]

Nonetheless, on June 3, 1943, Steinbeck departed on a troop ship for England, the first stage of a remarkable adventure in his life and some remarkable, if overlooked, writing collected in *Once There Was a War*. Sections of this work have the immediacy and power of some of the best war journalism:

The men slept in their pup tents and drew their mosquito nets over them and scratched and cursed all night until, after a time, they were too tired to scratch and curse and they fell asleep the moment they hit the blankets. Their minds and their bodies became machine-like. They did not talk about the war. They talked only of home and of clean beds with white sheets and they talked of ice water and ice cream and places that did not smell of urine. Most of them let their minds dwell on snow banks and the sharp winds of Middle Western winter. But the red dust blew over them and crusted their skins and after a while they could not wash it all off any more. The war had narrowed down to their own small group of men and their own job. It would be a lie to suggest that they liked being there. They wish they were somewhere else.[7]

Several of the pieces collected in *Once There Was a War* have the narrative, thematic, and character unity that would enable them to stand as independent short stories. "The Cottage That Wasn't There" tells a tight little ghost story through the mind and eyes of a weary sergeant. "A Hand" provides a brief sketch of a wounded soldier with a surprise ending. Big Train Mulligan appears several times as a unifying character. And Mulligan serves as the source for the one sketch published independently as a short story under the title "The Crapshooter" in the Avon publication *Various Temptations*.[8]

Eddie the crapshooter always wins on Sunday, "a fact he attributed to a clean and disinterested way of life." As he plays on the troopship, Eddie's pile grows steadily until he loses:

> "No," he said, "somepins wrong. I win on Sunday, always win on Sunday."
> A sergeant shuffled his feet uneasily. "Mister," he said. "Mister, you see, it ain't Sunday. We've went and crossed the date line. We lost Sunday."[9]

Steinbeck concludes the story with a note, "Anyway, it's one of Mulligan's lies."

In the same way, other sketches might be considered short stories. For example, the delightful episode of McKnight's turkey in "Positano"[10] could stand independently as a short story, as could "I Go Back to Ireland,"[11] a first-person account of Steinbeck's search for his ancestors, but told with the plotting and suspense of a short story. Another sketch commonly considered a short story is "Case of the Hotel Ghost—Or . . . What Are You Smoking in That Pipe, Mr. S?" Based upon a visit he and Elaine made to England in 1952, it was first published in the *Louisville Courier-Journal*, June 20, 1957, and later with some revisions in the London *Evening-Standard*, January 25, 1958. The story begins by comparing ghosts in England and Italy, and the narrator, who is Steinbeck speaking in the first person, undisguised by any narrative conventions, observes,

> Even I have—or had—my own shoddy ghost in London. It's an unlikely story, so preposterous on the face of it that I hesitate to put it down for an intelligent public. For my own peace of mind, I am glad my wife was with me when it happened. It gives one a feeling of mental security to know that someone else saw it too.[12]

The narrative presence in the story tends to mark the piece as a journalistic document focusing upon a present experience rather than a short story evoking a fictional world. Actually it is a hybrid, with Steinbeck serving as undisguised narrator recounting journalistically a fictive event.

In the story the narrator and his wife return six years

after the war to a hotel he stayed in as a correspondent before leaving to cover the Italian invasion. The narrator awakens at night dreaming of bombs. He tries to work in the morning but is distracted by his wife's increasing restlessness. They go to the White Tower for lunch, then walk back to the hotel to find "just a deep dark hole with rubble piled neatly around its edges." It is an effective little sketch, evoking well the disturbing emotional play of a postwar scene.

Story-like qualities mark this essentially journalistic piece, but good journalism will place a character in a setting, evoke a mood, have a plot of sorts. Nonetheless, the characters and place here are not fictional. The plot is a supposed event, but not a controlled sequence of events revealing a thematic purpose. The line between journalism and fiction is often a hazy one, meandering through gray areas that are not clearly defined. The safest judgment is that Steinbeck, as a fiction writer, wrote journalism that had many of the qualities of fiction.

It is also true, despite the very few short stories published after the *Long Valley* collection, that he wrote far more stories than he submitted for publication. He continued to write short stories, though several of them, as Jackson Benson noted, were "really just finger exercises" that underlined his frustration at times of acute stress in his life.[13] Most intriguing of the short stories that failed to see publication is one that he wrote in the bleak time during his divorce from Gwyndolyn. Steinbeck wrote in an October 26, 1948, letter,

Tonight I couldn't sleep and I wrote a little story that was so evil, so completely evil that when I finished it I burned it. It was effective, horribly effective. It would have made anyone who read it completely miserable. I don't mind evil if anything else is accomplished but this was unqualifiedly murderous and terrible. I wonder where it came from. It just seemed to creep in from under the door. I suppose the best thing was to write it and the next was to burn it. [*SLL,* pp. 336–37]

Noting such facts as these—that the intensive period of early short-story writing achieved many of the ends Steinbeck wished, that he was indeed a streaky writer compelled by new projects, that there exists a story-like quality to nearly everything he wrote—one locates only a handful of short stories designed and written as such after *The Long Valley*. Nonetheless, written at a time when his artistic power was at its peak, they form an important part of Steinbeck's legacy.

THE FORGOTTEN VILLAGE AND "THE MIRACLE OF TEPAYAC": THE MEXICAN STORIES

They seem at first entirely dissimilar works. *The Forgotten Village* was Steinbeck's first film script, a very slight work written quickly under pressure and finished on June 20, 1940. "The Miracle of Tepayac" is a retelling of the Image of Guadalupe story, its roots stretching back to 1531, written for the Christmas issue of *Collier's* in 1948. Nonetheless, fundamental similarities do exist. Furthermore, it is not improbable to label *The Forgotten Village* as a short story, if only in length. It is nearly the same length as any of Steinbeck's stories and only slightly longer than "The Miracle of Tepayac."

Although Steinbeck had visited Mexico during earlier years, his visits grew more frequent and his interest grew more intense during the 1940s. Mexico increasingly began to represent an escape and freedom for him. When he returned from his coverage of World War II in October 1943, he was physically and emotionally exhausted. However poor his condition, by January 11, 1944, he was on his way to Mexico again. He planned to work on *Cannery Row* and *The Pearl*, but work eluded him. The solace he was unable to find either in his work or in his marriage was sought in relentless travel, and over and over his travels led back to Mexico. The restlessness of spirit is mirrored in the relative shallowness of his work during this decade, in which he produced little that could be considered of major significance. Only *The Pearl*, thin volume that it is, can stake a fair claim to that significance.

Steinbeck's interest in Mexico during the 1940s is also reflected in his writing. Although *The Sea of Cortez* was a travel account of his voyage in the Gulf of California, loosely tied together with speculations on marine biology and the state of life, his first fictional piece with a Mexican setting was *The Forgotten Village*. It was an ill-fated filming venture, and by the time it was nearing completion Steinbeck had already distanced himself from it as much as he could. Although there were other Mexican works during the 1940s—*The Pearl, The Wayward Bus*, and *Viva Zapata!*—"The Miracle of Tepayac" closed the influence. The first work in many ways anticipates the last.

To say that *The Forgotten Village* is a story demonstrating the clash between ancient superstitions and spirituality versus technical knowledge and modern medicine is accurate, but also misleading. As he demonstrated in *Tortilla Flat*, Steinbeck was sensitive to the religious beliefs of people. While he loathed religion when it was used to keep a people under submission, Steinbeck considered it a warm and vital part of a people's way of life when it sprang naturally from their daily patterns of belief. The excessive superstition in *The Forgotten Village* is not there as the subject of satire or ridicule. This is the way people are, the way he found them.

The story opens with Juan Diego taking his pregnant wife, Esperanza, to the Wise Woman, Trini, who makes a prophecy about the child in exchange for a chicken. Trini's magic is severely tested, however, when the boy, Paco, suddenly becomes ill. According to Trini, the sickness is an evil in the air, and she tries to withdraw the evil spirit from Paco with an egg. But soon others in the village fall ill:

Juan Diego went to see his friend the teacher, the only man in Santiago who had been to the outside world. And Juan Diego said, "You know many children are sick." "I know it," the teacher

said. "They say it is in the air, the evil little spirits," Juan Diego
said. "No, I think it is the water," the teacher said. "I think the
germs are in the pueblo well. I can try to help, but I do not know
enough. I can only try to help them." And he gathered his medi-
cines and his books.[14]

When the teacher confronts Trini, she exclaims, "'What is
this nonsense—these new things—these young men who
tell their elders? You will kill the people with your new foolishness. This for your nonsense!' And she threw his medi-
cines to the ground" (p. 57). Thus the essential conflict: the
steadfast traditions rooted in a sense of superstition and
magic and the introduction of knowledge and medicine.
     But the teacher's practices are as ineffectual as Trini's.
Paco dies during the night. Others, particularly the children, fall ill. When the possibility of a cure through inocu-
lation is presented, the people protest: "'We do not want
horses' blood. Are we horses?' And another said, 'Truly,
some of the children die and go to heaven. Perhaps it is intended that way. We do not like these new things'" (p. 89).
It falls upon Juan Diego, as the only believer in the efficacy
of science to help his people, to take a letter to the authorities beseeching their aid. When the doctors do arrive to
help, however, the people hide their children, refusing
the help:

The father was courteous, but he said, "We do not want horses'
blood here." "But she will die without the injection," the doctor
warned. Ventura said, "Then she will die by God's will, not by
horses' blood. You may not enter my house nor poison my children." [pp. 116–17]

In desperation, the doctors treat the water at the village
well, but Trini sees them doing so, and leads a revolt to
have Juan Diego cast out of the village. Juan Diego returns
to the doctor:

"Do not worry about your sister—she will get well," the doctor
said. "The teacher has medicine enough until our regular medical

service truck gets back to the village. When the people see that your sister is well, they will accept the medicine. Do not blame them. It is the young people who will change them," the doctor said. "They come from the villages to learn, boys like you, Juan Diego, and girls. They learn not for themselves, but for their people. It will not be quick, Juan Diego; learning and teaching are slow, patient things." [pp. 138–39]

The story tells of great loss, but also of great hope. A new generation will rise up to bring knowledge. The old ways will pass. Juan Diego of *The Forgotten Village*, then, is much the same as Juan Diego of "The Miracle of Tepayac," as one who receives a great vision, is frustrated in fulfilling it, and ultimately perseveres.

"The Miracle of Tepayac" is based upon the legend of Our Lady of Guadalupe, in which the Virgin Mary's image was impressed upon a cloak to convince a bishop of her will.[15] The image is still preserved today, kept behind bulletproof glass in the basilica of Our Lady of Guadalupe in Mexico City. Each year, approximately ten million pilgrims genuflect before the shrine, approaching to within twenty-five feet of the revered image. Jody Brant Smith describes the image in his historical study, *The Image of Guadalupe: Myth or Miracle?*:

Her head is tilted to the right, her greenish eyes are cast downward in an expression of gentle concern. The mantle that covers her head and shoulders is of a deep turquoise, studded with gold stars and bordered in gold. Her hair is black, her complexion olive. She stands alone, her hands clasped in prayer, an angel at her feet.

She is Our Lady of Guadalupe, a life-sized image of the Virgin Mary that appeared miraculously on the cactus-cloth tilma, or cape, of Juan Diego, an Aztec peasant, in 1531, a mere dozen years after Hernan Cortes conquered Mexico for the King of Spain. For four hundred and fifty years the colors of the portrait have remained as bright as if they were painted yesterday. The coarse-woven cactus cloth, which seldom lasts even twenty years, shows no signs of decay.[16]

According to the earliest testimonies, preserved in the Aztec language, Juan Diego and his family were among the first converts to Christianity among the Aztecs. Steinbeck is faithful to the historical circumstance in the opening paragraphs of his story:

> The Spaniards came to Mexico with war and pestilence and ruin but they brought also the faith of Jesus Christ and his Mother Mary. Many of the Indian people were baptized, and among the first of them Juan Diego and his wife Maria Lucia. They were humble people and they lived in the little town of Cuautilan, to the north of Mexico City.
>
> For many years they had lived together in felicity. They had no children, so that their dependence on each other was very great. Their dwelling was a one-room hut of mud bricks, and they tended a garden and they were happy. Then one dawn Maria Lucia was feverish and at mid-morning her eyes were swollen and her breath labored. At noon she died.[17]

According to the Aztec records, Juan Diego's first vision occurred on Saturday, December 9, 1531, as he left his village to hear mass celebrated in Santiago, which, incidentally, is also Juan Diego's home village in *The Forgotten Village*. While walking past the hill, Juan Diego hears his name called out of a bright light emanating from the top of the hill, a pattern in keeping with biblical theophanies in which God reveals himself in a vision of light and by calling the recipient's name.

Juan Diego is told by the Virgin that a temple should be erected at the hill of Tepayac. The implication is that religion belongs among the common people and is not the exclusive province of city officials. Juan Diego's beseeching of the bishop is rebuffed twice. The third time he brings a sign of the Virgin's will by carrying to the bishop a bouquet of roses of Castille, growing out of season, that he picked from the hill of Tepayac and carried in his cloak. When he unfurls the cloak, the roses are still fresh, and the Virgin's image appears in the weave of the cloth.

Although Steinbeck adds the fiction writer's touch to the

legend by relaying the troubled emotions and the adamant persistence of Juna Diego in pursuing the Virgin's request, his rendition is completely loyal to the original. He refuses to pursue larger implications, ending the story with the character, Juan Diego, rather than the larger religious significance of the event:

At Tepayac they raised a simple hermitage on the place where She had appeared, to serve until the temple could be fashioned. And Juan Diego built a new mud house near by and planted a garden. He swept out the chapel and cared for it until he died. He was very happy. And it is possible he did not know that through his heart Our Lady of Guadalupe had become the Holy Mother of his people. [p. 23]

In historical fact, the revelation was instrumental in the missionizing of Mexico. Jody Smith points out,

News of the miraculous appearance of the Virgin's image on a peasant's cloak spread quickly throughout New Spain. Indians by the thousands, learning that the mother of the Christian God had appeared before one of their own and spoken to him in his native tongue, came from hundreds of miles away to see the image hung above the altar of the new church.

The miraculous picture played a major role in advancing the Church's mission in Mexico. In just seven years, from 1532 to 1538, eight million Indians were converted to Christianity. In one day alone, one thousand couples were married in the sacrament of matrimony.[18]

Although the plots differ, a thematic parallel may be found between Steinbeck's first and last Mexican stories. Like Juan Diego of *The Forgotten Village,* Juan Diego in "The Miracle of Tepayac" receives a great vision—the one for the physical health of his people, the other for the spiritual health of his people. The first Juan Diego "walked through the village and he heard the talk at the well, heard how the children were sickening with the same pain as little Paco had. The women were frightened for the children" (p. 510). Responding to the suffering of his people, he engages his quest for help. The second Juan Diego's heart is also full with sorrow for the suffering of his people, and the Virgin tells him, "I wish that here on this bleak hill a temple may be built in witness of my love for your people. I have seen the suffering of your people and I have come to them through you" (p. 22). Both receive these visions from people in authority over them, and the authorities—the doctor and the Virgin—come from a great distance to direct the recipient. Both stories are thus predicated upon acts of grace. Both Juan Diegos must battle great odds and great skepticism of their visions to ultimately succor their people. Both persevere in the effort, overcoming the odds, and bring hope for the future.

It is interesting, furthermore, that both stories were written during periods when Steinbeck underwent intense periods of loss and bleakness. *The Forgotten Village* was written when the marriage to Carol was unraveling, "The Miracle of Tepayac" during the dissolution of his marriage to Gwyn. Both were written during periods of hectic busyness and personal depression. Both were written during periods of indirection in his artistry, when he was looking for a larger project that would satisfy his restlessness. Yet, both of them signal some larger hope, some elusive goal that at the time Steinbeck seemed capable of finding only in the fiction. And both locate that hope in the struggle of one man against an implacable universe. The stories were as much incarnations of Steinbeck's spirit as they were of Juan Diego's.

"HIS FATHER" AND "THE SUMMER BEFORE": PRESENT AND PAST EXPERIENCE

Steinbeck's acute disconsolation in the later 1940s grew out of and focused upon the dissolution of his marriage. To be sure, there were artistic concerns. His work of the 1940s had not been well received critically. *Cannery Row* especially had been devastated by reviewers. His editor and agents, moreover, were applying pressure for him to pro-

duce a "big book," another *The Grapes of Wrath*. Too
much of his energy had been expended on quick writing
and slight books. For a writer whose work was so closely
allied with personal experience, feeling, and temperament,
however, the artistic difficulties have to be linked with personal ones. In this case, the dissolution of the marriage
with Gwyn was complicated by the fact that they had two
children born of that mariage, sons Thom and John.

The final breakdown of the marriage, which had been
unraveling almost from the beginning, occurred in a cruel
combination of circumstances. On May 7, 1948, Ed Ricketts drove his old Packard down Cannery Row toward a
blind railroad crossing and collided with the Del Monte Express coming in from San Francisco. He died four days
later, on May 11. After an agonizing flight to California, be-
set by long delays, Steinbeck arrived in Monterey shortly
after his dearest friend died.

After the funeral and the deposition of certain personal
items from the small estate, Steinbeck returned to New
York. Jackson Benson reports,

With the sense of timing that only someone with show-business
experience could have developed, Gwyn confronted John upon
his return from California and told him that she wanted a divorce. She gave familiar reasons: he was gone too much, and he
was smothering her creativity. She added a new, more painful
reason: she had not been in love with him for several years. The
request for a divorce was not totally unexpected, but the combination of the two events together with the announcement that
she had not loved him for years was devastating.[19]

During the separation, Gwyn moved to Los Angeles with
the children, and Steinbeck, once again, visited Mexico for
much of the summer. Ostensibly he was to write about
Zapata; in reality his life was a careening whirlpool of days
clouded by alcohol and quick relationships. It was a self-
destructive life, and one Steinbeck seemed to have little
control over. From the romantic intensity of his love for
Gwyn, he spun into a wasteland of unfettered passions. It

was almost as if he were enacting Lancelot—losing his Guinevere, he went mad in the nightmare forests.

There is little reason to dwell on the peculiar cruelties of the divorce here, but the biographical details are essential to understanding the very brief short story, "His Father." It is a sketch that erupted viscerally from the reality of Steinbeck's life, especially his acute sense of failure as a father and the sense that he had abandoned his own sons.

Although Steinbeck was for the most part remarkably restrained about the situation in his letters to others,[20] his concern for his children surfaces frequently. He could not, by any stretch of the imagination, have been considered a doting, careful parent to this point, but his love and concern for his boys was genuine. Now that too seemed threatened. Almost from the start of the marital breakdown, this large fear is present in his letters, and it intensifies whenever he thought about his periodic visits with them:

My boys will be with me in another two weeks and I will be glad. I deeply resent their growing and me not there to see. That is the only thing I resent now. The rest is all gone. But imagine if you couldn't see your daughter for months at a time when every day is a change and growth and fascination. [*SLL*, pp. 360–61]

For each visit, however, there was also the immediate prospect of renewed separation.

In one such letter, we are able to date the composition of "His Father" and observe it growing directly out of his life. To Bo Beskow on May 9, 1949, Steinbeck wrote,

Three weeks ago I had a compulsion to go to New York to see my children and I did so thinking I was more well than I was. It struck me hard, all of the unhappiness arose again but it will not be very long before I am back where I was so that will be all right. My boys were well and healthy. I shall have them with me this summer and get to know them again.

Coming home wrote three short stories and I don't know whether they are any good or not. It is long since I have worked in that form. I promptly tore up two of them because I am sure they were not very good and I don't have to put up with my own mediocrity any more. [*SLL*, p. 352]

The one short story he did not destroy was "His Father," which two weeks later was purchased by *Reader's Digest* for $2,500.

The unnamed protagonist is a six-year-old boy identified only in the third person. (Thom Steinbeck was born August 2, 1944, and was not quite five when the story was written.) The narrator is omniscient, looking upon the boy's feelings as he wonders when his father will come home:

He could feel Alvin [his chief tormentor] when he turned the corner two blocks away and a shuddering went over his skin. Alvin wouldn't say anything. None of the kids said anything, but it was in their eyes; it was always in their eyes looking out at him, and the look was shame, a burning, guilty shame. At first he had run away and stayed by himself, but you can't run away all the time and besides you get lonesome.[21]

As his friends taunt him, excuses for his father flood his mind:

"Where's your father?"
What he should have said was, "He's away on a trip," but he didn't. The question caught him in the pit of his stomach up under his ribs. He could feel the question and he knew that it was pure cruelty. The kids weren't asking, they were telling, taunting, hurting, and that was the way they wanted it. [pp. 19–20]

The jeers of the children rise to a tormenting chant: "Where's your father—where's your father—where's your father?" And the boy finally responds, "He's in the house. . . . He's in there working. He don't have to come out if he don't want to" (p. 20). This is the wish, that his father will be in the house. His emotions have shaped the reply, not reality.

The boy's anguish reaches a climax one day when he can no longer avoid Alvin. He sees him coming down the street and thinks of hitting him. But then, "There was a curious feeling—a strange explosive feeling in his chest. Something half noticed had caused it. He looked sharp right and it was true. His father had turned the corner and was walking rapidly toward him with his shoulders swinging the way they did" (p. 21). In this case, the father arrives at the right moment, a heroic deliverer. The boy screams out, *"He's here! You want to see him?"*

"His Father" is no more than a character sketch, but Steinbeck manages to penetrate the boy's yearning so deeply in so few words that the story also evokes a sense of profundity. The anguish is genuine, but relief over the father's return allays it. The boy dares outrage and defiance with his father beside him. He is no longer alone in the world. Totally missing from the story, its third person intimate point of view limiting our knowledge to the boy, is the father's reaction. One can't help wondering at his anguish as the boy screams out, "He's here! You want to see him?"

The turbulence of the 1940s, both personally and artistically, was laid to rest by Steinbeck's marriage to Elaine and his writing of *East of Eden*. Both were restorative for him. He had achieved the "big" book that he had been thinking of for much of his life, and his personal life achieved a measure of stability. That return to stability may also be seen in his lovely short story "The Summer Before," with its evocation of youth and Salinas.

Steinbeck had by now irrevocably moved his home from California, and even though he realized that fact fully in *Travels with Charley*, it was impossible ever to fully remove it from his heart. This was the land that had birthed and nourished him, launched his career, and compelled so many stories. In a series of articles by famous authors on their home towns, *Holiday* published "Always Something to Do in Salinas" in June 1955. "The Summer Before" had been published the month prior, in the May 1955 issue of *Punch*, but there is a connection in tone and setting between the two pieces.[22]

"Always Something to Do in Salinas" is one of those warm pieces of nostalgia, but one tempered here by Stein-

beck's inverterate realism. He points out the darker side of
life in Salinas as well as the bucolic:

Salinas was never a pretty town. It took a darkness from the
swamps. The high gray fog hung over it and the ceaseless wind
blew up the valley, cold and with a kind of desolate monotony.
The mountains on both sides of the valley were beautiful, but Salinas was not and we knew it.[23]

As he did so often in his fiction, here too Steinbeck probed
that darkness, which lay just out of sight beneath surface
appearances:

I wonder whether all towns have the blackness—the feeling of
violence just below the surface.
   It was a blackness that seemed to rise out of the swamps, a
kind of whispered brooding that never came into the open—a
subsurface violence that bubbled silently like the decaying vege-
tation under the black water of the Tule Swamps.[24]

Among the stories of Salinas demonstrating this subsurface
violence is that of Andy, who gives the fourth-grade teacher
whom he loves his severed ear as a present.
   "The Summer Before" is also a probing reflection. It begins with the bright wanderings of children on long summer days but uncovers a mystery that confounds them for
days to come. It is a sensitively told and very moving story
with a genuinely startling ending. In it we find many bits
and pieces of Steinbeck's own life. For example: "My pony
Jill, who was only a pony by courtesy, being half shetland
and half cayuse, had grown a raggedy coat and her forelock
was so long that she peered through it, and she was fat from
the spring grass so that we had hopes for a colt."[25] The autobiographical nature of the story admits many of Steinbeck's
boyhood friends—Glen Graves (who actually spelled his
name *Glenn*), Jackie Berges, Ernie Wallet, Max Wagner.
And then there is Willie Morton, the puzzling one, the son
of a poor, single mother and the undeniable town bully.
   It is a nice irony that the narrator's own champion in ju-

venile warfare is his kid sister Mary, for she has the gump-
tion to tackle the narrator's antagonists and metes out to
them a most unusual punishment:

I had a secret weapon in my sister Mary who was younger and a
girl. She was a rough little monkey with wild eyes looking out of
tangled yellow hair. When I was very angry at a boy I would turn
my sister Mary on him. She would then wait her chance, throw
him down and kiss him, which cost him face and social position so
that all he could do was to creep away until his shame evapo-
rated. [p. 647] [26]

The irony lies in the surprise ending, in which the tough
little girl, Mary, is compared to the tough little boy, Willie
Morton.

The commemorative nature of this semiautobiographical
story gives many insights into Steinbeck's boyhood world.
The recollection of those halcyon days of free and easy youth
flows smoothly from the author's pen. It is the great temptation of an author to romanticize the past, particularly
when, like Dylan Thomas, he has begun to understand,

As I was young and easy in the mercy of his means,
    Time held me green and dying
Though I sang in my chains like the sea. [27]

Under the wraps of this recollection, however, is the body
of a potent short story—the revelation of Willie Morton,
the toughest kid in town.

Willie has a reputation for being just plain mean, a true
tough guy. It is nurtured in part by Willie's mother, a neurotic woman, we discover, who invests her lost husband in
her child. The mother calls stridently from her doorway,
"Willie—Oh! Willie, Where's my man?" The call cuts two
ways: Where is her man who has forsaken her, and where is
her man Willie? It is a trick of rhetoric, but also a cruel trick
on Willie, as the story's ending reveals.

On one of the last days of summer the children plan a
frankfurter roast by the river instead of their routine lunch

STEINBECK'S SHORT STORIES

of packed sandwiches. This is to be a day of freedom and frolic: "We knew we didn't have much more river time. We knew we had to go to school and suddenly we knew there were some good things about being a little kid. We'd always hated it before"(p. 650). Once at the river, the gang enjoys all the festivities of youthful indulgence: "Max got out a great big cigarette butt he had found and lighted it with a burning stick and passed it around. Everybody got a puff but Glen. He said it was a sin and he wouldn't do it. We knew then he was going to tell on us but we couldn't hit him until after he told" (p. 651). This a Mark Twain kind of reminiscence, sweetly calling forth the innocent evils of youth.

After a satisfying round of smoking, the gang decides on an end-of-season swim in the Salinas river: "We took our time getting our clothes off. Mary had to swim in her pants because she was a girl. Nobody told her she had to. She was just a girl and that's what they do" (p. 651). Willie, however, refuses to swim, watching from the bank as the boys tease him. Finally Willie jumps in with all his clothes on.

Under the river's calm surface, traps lurk. Old limbs of fallen trees still reach out to snag the unwary. One has to know the safe spots. Willie does not. The boys spot Willie underwater with the straps of his overalls snagged on a branch of sunken cottonwood. Mary climbs on the pony to get a Japanese farmer working nearby: "The Jap waded out and leaned down and pulled and yanked. Willie's overall strap broke and his pants came off. The Jap carried him out and laid him on the sand" (p. 651). Only then does the gang discover that Willie Morton, meanest boy in town, the one called "Willie, my man" by his mother is in fact a girl.

The revelation comes with a sharp kick of surprise because expectations have been so carefully prepared otherwise. But throughout the story, Steinbeck has laced clues:

She called Willie her man—her only man. She would grab him and hug him and her face would be hungry and angry. [p. 649]

She was crazy on the subject of toilets. Didn't want any two of us to go at once. She said it was dirty. [p. 649]

We knew he was a poor kid and so we tolerated him perhaps more than we would have if he had been normal. But we knew he was strange just by the way he stood off and looked at us. [p. 649]

"The Summer Before" is a poignant little piece, wistfully evocative, touched by deft description and a fidelity to the child's point of view. It nicely captures Steinbeck's yearning for a simpler time now long past, receded into the well of memory. But those times, in retrospect, were really not so simple or sweet. Then too, there was anguish and turmoil. That realization is perfectly captured in the awful torment of Willie Morton, desperately playing a game his mother had designed for him.

"THE AFFAIR AT 7, RUE DE M———," "HOW MR. HOGAN
ROBBED A BANK," AND "THE SHORT-SHORT STORY OF
MANKIND": THE MYSTERY OF MORALITY

Steinbeck's initial interest in the detective story was purely commercial. The year 1930 had placed him at artistic cross-roads. One direction he took, albeit tentatively, was the hasty drafting of "Murder at Full Moon by Peter Pym," a work assessed by Jackson Benson as "Jungian-flavored mumbo jumbo." Wavering unsteadily among the comic burlesque, the trappings of rational analysis of clues, and some fog-wrapped marshlands of the hypothetical Cone City, the work is a hodge-podge of formula fiction. But for-mula fiction needs some artistic control as well, and "Mur-der at Full Moon" has little. The experiment itself, how-ever, was significant to Steinbeck. At least it steered him away from one direction this crossroads to his life may have pointed him. Henceforth he would write his own stories. Nonetheless, for nine days in late 1930, and for a few months of attempted sales thereafter, the mystery story exercised a powerful tug on his imagination.

Steinbeck first announced the work, and his effort to write it to pay off a debt, in a December 1930 letter to Amasa Miller, who was informally acting as his agent. Observing the people "do not want to buy the things I have been writing," Steinbeck confesses that "to make the money I need, I must write the things they want to read." Steinbeck cautions Miller that the manuscript might make him sick and goes on to describe it:

> It was written complete in nine days. It is about sixty two or three thousand words long. It took two weeks to type. In it I have included all the cheap rackets I know of, and have tried to make it stand up by giving it a slightly burlesque tone. No one but my wife and my folks know that I have written it, and no one except you will know. I see no reason why a nom de plume should not be respected and maintained. The nom de plume I have chosen is Peter Pym.
>
> The story holds water better than most, and I think it has a fairish amount of mystery. The burlesqued bits, which were put in mostly to keep my stomach from turning every time I sat down at the typewriter, may come out. [*SLL*, p. 32]

Miller peddled the manuscript around, hoarding the rejections, which he would send to Steinbeck in a lot from time to time. By June Steinbeck was wondering about the fate of the manuscript: "On what grounds was the murder story rejected? Was it the sloppiness of it or just that it wasn't a good enough story? Do you think there is the least chance of selling it?" (*SLL*, p. 39). At the same time, Steinbeck was beginning contact with Mavis McIntosh for her to represent him. He listed "Murder at Full Moon" as one of the possible works for her to consider, adding, "The quicker I can forget the damned thing, the happier I shall be" (*SLL*, p. 42).

"Murder at Full Moon," however derogatorily Steinbeck himself spoke of it, represented more than a simple commercial effort to peddle a story. In the 1930s, detective stories experienced a heyday of popularity, rivaling westerns and romance confessionals for a share of a huge audience. It seemed an easy commercial ploy, this writing of a formula piece for a quick market. But Steinbeck left his own peculiar impress on the story, not allowing it to be pure detective, nor pure gothic, nor yet again pure burlesque. In January 1933, still with the idea of peddling "Murder at Full Moon," he wrote Mavis McIntosh, "We live in the hills back of Los Angeles now and there are few people around. One of our neighbors loaned me three hundred detective magazines, and I have read a large part of them out of pure boredom. They are so utterly lousy that I wonder whether you have tried to peddle that thing I dashed off to any of them. It might mean a few dollars" (*SLL*, p. 67). Not long thereafter he crafted his short story, "The Murder," which won the O. Henry Prize for 1934.

Perhaps the primary influence upon Steinbeck in composing "Murder at Full Moon" was not the 300 detective magazines he read, but the first master of the genre, Edgar Allan Poe. The pseudonym for the story is, of course, a combination of Dirk Peters and Arthur Gordon Pym, but beyond that there is something about the logic of the detective story, the cerebral triumph over emotional torment, that was deeply appealing to Steinbeck in the early 1930s and again in the 1950s. By 1920 Steinbeck had read several of Poe's works, including "The Murders in the Rue Morgue" and "The Purloined Letter."[28] While it would be patently unfair to call Steinbeck a champion of the detective story, after the dismal experience of "Murder at Full Moon" and the decidedly low view of the genre he evidenced in later years, the influence resurges again in the construction of "The Affair at 7, Rue de M——."

"The Affair" was written in May 1954, when Steinbeck was living in Paris. France had by now replaced Mexico as his favorite retreat abroad, and he had decided to write for the French papers after they had demonstrated an avid interest in his work. In a May 27, 1954, letter he wrote of having "made a good start on my first short story of the series" (*SLL*, p. 480), and within two weeks wrote of having completed two pieces. "The Affair," originally published as "L'Affaire du l'avenue de M——" in *Figaro* (August 28, 1954), was published under its present title in *Harper's Bazaar* (April 1955).[29]

"The Affair" may be built on the foundation of a mystery, modeled as it is in tone upon Poe's "The Murders in the Rue Morgue," but it grows quickly into farce. Appropriately for the Poesque ratiocinative detective, the narrator is at first detached from the events: "I had hoped to withhold from public scrutiny those rather curious events which have given me some concern for the past month" (p. 619). The narrator uses refined diction uncharacteristic of Steinbeck, punctuated by such French words as *arrondissement* and *bizarrerie*. With the dispassionate calm of the empiricist, the narrator says, "I shall set down the events as they happened without comment, thereby allowing the public to judge of the situation" (p. 619).

This detached, rational tone changes dramatically several paragraphs into the story. The sentence describing the narrator's son John is pure Steinbeck, both in the nature of the boy (John IV was born on June 12, 1946, and like the character was eight years old) and the language used to describe him: "If one must have an agency in this matter, I can find no alternative to placing not the blame but rather the authorship, albeit innocent, on my younger son John who has only recently attained his eighth year, a lively child of singular beauty and buck teeth" (p. 620). From this point on the narrator and Steinbeck seem to fuse; pretenses are for the most part set aside, and a slapstick plot abetted by puns and asides develops. The narrator happens to be a scholar working on an essay, "Sartre Resartus," a pun on Carlyle's *Sartor Resartus* and French existentialist Jean-Paul Sartre. When father and son examine the blob of bubble gum which is now chewing the boy, the narrator observes, "I regarded it with popping eyes."

The plot balloons into pure farce. The boy, who is inordinately fond of bubble gum, has to do without his addiction while living in France. However, a visiting friend brings a new supply, and once again, "The jaws were in constant motion, giving the face at best a look of agony while the eyes took on a glaze like those of a pig with a recently severed jugular" (pp. 620–21). This particular wad takes on a life of its own. It lodges in John's mouth, not like an alien invader but like a friend come home, pulsating there like a primitive heartbeat. The subject of the detective's analysis is the remarkable life-form of this bubble gum:

> "I must think," I said. "This is something a little out of the ordinary, and I do not believe it should be passed over without some investigation."
> As I spoke a change came over the gum. It ceased to chew itself and seemed to rest for a while, and then with a flowing movement like those monocellular animals of the order Paramecium, the gum slid across the desk straight in the direction of my son. [p. 623]

To this task the narrator bends all of his considerable intellectual powers.

In the development of this farce, which as a genre is generally free from ethical investigation, one curious moral interpretation enters that has implications beyond the story. The narrator studies the blob under a microscope, examining it physically but also spiritually. In terms of Steinbeck's earlier distinction between nonteleological and teleological experience, the narrator is forced to consider the *why* and *how* of this phenomenon. He cannot remain the objective observer when the life of his son is threatened:

> The background I had been over hurriedly. It must be that from constant association with the lambent life which is my son, the magic of life had been created in the bubble gum. And with life had come intelligence, not the manly open intelligence of the boy, but an evil calculating wiliness.
> How could it be otherwise? Intelligence without the soul to balance it must of necessity be evil. The gum had not absorbed any part of John's soul. [pp. 626–27]

The comment also applies to Cathy Ames of *East of Eden*, another soulless intelligence, and therefore evil.

The story does not linger over such speculations, however. Firing up his pipe in the manner of Poe's narrator in "The Murders in the Rue Morgue," this narrator also puffs his way to a conclusion. He glues the blob to a dish, where it dies a prolonged death, and then buries it in the garden:

I am now in the seventh day and I believe it is almost over. The gum is lying in the center of the plate. At intervals it heaves and subsides. Its color has turned to a nasty yellow. Once today when my son entered the room, it leaped up excitedly, then seemed to realize its hopelessness and collapsed on the plate. It will die tonight I think and only then will I dig a deep hole in the garden, and I will deposit the sealed bell jar and cover it up and plant geraniums over it. [p. 628]

"The Affair at 7 Rue de M——" is a delightfully farcical piece. It is in the pattern of *Sweet Thursday* and the novel written at this same time, *The Short Reign of Pippin IV*. Farce may indeed entertain serious matters, as *Sweet Thursday* does in the relentless loneliness of Doc. But for all its broken tone, cluttered structure, and narrative posturing, "The Affair" is simply a pleasant piece of diversionary reading—rather as detective stories were for Steinbeck.

His other quasi-mystery story, "How Mr. Hogan Robbed a Bank," however, is quite a serious matter. This unusual story turns the expected trappings of the crime story upside down. That, in part, accounts for its peculiar charm and its salient moral theme. Steinbeck selects as protagonist an unassuming grocery store clerk, a man so plain and common that he blends easily into the background of the grocery shelves like one more piece in trade—which he is in a sense. But this unpretentious little man hatches a grand scheme to rob the bank next door. It is all so easy when planned carefully. Mr. Hogan's cardinal rule is, "To successfully rob a bank, forget all about hanky-panky."

That ordinariness of Mr. Hogan and his idea, right down to the split infinitive of his rule, is balanced artistically by close attention to detail. From the first sentence—"On the Saturday before Labor Day, 1955, at 9:04 1/2 A.M., Mr. Hogan robbed a bank."—precision of detail marks the narrative. The opening paragraph describes the Hogan family like a fact sheet on the police blotter, where Mr. Hogan's name will never appear. Throughout the heist, detail governs every step. At the precise moment, Mr. Hogan prepares his mask, a ludicrous touch of Disneyland but a fitting one for the thematic development:

At ten minutes to nine, Mr. Hogan went to a shelf. He pushed a spaghetti box aside and took down a cereal box, which he emptied in the little closet toilet. Then, with a banana knife, he cut out the Mickey Mouse mask that was on the back. The rest of the box he took to the toilet and tore up the cardboard and flushed it down. He went into the store then and yanked a piece of string loose and tied the ends through the side holes of the mask and then he looked at his watch—a large silver Hamilton with black hands. It was two minutes to nine. [p. 635–36]

This is a thoroughly ordinary person exercising an extraordinary plot.

Steinbeck supplies other details testifying to the precision of the exercise, for that is essentially what it is, somehow divested of moral significance: "Mr. Hogan opened the charge account drawer and took out the store pistol, a silver-colored Iver Johnson .38. He moved quickly to the storeroom, slipped off his apron, put on his coat, and stuck the revolver in his side pocket" (p. 636). The entire act is completed, Steinbeck tells us, by 9:07 1/2. Only after the crime do the details begin to haze a bit: "It was 9:05, or :06, or :07, when he got back to the brown-shingle house at 215 East Maple" (p. 638). Mr. Hogan is back to his routine now; life slips into its informal way.

The story, however, leaves a jarring sense of moral dislocation. While Mr. Hogan's son John is winning honorable mention in the "I Love America" contest, Mr. Hogan executes his bank heist, untouched by any moral recrimination. The many stylistic parallels between "How Mr. Hogan Robbed a Bank" and *The Winter of Our Discontent* have been thoroughly analyzed,[30] but it should also be clear that the moral concerns that sparked the novel are implicit in the short story. There is this important difference between the two: While Mr. Hogan snaps two five-dollar bills off his

pile of $8,320 as gifts for his children, and thereby allows
life to go its way, Ethan Hawley's moral debentures are
called in at the expense of his life. For Mr. Hogan, we have
no *why*, no motivation for the action. It can be done, so he
does it. His is a thoroughly nonteleological action. Any
moral speculation comes from the reader, not from the
plot. For Ethan Hawley, however, the *why* becomes a roar
of confusion. His life is a crooked path that wanders inevitably to the cave by the sea. The moral concern threads
through every strand of the novel.

While living abroad, Steinbeck had placed himself in a
unique perspective from which to view his own country.
Once apart from it, he grew increasingly critical of it. The
sense of America's moral failure becomes acute during his
last decade and forms the artistic underpinnings of his late
work. His letters too are increasingly marked by his concern. To Pascal Covici in July 1961, he wrote,

> Through time, the nation has become a discontented land. I've
> sought for an out on this—saying it is my aging eyes seeing it, my
> waning energy feeling it, my warped vision that is distorting it,
> but it is only partly true. The thing I have described is really
> there. I did not create it. It's very well for me to write jokes and
> anecdotes but the haunting decay is there under it.
>
> Well, there was once a man named Isaiah—and what he saw in
> his time was not unlike what I have seen, but he was shored up
> by a hard and durable prophecy that nothing could disturb. We
> have no prophecy now, nor any prophets. [*SLL*, p. 703]

What is merely implicit in "How Mr. Hogan Robbed a
Bank" becomes increasingly explicit as Steinbeck donned
the mantle of Isaiah and proclaimed a message of moral failure to his own nation.

That message is treated allegorically in his last pure short
story, "The Short-Short Story of Mankind: An Improbable
Allegory of Human History Compressed for a Very Small
Time Capsule."[31] Steinbeck believed that the nation had
sunk into a quagmire through moral devolution: Values had
been replaced by a rage for things; the bank vault had be-

come the modern Bible; the aim of the church, as in *The Winter of Our Discontent,* had become power over humanity. This devolution is traced allegorically in "The Short-Short Story of Mankind." As an allegory of humankind, it begins in the early age of humanity: "It was pretty drafty in the cave in the middle of the afternoon. There wasn't any fire—the last spark had gone out six months ago and the family wouldn't have any more fire until lightning struck another tree" (p. 443). In the cave a family quarrels over a chunk of mammoth meat. Here is the urge that can spin out of control: From the start humans have focused upon individual rather than corporate needs. Selfishness conflicts with the essential action of morality—the setting aside of self for the larger interests of the corporate body.

The cave dwellers see people move in down in the copse. They are fearful of and instinctively loathe these foreigners. Yet, the foreigners have some interesting attributes. For one thing, they eat better than the cave dwellers. Son Joe asks, "Pa, why don't we join up with those tree people? They've got a net kind of thing—catch all sorts of animals." And his father, old William, replies, "They're foreigners, that's why. They live in trees. We can't associate with savages. How'd you like your sister to marry a savage?" Joe responds, "She did!" (p. 443).

What begins as a battle of cravings and prejudices naturally develops into a religion in order to sanctify those very cravings and prejudices. The cave dwellers kill Elmer for being so different as to build a house, but when they move in and realize its advantages, they decide to make him a god: "Used to swear by him. Said he was the moon."

At this point the narrator steps in to comment, "You can see from this that things started going to pot right from the beginning. Things would be going along fine—law and order and all that and the leaders in charge—and then some smart aleck would invent something and spoil the whole business" (p. 445). The comment is redundant to the allegory itself, for the point is clear enough.

In time the people enter a new stage in human evolution

and moral devolution. Wherever a group of people locate and begin to enjoy a time of prosperity, a leader of the people emerges. Here "Strong Arm Bugsy" takes over, a mix of ruthless dictator and 1920s gangster who ardently believes that might makes right. And the people are an easy mark for him: "By now the elders had confused protection with virtue because Bugsy passed out his surplus to the better people. The elders were pretty hard on anybody who complained. They said it was a sin" (p. 446). Thus the people have developed the religion of politics; the greased palm is raised to hail the leader. Any dissenting voice is drowned out by those proclaiming that dissent is a sin.

Bugsy turns any moral concept of ruling on its head. Instead of the leaders being responsible to the welfare of the people, the people become responsible to the welfare of the ruler. Bugsy insists that it is the task of the people to protect him. Perhaps no other political concern was so keen for Steinbeck as this conflict between public welfare and personal gain. It roots in his work among the migrants in the 1930s and flowers actively in his political involvement in the 1950s and 1960s. Louis Owens describes one case in point—Steinbeck's attitude toward Richard Nixon.

Nixon would bring about his own downfall, Steinbeck prophesied, declaring, "Perhaps it is an accident that the names are the same—but the theme of *Richard III* will prove prophetic." It is surely a painful awareness of the political cynicism Steinbeck saw in both Nixon and Joseph McCarthy that informs the dark side of *The Short Reign of Pippin IV*, and just as surely when Steinbeck chose his title for *The Winter of Our Discontent* from the play featuring literature's most famous deep dissembler, he was thinking of Nixon.[32]

But Steinbeck's contempt was not reserved for Nixon alone. Indeed, all of Washington seemed to have sunk into a murky world where the true values of government had been lost. Steinbeck's letters over a half-dozen years insistently announce his judgments. To Adlai Stevenson on November 5, 1959, he wrote,

Back from Camelot, and, reading the papers not at all sure it was wise. Two first impressions. First a creeping, all-pervading, nerve-gas of immorality which starts in the nursery and does not stop before it reaches the highest offices, both corporate and governmental. Two, a nervous restlessness, a hunger, a thirst, a yearning for something unknown—perhaps morality. [*SLL*, pp. 651–52]

And to James S. Pope on March 28, 1960, he wrote,

Maybe the country has been in as bad a state before but the only times I can think of are the winter of Valley Forge and the glorious days of Warren Harding. The candidates are playing them so close that they have Ace marks on their shirt fronts. The mess in Washington now resembles a cat toilet in Rome. [*SLL*, p. 663]

Such concerns also surround the allegorical testament of "The Short-Short Story of Mankind." But what vindicates the moral dissolution in the mind of the people? The Gospel of Free Trade. So too in the story. A kind of free trade capitalism arises, but only after the man who thought of it is hanged head down over a fire. Bugsy himself assesses the reaction of the people: "Makes folks restless—why, it makes a man think he's as good as the ones that got it a couple of generations earlier" (pp. 446–47). The essence of the Gospel of Free Trade is the belief in feeling good. If a deed, however dark, engenders prosperity, it must be good. Based upon this philosophy, the community expands to a nation predicated upon capitalism. The expansion is stopped by natural barriers, but missiles are invented to overcome those barriers. Once more the narrator, who cannot quite leave his allegory alone, intrudes:

When people are finally forced with extinction, they have to do something about it. Now we've got the United Nations and the elders are right in there fighting it the way they fought coming out of caves. . . . It'd be kind of silly if we killed ourselves off after all this time. If we do, we're stupider than the cave people and I don't think we are. I think we're just exactly as stupid and that's pretty bright in the long run. [p. 447]

"The Short-Short Story of Mankind" is a rather bleak piece, the story of humankind viewed through a jaded eye. In an odd way, however, it may be seen as an outgrowth of Steinbeck's two quasi-detective stories. At its best, the detective story demonstrates the logical progression of human actions—even the most grisly and macabre, and the supersession of logic over emotions through the one who solves the case. "The Short-Short Story of Mankind" may well represent the logical consequence Steinbeck perceived of the emotional dispassion and the unflinching immorality in "How Mr. Hogan Robbed a Bank." Like the narrator in "The Affair at 7 Rue d M——," Steinbeck examines the modern moral temperament and discovers that he can neither throw it away nor bottle it up and bury it. The little allegory here shows how immorality can possess a people, so that every step in humanity's evolution as a race is accompanied by a moral devolution in spirit.

8

East of Salinas

THE HAWK DROPPED as silently as light. One moment the
empty field; the next the spray of brown and red wings,
arched like fans, hurling light from their tips like beads of
moisture. It landed not with the impact of the hunter, in
the sudden strike and slash of talons, but with the grace of
the parachutist, in expert control of weight and wind. The
wing feathers fanned, each rigid against the golden field.
The tail feathers fanned, arched downard against the drafts.
The raptor played against a sky so blue it hurt the eye.

This was in a field east of Salinas, one of the fields strad-
dled by the Gabilan Mountains, which Steinbeck called the
warm lap of a beloved mother. To the west lie those other
mountains. The crooked spine starts in the tangle of hills in
San Francisco, warps southward where the Pacific beats
against shaggy cliffs, breaks north of Salinas, and then starts
its crooked maze in the Santa Lucias. These are the dark
ones, the brooding ones, home of the Dark Watchers.

Like a child's tower of building blocks, the road through
the Santa Lucias stacks turns and angles upon each other.
One wonders whether they will stay balanced all the way to
the top. Towering redwoods hold the road in place. It is no
wonder the cars hurry; the dark mountains hold their gloom
right to the top.

In between the Gabilan Mountains, full of bright splashes
of sun, and the Santa Lucias, full of an arching gloom, lies
the Salinas Valley, a bowl of green. Green avocado plants in
the north, green pumping arms of the oil stations south of

King City, green mists in the air from irrigation. It is a band of fertility between two high, opposing places.

It is little wonder that Steinbeck located his major metaphor for life, as well as most of his short stories, in this valley. Both metaphor and art were nourished by it, twin offspring of a mind homed by this land. In another sense, the dramatic variations of the land are also a bit like Steinbeck's short stories, opening artistically and thematically in different directions, different contours of storytelling, different heights and depths of human personality in the characters.

Steinbeck's considerable body of short stories has long suffered from critical neglect and, not infrequently, from misunderstanding. This state exists despite the recognition they earned him. Four of them received the O. Henry Memorial Award: "The Murder" in 1934, "The Promise" in 1938, "How Edith McGillcuddy Met R. L. Stevenson" in 1942, and "Affair at 7, Rue de M——" in 1956. This prestige, in addition to the reprinting of several short stories in collections of American short story masterpieces and college anthologies, marks a pattern of excellence. But it is clear that Steinbeck's work in short stories has been overshadowed by the meteoric rise of his career with the great novels of the 1930s and the major works that followed. His success as a novelist left the achievement of the short stories in its wake.

The stories merit close critical attention, first of all, simply for their aesthetic merit. While it is clear that he wrote a number of works of inferior quality, especially some of the unpublished works, it is also clear that he crafted works of enduring brilliance, marked by masterful use of narrative points of view, complex patterns of imagery, strong plots, and memorable characters. As works of literary art, Steinbeck's short stories bear a place of significance in American literature.

The best known of them all, the stories collected in *The Red Pony,* evoke a boyhood world with wonder and grace, and poignantly unveil their theme of maturation through suffering. The prophetic insights of "The Chrysanthemums" anticipate issues of human worth and freedom to express individual gifts that achieved currency many years later. Similarly, the story of Molly Morgan probes, like a session of psychotherapy, the convoluted forces that shape her character. The haunting imagery and the dire quest of "Flight" challenge readers now no less than in the 1930s.

A number of lesser-known works are no less successful in artistic achievement. "Johnny Bear" provides one of the more forceful revelations of Steinbeck's view of the artist, and that in a powerfully moving story. It is unimaginable that one would presume to know Steinbeck's artistic mind without a thorough consideration of this story. "The Summer Before," possibly the best of the stories not generally collected, achieves surprising suspense and power through a seemingly innocent reminiscence of youth. "The Lopez Sisters," often written off as a harmless bit of comedy, was written as a brief tragicomedy, unveiling the twisted grimace of pain behind the mask of humor.

If such stories are often artistically overshadowed by the novels, however, they may well bear even more significance as a revelation of the developing mind of the artist. Of course the novels may be well understood apart from the short stories. But one is mindful of Steinbeck's often repeated warning that his novels were crafted with several layers of meaning. A careful study of the short stories helps the reader penetrate those layers and, at the same time, learn a great deal about the development of Steinbeck's artistic techniques.

In retrospect, after one surveys the long list of achievements, the very early works such as "Fingers of Cloud" and "Adventures in Arcademy" may seem like hopelessly fumbling efforts. In a sense they were. But Steinbeck was fumbling *toward* something, and one sees the germ of his achievement there already. The harsh satirical voice would eventually turn into outrage at the oppressive powers of society. The wandering iconoclast would develop into characters such as the migrants, the paisanos, and the Mexican Indians with their search for leaders who would liberate them. The heartache and loneliness of the New York stories would develop into George and Lennie of *Of Mice and Men* and the inimitable Doc of *Sweet Thursday.*

One thematic pattern threaded through several of the short stories and bearing tremendous relevance both to his novels and to contemporary critical issues has to do with the personhood of the protagonist. Although not the province of the critical method of this study, it can be argued that several of the short stories must be approached with some kind of gender studies methodology. Pepe's quest for manhood in "Flight" is one sort of proving ground, one that Steinbeck himself experienced in *Travels with Charley in Search of America.* Moreover, the complex psychological studies of the female protagonists Helen Van Deventer, Molly Morgan, Elisa Allen, Mary Teller and even Jelka of "The Murder" raise issues of gender and character that have acquired serious critical attention only in the last decade. As he so often did in the novels, in the short stories also Steinbeck seemed to anticipate themes that became trenchant concerns in later years.

The short stories were a proving ground for ideas and themes, but also for skills. If the imagery patterns sometimes seem to acquire a life of their own and virtually dominate the story, Steinbeck was learning the complex revelation of theme through image. One sees this fulfilled in the late novels also, in the serpentine imagery of the temptress Cathy Ames, for example. Steinbeck is duly noted as one of America's great orchestrators of imagery patterns, and the complex patterns in such works as *East of Eden, The Pearl,* and *The Winter of Our Discontent* were proven first in the short stories.

Furthermore, the short stories were a proving ground for narrative points of view. A few of the experiments, "The White Sister of Fourteenth Avenue," for example, may be unfortunate. They led Steinbeck, however, through trial and error and triumph to a skillful use of varying points of view. The positions by which a narrator reveals the event of the story to the reader is of incalculable significance. To what degree is the reader admitted to the mind of the character? How much does the narrator reveal? These are the tough artistic questions that Steinbeck was working through. One sees the answers dramatically in such works as "Helen Van Deventer," "The Snake," "The Raid," "Breakfast," and the late work, "His Father."

Finally, Steinbeck was mustering the less specifiable artistic skill of self-confidence. The early notes to himself in the ledgers, lamenting a lack of sureness of touch, disconsolate with a sense of repeated failure and bitterly lonesome, were also driving him relentlessly toward a confident sureness of touch. He revised mercilessly, slashing verbal fat into lean prose. The most notable example is "The Vigilante," which turns the windy philosophical dissertation of "Case History" into a gripping story. The short stories, often written in wavering doubt and self-questioning, toughened his artistic muscle. His early goal to be a writer, often stated as a kind of adolescent wish, came true largely through the hard, journeyman labor over the short stories.

"What I complain of," says Mark Rampion in Aldous Huxley's *Point Counter Point*, "is the horrible unwholesome tameness of our world." Steinbeck's ideas and themes and style were never tame. He wanted to go his own way, and he sometimes went there, as he once wrote, like "a grazing elephant, knocking down trees I am too stupid to consider formidable (*SLL*, p. 35). When enough trees are laid low, however, one has to pay attention to the elephant itself, its brute strength an undeniable thing of beauty. In the short stories, that strength sometimes rampages wildly, but when brought under control, it evinces a stunning power.

In this remarkable body of short stories, then, Steinbeck left works of enduring artistic significance and a legacy of his own growth as an artist. Finally, however, what calls us to the short stories, again and again, is the undefinable gift of the writer, which provides the sense of sheer enjoyment from a tale well told. Our pleasure taken as readers is the final criterion of value. That pleasure places the highest value upon the work.

Appendix

Steinbeck's Notebooks

THE *PASTURES OF HEAVEN* NOTEBOOK (*POH-1*)

The *Pastures of Heaven* notebook, held by the Harry Ransom Research Center of the University of Texas, Austin, is a "Reliable Composition Notebook" measuring approximately six by eight inches and originally purchased from Holman's for twelve cents. The notebook is an oddity in that Steinbeck wrote only on the recto leaf, as he usually did, but when he came to the end of the notebook he flipped it upside down, again to write on the recto, formerly the verso, from the back cover to the front. After filling the notebook, Steinbeck later entered a title on page one:

> *Pastures of Heaven*
> I hope. And quite a lot of other
> nonsense.
>
> > John Steinbeck
> > Los Gatos, 1937

A list of stories for *The Pastures of Heaven* follows, and then complete and incomplete drafts, interspersed with notes, of the following stories, in order, with Steinbeck's working titles: "Shark Wicks," "The Munroes," "Coyote Tularecito," "Molly Morgan," "The Origin and History of Las Pasturas del Cielo," "The Battle Farm," "Raymond Banks," "The Maltbys." Several of the incomplete stories and rough starts were completed in the second *Pastures of Heaven* notebook.

THE SECOND *PASTURES OF HEAVEN* NOTEBOOK (*POH-2*)

This notebook, held by Stanford University, is titled *The Record Book* in *A Catalogue of the John Steinbeck Collection at Stanford University*, comp. and ed. Susan F. Riggs (Stanford, CA: Stanford University Libraries, 1980). The catalogue description is as follows:

287

Ink and pencil manuscripts in hardbound record book. ND [1929–31]. 300 pages, of which pp. 99–102 and 123–36 have been cut out. Pp. 16, 48, 54, 70, 116–18, and 261–99 are blank. Some water damage. Notes addressed to Carlton Sheffield appear on pp. 115, 122, 157, 159, 168–69, 183, and 260, written during the progress of the work. Some draft notes for plots and one paragraph of a story are on pp. 300 and [301].

Contents:

THE *TORTILLA FLAT* NOTEBOOK (*TFN*)

This notebook, held by the Harry Ransom Research Center of the University of Texas, Austin, is one of the more fragile manuscripts of Steinbeck's work. It begins with a start on "The Leader of the People" and "The Promise" and then a complete draft of *Tortilla Flat*. In the *Tortilla Flat* draft the protagonist is first identified as Bennie, then Benny. The "Señora Terrasina Cortez" episode from *Tortilla Flat* was written after the main body. This is followed by "The Murder," then the various starts and the full draft of "The Chrysanthemums," and the notebook concludes with full drafts of "The Leader of the People" and "The Promise."

On one of the last pages is the following note:

> Note to Pat Covici
> Who is curiously fitted to live
> on Tortilla Flat con las otras paisanos.

THE *IN DUBIOUS BATTLE* NOTEBOOK (*IDBN*)

This notebook, held by the Harry Ransom Research Center of the University of Texas, Austin, is actually a diary bound in black covers and bearing the words, "Standard Diary 1905 No. 362." This is one of the slightly used notebooks Steinbeck borrowed from his father's office. The first eight leaves have been cut out, and penciled notations pertaining to court cases, lightly erased, appear throughout. The volume has many blank pages, indicating that Steinbeck worked in this notebook at various times rather than straight through. The major contents, again interspersed with personal notes and other matter, include, in order: a partial draft of "The Great Mountains" broken by two short poems; "How Edith McGillcuddy Met Robert Louis Stevenson"; a rough beginning to *Tortilla Flat* over 1½ pages; a list of chapter headings for *Tortilla Flat;* the first draft of *In Dubious Battle*, including random notes and starts. The notebook concludes with this note:

> I can't imagine why any one would
> want this but here it is—
> A number of stories and the first
> draft of In Dubious Battle
> John Steinbeck
> Los Gatos 1937

Shortly after that inscription, Steinbeck added another note, also written in 1937: "It is some years now since Junius Maltby and Robbie climbed on the bus to go back to San Francisco to get a job. I've often wondered about him, whether he got it and whether he kept it."

THE *LONG VALLEY* NOTEBOOK (*LVN*)

This ledger, held by the Steinbeck Research Center of San Jose State University, which identifies it as "The Ledger Notebook," measures 188 by 305 mm and includes the stories written in the spring and summer of 1934. In addition to many notes, the ledger contains drafts of the following, in order: "The Raid"; "The Fool" (a draft of "The Harness"); "Man Hunt" (a draft of "Flight"); "Case History"; "The White Quail"; "Addenda to Flight"; "Johnny Bear"; "The Cow"; "The Vigilante"; "The Snake"; fragments of drafts for *Of Mice and Men;* and some notes for a dramatization of *In Dubious Battle*.

The Steinbeck Research Center holds a second ledger book that contains several pages of writing for "The Wizard" and a note referring to "The Chrysanthemums."

Notes

CHAPTER 1

1. Quotations from Steinbeck's letters to Katherine Beswick are by permission of the Stanford University Libraries and the John Steinbeck estate. The letters are located in the John Steinbeck collection, M263, box 1, folder 2.

2. Preston Beyer, "The Current Status of John Steinbeck Book Collections," *Steinbeck Quarterly* 17, no. 3–4 (Summer–Fall 1984): 92.

3. *Steinbeck: A Life in Letters*, ed. Elaine Steinbeck and Robert Wallsten, p. 51. Hereafter all references to *Steinbeck: A Life in Letters* will be cited parenthetically with the abbreviation *SLL*.

4. Steinbeck's academic career at Stanford was less than impressive. In *Steinbeck's Reading: A Catalogue of Books Owned and Borrowed*, Robert DeMott provides details gleaned from the office of the registrar:

The first half of his academic career was dismal: out of eight possible academic semesters from Spring, 1920, through Fall, 1923, he was enrolled twice in a total of eight courses. He withdrew from all of them, preferring instead nomadic stints as a laborer and farm hand in the country below Salinas. His second stab at college was more consistent and respectable. From Winter semester, 1923, through Spring semester, 1925, he was enrolled seven out of ten possible semesters, and earned grades or credit in 32 of 35 courses. [p. xxiii]

Of these courses, many of which were in writing, journalism, and English literature studies, Steinbeck has six grades of A recorded.

5. Jackson J. Benson, *The True Adventures of John Steinbeck, Writer*, p. 68.

6. Carlton Sheffield, "Introduction," in *Letters to Elizabeth: A Selection of Letters from John Steinbeck to Elizabeth Otis*, ed. Florian J. Shasky and Susan F. Riggs, p. x.

7. John Steinbeck, "On Learning Writing," *Writer's Yearbook* 34 (1963): 10.

8. Ibid.

9. Edith Mirrielees, *Story Writing*, pp. 3, 15, 210, respectively.

10. Ibid., p. 4.

11. *"Your Only Weapon Is Your Work": A Letter by John Steinbeck to Dennis Murphy*, ed. Robert DeMott.

12. In letters to his friends Steinbeck often wrote candidly and movingly about friendship itself, a frequent theme of the fiction also. To Webster Street, whose friendship Steinbeck agonized over for years, he wrote in 1940, "But we've become such strangers and no seeming way out of it. You're surrounded with things and I am too" (*SLL*, p. 218). Eight years later, as his marriage with Gwyndolyn was breaking up, he wrote again to Street: "I think you know that I put a high value on friendship. I have been kicked in the behind quite a bit on this account" (*SLL*, p. 315).

13. The snide thrust against Stanford's position on alcohol is revisited in "Adventures in Arcademy." Stanford President Ray Lyman Wilbur inveighed frequently against alcohol, particularly against drinking and driving, and saw the university as a kind of mecca free from the ills of a prohibitionist era. In "Arcademy" a voice wails, "Gasoline and alcohol will not mix," a wail that only incites the workers to demonstrate that they will.

14. John Steinbeck, "Always Something to Do in Salinas," *Holiday* 14 (June 1955): 152.

15. Steinbeck was frank in his dislike for Stanford, where he often felt repressed by rules and snobbishness. In a December 1929 letter to A. Grove Day, he wrote, "I don't like Stanford and never did. Prigs they are there and pretenders" (*SLL*, p. 20).

16. Benson, *True Adventures*, p. 69.

17. Ibid., p. 72.

18. Ibid., p. 75.

19. R. S. Hughes, *Beyond "The Red Pony": A Reader's Companion to Steinbeck's Complete Short Stories*, p. 11.

20. See Clifford L. Lewis, "Four Dubious Steinbeck Stories," *Steinbeck Quarterly* 5 (1972): 17–19.

21. From an unpublished letter reprinted by permission of the John Steinbeck estate and the Steinbeck Research Center, San Jose State University.

22. John Steinbeck, "The Making of a New Yorker," in *The Empire City: A Treasury of New York* (reprinted from the *New York Times Magazine*, Feb. 1, 1953), ed. Alexander Klein, pp. 469, 470, 471, respectively.

23. The theme is evident in Steinbeck's *America and Americans:* "But we are also poisoned with things. . . . We have the things and we have not had time to develop a way of thinking about them" (p. 172).

24. The untitled Christmas story manuscript is held by the Steinbeck Collection of Stanford University Libraries and is quoted by permission of Stanford University and the John Steinbeck estate.

25. The "Days of Long Marsh" manuscript is held by the Houghton Library of Harvard University and is quoted by permission of Harvard University and the John Steinbeck estate.

26. The "White Sister of Fourteenth Street" manuscript is held by the John Steinbeck Collection of Stanford University and is quoted by permission of Stanford University Libraries and the John Steinbeck estate.

27. From an undated (c. 1927–28) letter to Katherine Beswick, reprinted by permission of the John Steinbeck estate and the Stanford University Libraries.

28. DeMott, *Steinbeck's Reading*, p. 21. In *John Steinbeck: The Good Companion,* Carlton Sheffield remarks, "A stronger literary influence on John's developing style was the work of James Branch Cabell, whose delicate ironies and stylistic arabesques for a time hypnotized many of the would-be writers of the 1920s. We read and admired *Jurgen* together and in our letters and literary experiments, we strove to emulate the polished frivolities" (p. 80). R. S. Hughes has observed, "The setting and characters of 'The Gifts of Iban' are nearly identical to those in chapters three and four of Cabell's *Jurgen*" (*Beyond "The Red Pony,"* p. 26).

29. John Steinbeck, "The Gifts of Iban," *The Smokers Companion* 1 (Mar. 1927), p. 72.

30. Benson, *True Adventures*, p. 14.

31. John Steinbeck, *Cup of Gold*, p. 19.

32. Ibid., p. 108.

33. William Barrett, *Irrational Man: A Study in Existential Philosophy*, p. 23.

34. See DeMott, *Steinbeck's Reading*, p. 140. DeMott is entirely correct in his assessment of influences upon Steinbeck: "Steinbeck was not above pilfering from the library of available material. Generally—and this is what matters most—he asserted imaginative dominion over those appropriated elements by transmuting them in such a way that they became his own fictive property" (p. xx).

35. Joseph Epstein, *Plausible Prejudices: Essays on American Writing*, p. 18.

36. Ibid., p. 19.

CHAPTER 2

1. John Steinbeck, "A Primer on the Thirties," *Esquire* 80, no. 479 (Oct. 1973): 127.

2. Years later Steinbeck was to state directly what he discovered intuitively in the 1930s. In a January 29, 1963, letter to Pascal Covici he wrote, "Fiction, it seems to me, in its inception was an attempt to put experience in a form and direction so that it could be understood. Not that fiction could be understood but that reality could" (*Steinbeck and Covici: The Story of a Friendship*, ed. Thomas Fensch, p. 227).

3. Edith Mirrielees, *Story Writing*, p. 191. In a letter to Robert Cathcart, Steinbeck observed of Mirrielees, "She does one thing for you. She makes you get over what you want to say. Her only really vicious criticism is directed toward turgidity, and that is a good thing" (quoted in Benson, *True Adventures*, p. 59).

4. Steinbeck's most consciously symbolic work was *East of Eden*. While writing the novel, Steinbeck wrote to Pascal Covici of having to change Carl Trask's name because the character had "changed his symbolic nature to a certain extent." Steinbeck adds:

Since these people are essentially symbol people, I must make them doubly understandable as people apart from their symbols. A symbol is usually a kind of part of an equation—it is one part or facet chosen to illuminate as well as to illustrate the whole. The symbol is never the whole. It is a kind of psychological sign language. . . . I want to clothe my symbol people in trappings of experience so that the symbol is discernible but not overwhelming. [*Journal of a Novel: The "East of Eden" Letters*, p. 27]

5. There is something of an irony in Steinbeck's playful speculation here, because his writing instruments, including the color of ink, were psychologically important to him. Usually he wrote with black ink. While working on the first draft of "The Chrysanthemums" he happened to run out of black ink and had to switch to a very light, almost indecipherable purple ink. He broke off the story to reflect on the ink: "Purple ink again. Apparently it doesn't make much difference in the writing. I'll give it a try. It looks pretty pale to me though. But it was a bargain not to be overlooked" (*TFN*). He picked up the writing again, and the purple ink became very thin. Steinbeck observed, "Purple, if it were a little bit stronger, would be a good color for the story." Soon he switched back to black ink and stated that he felt ready to go on working. In fact, he had difficulty retracing the thread of the story.

6. According to Carlton Sheffield, Steinbeck composed long passages of *Cup of Gold* while listening to Dvorak's *New World Symphony*, allowing the musical work to subconsciously shape prose patterns. See *John Steinbeck: The Good Companion*, p. 138–39.

7. Warren French, "Introduction," in *Steinbeck's "The Red Pony": Essays in Criticism*, ed. Tetsumaro Hayashi and Thomas J. Moore, p. xiii.

8. Quoted from *The Grapes of Wrath* journal by permission of Harry Ransom Research Center, University of Texas, Austin, and the John Steinbeck estate.

9. Brian M. Barbour, "Steinbeck As a Short Story Writer," in *A Study Guide to Steinbeck's "The Long Valley,"* ed. Tetsumaro Hayashi, p. 121. Barbour writes in curious ignorance of the historical backgrounds and chronology of the composition of the stories. For example, Steinbeck did not write any short stories in 1938. The first few months of the year were spent working on "L'Affaire Lettuceberg," and from late May until the end of the year he worked on *The Grapes of Wrath*.

CHAPTER 3

1. See Benson, *True Adventures*, pp. 208–9. Another source for the stories was Steinbeck's Aunt Molly, who resided in the Corral de Tierra. See Brian St. Pierre, *John Steinbeck: The California Years*, p. 50.

2. Technically the firm was still called Cape and Smith at this time. The parent firm was Jonathan Cape in England. By 1932, when the actual contracts for *The Pastures of Heaven* were signed, the firm had been reorganized as Jonathan Cape and Robert Ballou, Inc. Robert Ballou, who had been the literary editor of the *Chicago Daily News*, was now the editor of the firm. Shortly after the contract was signed, the firm went bankrupt. Ballou moved to Brewer, Warren and Putnam, which issued a new contract and published the book in late 1932.

3. In a letter to Amasa Miller, Steinbeck indicated his intentions by the title: "I think the ironic name the Pastures of Heaven and the nebulous parallel of the M——s with the Miltonic Lucifer is fairly good." See Benson, *True Adventures*, p. 201.

4. In a letter to Pascal Covici written while he was working on *East of Eden*, Steinbeck remarked that the story of Cain and Abel "has made a deeper mark in people than any other save possibly the story of the Tree of Life and original sin" (*Steinbeck and Covici*, p. 148).

5. George Battle was draft age when he arrived in 1863. Assuming that to be eighteen, he died in 1910.

6. In *Steinbeck's Unhappy Valley*, Joseph Fontenrose details some of the chronology of the valley residents:

The dramatic time of the central sequence, from the coming of the Munroes (early spring) to the burning of the Whiteside house (October) covers about one year and a half. But there is an inconsistency about the calendar years in which these events are supposed to have occurred. In the Introduction we are informed that the Battle farm had been unoccupied for five years (p. 12) when the Munroes took it over. That seems to indicate 1928, since the Mustrovics had taken the place in 1921 and had stayed for two years (pp. 15–16). Bert Munroe became a school trustee in six months (p. 23); he was elected early in the fall (p. 124) and made his first visit to the schoolhouse on December 15 (p. 91). Now Molly Morgan was the teacher, and Robbie Maltby was in his first year of attendance. Robbie was born late in 1917 (p. 76). He was required by law to go to school at the beginning of the school year following his sixth birthday (p. 82), which should be in September of 1924. Molly Morgan taught less than a full year in the Pastures, so that the year of her tenure should be 1924–1925. Probably we should accept 1928–1929 as the dramatic date and suppose that Steinbeck never noticed the discrepancy in the date indications of the two stories. [pp. 6–7]

7. Benson, *True Adventures*, pp. 210–11.

8. Melanie Mortlock, "The Eden Myth as Paradox: An Allegorical Reading of *The Pastures of Heaven*," *Steinbeck Quarterly* 11, no. 1 (Winter 1978): 14.

9. *Tularecito* literally means "little frog," and his physical appearance—a squat, strong body, "short, chubby arms and long loose-jointed legs"—suggests the name. Tularecito is also very much like the coyote, however—the hunted one, the outsider. Bert Munroe is going out to inspect a coyote trap when he discovers the hole Tularecito has dug, which will be a kind of trap for him. Franklin Gomez calls him "Coyote," seeing in him "that ancient wisdom one finds in the face of a coyote."

10. In a foreshadowing of "The Snake," Steinbeck depicts Miss Martin ritualistically engaged in the beating, participating involuntarily in its action: "Then, while Tularecito smiled blandly at Miss Martin, Franklin Gomez beat him severely across the back. Miss Martin's hand made involuntary motions of beating" (p. 52).

11. Steinbeck used the water-birth pattern heavily in *To a God Unknown*, which had already been drafted at this time. When he had finished *The Pastures of Heaven* and taken up *To a God Unknown* again in early 1932, Pacific Grove received an unusually heavy

rain after a prolonged dry spell. Steinbeck elaborated the effects of drought and water upon people in a letter to Mavis McIntosh:

Gradually during the last ten years the country has been dying of lack of moisture. This dryness has peculiar effects. Diseases increase, people are subject to colds, to fevers and to curious nervous disorders. Crimes of violence increase. The whole people are touchy and nervous. . . . Then in December the thing broke. There were two weeks of downpour. The rivers overflowed and took away houses and cattle and land. I've seen decorous people dancing in the mud. They have laughed with a kind of crazy joy when their land was washing away. [*SLL*, p. 53]

Water functions symbolically for Steinbeck as rejuvenation, but in a biological rather than a Christian fashion. It reminds us, subconsciously, of birth and beginnings.

12. John Steinbeck, *Nothing So Monstrous*, n.p.

13. Howard Levant argues that the conclusion fits neither the story nor the larger work. See *The Novels of John Steinbeck: A Critical Study*, pp. 43–44. R. S. Hughes echoes Levant's view and adds, "Rosa and Maria become stereotypes, rather than unique characters" (*Beyond "The Red Pony*," pp. 41–42). Richard Astro believes the story does not quite fit the larger book because it was drafted earlier as part of Webster Street's "The Green Lady," which Steinbeck later developed into *To a God Unknown* (see *John Steinbeck and Edward F. Ricketts: The Shaping of a Novelist*, pp. 81–83). In fact, the story was fully revised and redrafted in the record book ledger with other stories of *The Pastures of Heaven*, clearly redesigned by Steinbeck to be a piece of the whole.

14. Louis Owens, *John Steinbeck's Re-Vision of America*, p. 81.

15. Ibid.

16. Although not fully informed by biographical data that have drawn tight the links in the chain between Steinbeck and Jung, several studies have successfully speculated on the influence. See Clifford L. Lewis, "Jungian Psychology and the Artistic Design of John Steinbeck," *Steinbeck Quarterly* 10 (Summer–Fall 1977): 89–97; Robert DeMott, "Toward a Redefinition of *To a God Unknown*," *Windsor Review* 8 (1973): 34–53; Charles E. May, "Myth and Mystery in Steinbeck's 'The Snake': A Jungian View," Criticism 15 (1973): 322–35; Donal Stone, "Steinbeck, Jung, and *The Winter of Our Discontent*," *Steinbeck Quarterly* 11 (Summer–Fall 1978): 87–96.

17. Benson, *True Adventures*, p. 207.

18. DeMott, *Steinbeck's Reading*, pp. 62–63.

19. Ibid., p. 63. In a number of letters Steinbeck mentions the influence of Jung on his phalanx theory. For example, to George Albee

he wrote, "Now in the unconscious of the man unit there is a keying mechanism. Jung calls it the third person" (*SLL*, p. 80). Other references occur on pages 75 and 87.

20. Carl Jung, "Archetypes of the Collective Unconscious," in *AION*, vol. 9, part 1, *The Collected Works of Carl Jung*, trans. R. F. C. Hull, pp. 284–85. Although some discussion of the shadow appears in nearly all of Jung's work, the key analyses appear in several works directly relating to the topic. These include, in addition to "Archetypes," the following: "The Structure and Dynamics of the Psyche," vol. 8; "The Fight with the Shadow," vol. 10; "Answer to Job," vol. 11; "The Meaning of Self-Knowledge," vol. 11; "Depth Psychology and a New Ethic," vol. 18; "The Symbolic Life," vol. 18; and "The Tavistock Lectures," vol. 18. The crucial work is *AION*, vol. 9, parts 1 and 2, which includes "Archetypes," "The Syzygy: Anima and Animus," "The Structure and Dynamics of the Self," and "The Shadow."

21. Carl Jung, "Depth Psychology and a New Ethic," in *Collected Works*, vol. 18, p. 620.

22. See, for example, Louis Owens in *John Steinbeck's Re-Vision of America:* "Molly's fondness for illusion also has a tragic effect on another inhabitant of the valley, Tularecito. Molly and the society of the Pastures are both responsible for Tularecito's imprisonment in the mental institution" (p. 81).

23. In *John Steinbeck's Fiction: The Aesthetics of the Road Taken*, I have developed this theme of the individual versus society in "Tularecito." See particularly pages 60–62.

24. Carl Jung, "Psychology and Religion," in *Collected Works*, vol. 11, p. 79. The golden period of Molly's teaching is roughly comparable to Jung's concept of the daylight period of the human personality in denial of the shadow: "Anyone who identifies with the daylight half of his psychic life will therefore declare the dreams of the night to be null and void, notwithstanding that the night is as long as the day and that all consciousness is manifestly founded on unconsciousness, is rooted in it and every night is extinguished in it" ("The Self," in *Collected Works, AION*, vol. 9, part 2, p. 30).

25. Carl Jung, "Archetypes of the Collective Unconscious," in *Collected Works, AION*, vol. 9, part 1, p. 123.

26. Ibid., pp. 20–21.

27. The careful pattern of colors in the Raymond Banks story—the interplay of white, red, and black—brings to mind the horrible visage Robin perceives in Hawthorne's "My Kinsman, Major Molineaux":

The forehead with its double prominence, the broad hooked nose, the shaggy eyebrows, and fiery eyes were those which he had noticed at the inn, but the man's complexion had undergone a singular, or, more properly, a twofold change. One side of the face blazed an intense red, while the other was black as midnight, the division line being in the broad bridge of the nose; and a mouth which seemed to extend from ear to ear was black or red, in contrast to the color of the cheek. The effect was as if two individual devils, a fiend of fire and a fiend of darkness, had united themselves to form this infernal visage. [*Complete Novels and Selected Tales*, p. 1216]

For Hawthorne, humanity is, as he put it in "Rappaccini's Daughter," a "lurid intermixture . . . of the infernal regions" (p. 1051).

28. Peter Lisca, *The Wide World of John Steinbeck*, pp. 63–64.

29. Fontenrose, *Steinbeck's Unhappy Valley*, p. 15. Fontenrose observes, "The Munroes are a precipitating factor, but not the true cause of catastrophe. The material cause in nearly every story is the principal himself or herself, or rather the illusions and evasions on which he has built his life."

30. John Steinbeck, *The Grapes of Wrath*, p. 577.

31. John Steinbeck, *The Pearl*, in the companion volume with *The Red Pony*, p. 60.

32. In the first draft of the story, Pat was twenty-one, a traditional threshold of manhood. The change to thirty emphasized the hold of his parents upon him, past the age where he might have chosen his own way.

CHAPTER 4

1. Benson, *True Adventures*, p. 262. In the ledger notebook Steinbeck entered a note that tied together his mother's illness and the theme of his stories. After observing the challenge "to know the sorrow in it and to feel it not in myself but in herself," he announces, "And that is the new theme. Curious that the greatest conceptions should come to me in this time of trouble. I wonder whether Carol can be right when she says it is because of the trouble. . . . Even a few lines written every night would make me feel better" (*LVN*).

2. "The Murder" and "The Chrysanthemums" were the first two stories written in the *Long Valley* collection. Both were completed and sent to George Albee for comment by February 25, 1934. Their probable dates of composition were December 1933 for "The Murder" and December–February 1934 for "The Chrysanthemums." On November 23, 1933, Steinbeck wrote of having finished the first draft of *Tortilla Flat* (*SLL*, pp. 89–90), dating the composition of that manuscript from August to November 1933. In the summer of 1934,

Steinbeck returned to the *Tortilla Flat* manuscript with a clearer concept of thematic unity (*SLL*, pp. 96–97).

3. Joseph Fontenrose, *John Steinbeck: An Introduction and Interpretation*, p. 63.

4. Joseph Warren Beach, "John Steinbeck: Journeyman Artist," in *American Fiction: 1920–1940*, p. 314. Steinbeck was very much conscious of a similarity between *The Red Pony* and *The Yearling*. In February 1941 he wrote Elizabeth Otis regarding the film production of *The Red Pony:*

> I wish you would read *The Yearling* again. Just a little boy named Jody has affection for a deer. Now I know there is no plagiarism on The Red Pony. But we are going to make The Red Pony, and two stories about a little boy in relation to animals is too much, particularly if in both cases the little boy's name is Jody. Will you see if we can't stop them from using the name and as much of the story as seems possible? If we don't want money we might easily get a court order. [*SLL*, p. 225]

Marjorie Rawlings began work on *The Yearling* in March 1936, over two years after "The Gift" had been published in the *North American Review*. Rawlings worked on the book for well over a year, at one point throwing out the manuscript altogether, finally restarting and completing it in December 1937. When it did appear in the spring of 1938, *The Yearling* became an immediate best seller, winning the Pulitzer Prize for that year. For details of Rawlings's composition, see A. Scott Berg, *Max Perkins: Editor of Genius* (New York: E. P. Dutton, 1978).

5. Arnold L. Goldsmith, "Thematic Rhythm in *The Red Pony*," *College English* 26 (Feb. 1965): 391–94.

6. Mimi R. Gladstein, "'The Leader of the People': A Boy Becomes a 'Mench,'" in *Steinbeck's "The Red Pony": Essays in Criticism*, ed. Tetsumaro Hayashi and Thomas J. Moore, pp. 27–37.

7. R. Baird Shuman, "Initiation Rites in Steinbeck's *The Red Pony*," *English Journal* 59, no. 9 (Dec. 1970): 1252–55.

8. Frederic I. Carpenter, "John Steinbeck: American Dreamer," in *Steinbeck and His Critics: A Record of Twenty-Five Years*, ed. E. W. Tedlock, Jr., and C. V. Wicker, p. 77.

9. Lisca, *Wide World*, p. 10.

10. See Donald E. Houghton, "'Westering' in 'Leader of the People,'" *Western American Literature* 4 (Summer 1969): 117–24, and Robert E. Morsberger, "In Defense of 'Westering,'" *Western American Literature* 5 (Summer 1970): 143–46. Houghton argues that Grandfather's "explanation of westering is an unfortunate, confusing, and unnecessary digression which tears at the emotional and

thematic unity of this story and of *The Red Pony* as a whole" (p. 124). Morsberger correctly takes some of the historical, critical, and philosophical errors of the essay to task.

11. Robert S. Hughes, Jr., "The Black Cypress and the Green Tub: Death and Procreation in Steinbeck's 'The Promise,'" in *Steinbeck's "The Red Pony": Essays in Criticism*, pp. 9–16.

12. French, "Introduction," in *Steinbeck's "The Red Pony*," p. xii.

13. Each of the *Red Pony* stories was published independently in periodicals. They first appeared together as a collection in a special issue by Covici-Friede in 1937, in which 699 copies were published and signed by Steinbeck, but the most convenient pagination occurs with their publication in *The Long Valley*. All page references in this study are to *The Long Valley*.

14. Goldsmith, "Thematic Rhythm," p. 392.

15. Ibid.

16. John Steinbeck, "My Short Novels," *Wings* 26 (Oct. 1953): 4.

17. In "Who *Is* 'The Leader of the People'?: Helping Students Examine Fiction," *English Journal* 48 (Nov. 1959), Alfred Grommen points out that Carl "is, ironically, unequal to the stature of his ten-year-old son and the old man"(p. 455). Except that Jody is nearer age twelve in this story, it is true that Carl and Jody's behavioral rules are reversed in the final story.

18. As the mice-hunt episode develops in the ledger, the significance of the mice themselves undergoes an interesting change. In the first mention of it, Steinbeck wrote, "Those fat sleek arrogant mice were doomed." After commenting, "They had grown smug in their security, overbearing and fat. But the time of disaster had come," he links the mice to certain social orders. A passage that originally read, "The [undecipherable word] of mother mice, the carcasses of political mice, the gossiping clicks of social mice, the young fiery mice, all would go to the death" was revised simply to "They would not survive another day."

19. John Steinbeck, *East of Eden*, p. 3.

20. In "Something That Happened: A Non-Teleological Approach to 'The Leader of the People,'" *Steinbeck Quarterly* 6 (Winter 1973), Richard Astro claims that Jody's concern for Grandfather arises from "his juvenile fantasies of adventure which distinctly prohibit him from understanding the true meaning of Grandfather's expression of the unifying aspirations of the 'group man'" (p. 22). Thus, in Astro's view Jody's attraction is to the sense of adventure rather than to his Grandfather and his dream.

21. Morsberger, "In Defense of 'Westering,'" p. 146.

22. Lev Shestov, *Athens and Jerusalem*, trans. Bernard Martin,

p. 76–77. Shestov argues that the apprehension of truth must be wrested from the grip of what he calls Necessity, the equivalent in Steinbeck's view of pragmatic reality, or civilization. Shestov comments, "Both men and gods must again learn it from the very Necessity which itself learns nothing, knows nothing, and wishes to know nothing, which is not concerned with any thing or any person and which despite this—without wishing or seeking it—has been reared so high above everything existing that gods and men all become equal before it, equal in rights or, more correctly, equal in the lack of all rights" (p. 126).

CHAPTER 5

1. Barbour, "Steinbeck As a Short Story Writer," p. 114.
2. Ibid.
3. Ibid., p. 120.
4. In his article "Steinbeck's 'The Murder': A Critical and Bibliographical Study," *Steinbeck Quarterly* 9 (Spring 1976), Roy S. Simmonds details the variants among the manuscript, the American edition, and the British edition of the story. He observes, "The Viking text, which one would normally assume should be the copy text, is unfortunately a somewhat debased text, including several obvious printing errors. There is some evidence that the Viking text may have been taken from the *Lovat Dickson's Magazine* text, for it incongruously . . . reproduces a number of Anglicizations, such as 'towards' instead of 'toward', 'colour' instead of 'color' and 'neighbour' instead of 'neighbor'" (p. 50).
5. According to Jackson Benson, Steinbeck insisted that "Saint Katy" be included in *The Long Valley:*

His attachment for the story can be measured by the fact that it was one of the few things (in its preliminary form) that he kept out of the manuscript fire of the previous spring, and by his persistence in trying to get it published. After several years of submissions without a nibble, he had finally arranged with his book publisher at the time, Covici-Friede, for separate publication as a gift book. Then he insisted on including it in his story collection *The Long Valley,* even though it is so different in kind from the other items that the reader hardly knows what to make of it. [*True Adventures,* p. 253]

6. Donald Friede, *The Mechanical Angel,* p. 131.
7. Sanford E. Marovitz, "The Cryptic Raillery of 'Saint Katy the Virgin,'" in Hayashi, *Study Guide,* p. 73.
8. Ibid.

9. Susan F. Riggs, "Steinbeck at Stanford," *Stanford Magazine* 4 (Fall–Winter 1976): 15. See also Benson, *True Adventures*, p. 253.

10. Benson, *True Adventures*, p. 83.

11. Robert Bennett, *The Wrath of John Steinbeck*. In Bennett's view, Steinbeck's wrath was directed at the preacher's otherworldliness and failure to address readily evident needs about him. For a discussion of Steinbeck's religious attitudes and beliefs, see my essay "John Steinbeck's Use of the Bible: A Descriptive Bibliography of the Critical Tradition," *Steinbeck Quarterly* 21 (Winter–Spring 1988): 24–39.

12. Two of the better discussions of the medieval fabliau are generally considered to be Joseph Bedier, *Les fabliaux: Etudes de littérature populaire et d'histoire littéraire du mayen âge* (Paris: Champion, 1925) and Robert Hellman and Richard O'Gorman's translation and notes in *Fabliaux* (New York: Thomas Y. Crowell, 1965).

13. In *The Art of The Canterbury Tales*, Paul Ruggiers writes that in the fabliau, "The story arises out of what is uniquely human: man is able to laugh, and what he laughs at in himself and in the actions of his neighbor emerges out of the very deep layers of the mind. . . . Man may be unique as a rational creature, but he is also perverse; the fact that he can laugh is his saving grace" (p. 64).

14. Warren French, *John Steinbeck*, p. 108.

15. Marovitz, "Cryptic Raillery," p. 75.

16. *Cup of Gold*, ironically, was plagiarized by Breton Braley in 1934 in his *Morgan Sails the Caribbean*. Harry Moore provides details and Steinbeck's response to the author in *The Novels of John Steinbeck* (Chicago: Normandie House, 1939), p. 17.

17. Hemingway's letters reveal an outrageous sense of competition with Steinbeck. After *The Grapes of Wrath* appeared, Hemingway speculated on the sales of his own next work: "There is a chance the book of the month will take the book. If they do they will print a hundred thousand and Scribner's a hundred thousand and we will be off in a cloud of Steinbecks" (*Ernest Hemingway: Selected Letters*, ed. Carlos Baker, p. 511). In 1959 he wrote his publisher, "I could give him a book every year like Steinbeck composed of my toenail parings . . . little fantasies about King Poo Poo or other author toe jam" (pp. 893–94). In light of this, one recalls Steinbeck's comment to Elizabeth Otis when Hemingway won the Nobel Prize: "News last night of Hemingway's Nobel Prize which pleased me greatly. He should have had it before this" (*SLL*, p. 500).

18. *Correspondence of F. Scott Fitzgerald*, ed. Matthew J. Bruccoli and Margaret M. Duggan, p. 483.

19. Ibid., p. 612.

20. The comparison of Steinbeck to D. H. Lawrence is one that Fitzgerald suggested several times in his letters, and a similarity between the two does exist in their concepts of nature and religion. If one were pressed to find an artistic tie, it would extend between Lawrence's *The Rainbow* and Steinbeck's *To a God Unknown*. This particular relationship has been examined by Reloy Garcia in *Steinbeck and D. H. Lawrence: Fictive Voices and the Ethical Imperative*. The primary relational basis, according to Garcia, lies in the authors' "clear conceptions of the nature of art and the function of the artist, conceptions often so strikingly similar that one might suppose a kinship or at least an extended correspondence; for this conviction impelled them both: art was moral" (p. 4). For other views on the Lawrence-Steinbeck relationship see Richard Peterson, "Steinbeck and D. H. Lawrence," in *Steinbeck's Literary Dimension: A Guide to Comparative Studies*, ed. Tetsumaro Hayashi (Metuchen, NJ: Scarecrow Press, 1973), pp. 67–82; and Marilyn Mitchell, "Steinbeck's Strong Women: Feminine Identity in the Short Stories," *Southwest Review* 61 (Summer 1976): 304–15.

21. Leonard Lutwack has argued in *Heroic Fiction: The Epic Tradition and American Novels of the Twentieth Century* that "the line of descent from *The Octopus* to *The Grapes of Wrath* is as direct as any that can be found in American literature" (p. 47). This is true, perhaps, in terms of general locale and theme, but there is little evidence of a direct influence. Steinbeck's style in the novel is distinct, and his subject matter, influenced by firsthand experience and Tom Collins's journals, is quite different.

22. Frank Norris, *McTeague*, p. 39. Further references to this work will be cited parenthetically.

23. In "Struggle for Survival: Parallel Theme and Techniques in Steinbeck's 'Flight' and Norris's *McTeague*," *Steinbeck Quarterly* 21 (Summer–Fall 1988), Elaine Ware demonstrates "that the plot of Steinbeck's 'Flight' clearly parallels the action of the last two chapters in *McTeague*" (p. 97). Her extensive comparisons justify her conclusion: "This knowledge about Steinbeck's reading as well as the internal evidence—that is, the parallel theme and techniques between Norris and Steinbeck outlined here—convince me that Norris was an influence on Steinbeck in 'Flight'" (pp. 102–3).

24. Benson, *True Adventures*, p. 280.

25. Roy S. Simmonds, "John Steinbeck, Robert Louis Stevenson, and Edith McGillcuddy," *San Jose Studies* 1 (Nov. 1975): 34.

26. Hughes, *Beyond "The Red Pony,"* p. 106.

27. DeMott, *Steinbeck's Reading*, p. 174.

28. John Steinbeck, "How Edith McGillcuddy Met R. L. Steven-

son," *Harper's Magazine* 183 (Aug. 1914): 252. All references to this story will be from this publication, and page numbers will be entered parenthetically in the text.

29. Benson, *True Adventures*, p. 274.

30. One of the major flaws in the otherwise excellent production of *Steinbeck: A Life in Letters* occurs in its confusion of "The Murder" and "Murder at High Moon by Peter Pym." The index, for example, lists only the former and regards all references in the letters to be to that work. In fact, the letters on pages 32 and 42 refer to "Murder at Full Moon." The January 1933 letter to Mavis McIntosh, which refers to Steinbeck's having read "three hundred detective magazines," and in which he asks, "I wonder whether you have tried to peddle that thing I dashed off to any of them" (p. 67) almost surely refers to "Murder at Full Moon," rather than "The Murder," as indicated by the editors in the text. Steinbeck's reading of detective fiction while living in Los Angeles during the winter of 1933 no doubt influenced his composition of "The Murder" the following summer. Similarly, the letter of February 11, 1933, to Robert Ballou (pp. 68–69) seems to refer to "Murder at Full Moon" rather than "The Murder," as the editors identify it. Steinbeck's letter to George Albee on February 25, 1934, refers to "The Murder" because Steinbeck had also sent him a draft of "The Chrysanthemums," which had been written shortly after "The Murder."

31. Robert Murray Davis, "Steinbeck's 'The Murder,'" *Studies in Short Fiction* 14 (1977): 63.

32. Hughes, *Beyond "The Red Pony,"* p. 86.

33. French, *John Steinbeck*, p. 86.

34. Katharine M. Morsberger and Robert Morsberger, "'The Murder'—Realism or Ritual," in Hayashi, *A Study Guide*, p. 70.

35. Ibid.

36. Louis D. Owens, "Steinbeck's 'The Murder': Illusions of Chivalry," *Steinbeck Quarterly* 17 (Winter–Spring 1984): 13.

37. Simmonds, "Steinbeck's 'The Murder,'" *Steinbeck Quarterly* 9 (Spring 1976): 47.

38. Owens, "Steinbeck's 'The Murder,'" p. 12.

CHAPTER 6

1. In a description of the Harry Valentine Collection in *John Steinbeck: A Collection of Books and Manuscripts*, "The Wizard of Maine" is described as follows: "*The Wizard of Maine* is divided into six sections, and is the story of a traveling elixir salesman and magician who has set out from his home in Maine and travels across the

country in hope of being discovered, so that he can perform his tricks on stage as a professional." The description states, "Composition date for the manuscript is unknown, but would seem to date from the 1940s based upon the style of the binder housing the paper." Jackson J. Benson dates the composition from the summer of 1944 (*True Adventures*, pp. 550–51).

2. See William R. Osborne, "The Texts of Steinbeck's 'The Chrysanthemums,'" *Modern Fiction Studies* 12 (Winter 1966–67): 479–84; and Roy S. Simmonds, "The Original Manuscripts of Steinbeck's 'The Chrysanthemums,'" *Steinbeck Quarterly* 7 (Summer– Fall 1974): 102–11.

3. Simmonds, "Original Manuscripts of 'The Chrysanthemums,'" p. 103.

4. Ibid., pp. 110–11.

5. Ibid., pp. 108–9. For other views on the sexuality and femininity of Elisa, see Mordecai Marcus, "The Lost Dream of Sex and Childbirth in 'The Chrysanthemums,'" *Modern Fiction Studies* 11 (Spring 1965): 54–58; Charles A. Sweet, Jr., "Ms. Elisa Allen and Steinbeck's 'The Chrysanthemums,'" *Modern Fiction Studies* 20 (June 1974): 210–14; and *Steinbeck's Women: Essays in Criticism*, ed. Tetsumaro Hayashi.

6. Hughes, *Beyond "The Red Pony,"* p. 64.

7. Arthur L. Simpson, Jr., "'The White Quail': A Portrait of an Artist," in Hayashi, *Study Guide*, p. 11.

8. In "Steinbeck's Strong Women," Marilyn L. Mitchell erroneously argues that the fuchsias represent Mary (p. 307). The fuchsias are specifically male in the story and clearly represent her displacement of a sexual and spiritual union with Harry to her garden.

9. C. M. Bowra, *The Romantic Imagination*, p. 3. Bowra points out the difficulty of the view he describes: "If a man gives free play to his imagination, what assurance is there that what he says is in any sense true? Can it tell us anything that we do not know, or is it so removed from ordinary life as to be an escape from it?" (p. 5).

10. Ibid., pp. 3–4. A convincing argument for the influence of Romanticism, and Blake in particular, upon Steinbeck has been provided by Duane R. Carr, "Steinbeck's Blakean Vision in *The Grapes of Wrath*," *Steinbeck Quarterly* 8 (Summer–Fall 1975): 67–73.

11. Roma A. King, Jr., *The Focusing Artifice: The Poetry of Robert Browning*, pp. xxii–xxiii.

12. Stanley Renner, "Sexual Idealism and Violence in 'The White Quail,'" *Steinbeck Quarterly* 17 (Summer–Fall 1984): 79.

13. Benson, *True Adventures*, p. 285.

14. Joseph Fontenrose, "The Harness," in Hayashi, *Study Guide,* p. 49.

15. The analogy between human and marine life forms is readily apparent in *Cannery Row*. In "John Steinbeck's *Cannery Row:* A Reconsideration," *Western American Literature* 12 (1977), Jackson J. Benson considers specific similarities between the tidal flats and life on the row. Also, Howard Levant explores the analogy in *The Novels of John Steinbeck*, pp. 169–70. Steinbeck made his perceived relationship between humanity and the sea explicit in *The Log from the Sea of Cortez*. There he argues, for example, "The ocean, deep and black in the depths, is like the low dark levels of our minds in which the dream symbols incubate and sometimes rise up to sight like the Old Man of the Sea" (p. 31). In *The Winter of Our Discontent,* Ethan Hawley says, "It's as though, in the dark and desolate caves of the mind, a faceless journey had met and decided. This secret and sleepless area in me I have always thought of as a black, deep, waveless water, a spawning place from which only a few forms ever rise to the surface" (p. 86). For studies of Steinbeck's relation with the sea, see Astro, *Steinbeck and Ricketts;* and Joel W. Hedgpeth, ed., *The Outer Shores, Part I: Ed Ricketts and John Steinbeck Explore the Pacific Coast* and *The Outer Shores, Part II: From the Papers of Edward F. Ricketts.*

16. Dan Vogel, "Steinbeck's 'Flight': The Myth of Manhood," *College English* 23 (1961): 226.

17. William M. Jones, "Steinbeck's 'Flight,'" *Explicator* 18 (Nov. 1959): item 11.

18. Walter K. Gordon, "Steinbeck's 'Flight': Journey To or From Maturity?" *Studies in Short Fiction* 3 (1966): 454.

19. Steinbeck, *Log from the Sea of Cortez,* p. 34.

20. Steinbeck, *The Grapes of Wrath,* pp. 204–5.

21. John M. Ditsky, "Steinbeck's 'Flight': The Ambiguity of Manhood," in Hayashi, *Study Guide,* p. 19. See also Walter K. Gordon, "Steinbeck's 'Flight.'" Gordon argues, "The story . . . portrays . . . man's moral deterioration and regression that inevitably results when he abandons responsibility for his actions. Pepe, then, begins as a child and becomes by running away less than an animal rather than a man" (p. 454). In Gordon's view, Pepe's loss of civilized tools represents the deterioration of Pepe in the wasteland.

22. Louis D. Owens, "Steinbeck's 'Flight': Into the Jaws of Death," *Steinbeck Quarterly* 10 (Summer–Fall 1977): 104.

23. John Antico, "A Reading of Steinbeck's 'Flight,'" *Modern Fiction Studies* 11 (Spring 1965): 50. See also Lisca, *Wide World.* Lisca

points out, "The whole action of the story goes to show how man, even when stripped of all his civilized accoutrements . . . is still something more than an animal" (p. 99). According to Lisca, Pepe faces "his inevitable death not with the headlong retreat or futile death struggle of an animal, but with the calm and stoicism required by the highest conception of manhood, forcing fate to give him a voice in the 'how' if not the 'what' of his destiny" (p. 100).

24. Ibid.

25. Michael Ratcliffe, "Cutting Loose," *Encore: The Sunday Times Book*, ed. Leonard Russell (London: Michael Joseph, 1963), pp. 153–54.

26. Antico, "Steinbeck's 'Flight,'" pp. 51–52.

27. One of the better studies applying the nonteleological premises to an analysis of Steinbeck's fiction appears in Antonia Seixas, "John Steinbeck and the Non-Teleological Bus," in *Steinbeck and His Critics: A Record of Twenty-Five Years*, ed. E. W. Tedlock, Jr., and C. V. Wicker, pp. 275–80.

28. Steinbeck's vision of the nonteleological artist anticipated the modern novel of narrative objectivity by many years. While the "new" novel of surfaces has never thoroughly invaded the ranks of leading American writers, it became particularly fashionable in France during the 1960s and influenced, perhaps, deconstructionism in literary criticism. One of the originators of the novel of surfaces in France was Alain Robbe-Grillet, who attracted considerable international attention with his novels *The Voyeur* and *Last Year at Marienbad*. Following the success of these, Robbe-Grillet published *For a New Novel: Essays on Fiction*. The essays are notable here for their similarities to Steinbeck's less systematic views on nonteleological versus teleological art.

Robbe-Grillet admits, "Objectivity in the ordinary sense of the word—total impersonality of observation—is all too obviously an illusion. But *freedom* of observation should be possible, and yet it is not" (p. 18). Nonetheless, the task of the artist is to render *what is* in prose: "But the world is neither significant nor absurd. It *is*, quite simply" (p. 19). The novelist is a kind of scientific anatomist, discovering the things that *are* there before him: "Around us, defying the noisy pack of our animistic or protective adjectives, things *are* there. Their surfaces are distinct and smooth, *intact*, neither suspiciously brilliant nor transparent" (p. 19). To do this artistically, Robbe-Grillet advises forsaking psychological character studies and presenting life through first-person experience of it without coloring commentary.

Perhaps the most important tenet in Robbe-Grillet's aesthetic,

however, is distrust of metaphor. Metaphor is the dangerous tool of
the artist, for it always suggests more than it describes. Robbe-
Grillet states, "Metaphor, which is supposed to express only a comparison, without any particular motive, actually introduces a subterranean communication, a movement of sympathy (or of antipathy)
which is its true *raison d'etre*" (p. 54). Like Robert Frost, Steinbeck
refused to give up metaphor. However objective he attempts to be in
these short stories, his patterns of imagery do signal a "subterranean
communication" and tell the reader how to view events that unfold.
The imagery of Steinbeck's most nonteleological stories finally provide them a teleological caste.

    29. John Steinbeck, "About Ed Ricketts," in *The Log from the
Sea of Cortez*, pp. xxii–xxiii.
    30. Webster Street, "Remembering John Steinbeck," *San Jose
Studies* 1 (Nov. 1975): 121.
    31. Ibid.
    32. Steinbeck, "About Ed Ricketts," p. xxiii.
    33. See Robert M. Benton, "'Breakfast' I and II," in Hayashi,
Study Guide, pp. 33–38, for a detailed comparison of the original
sketch and its incorporation into *The Grapes of Wrath*.
    34. Salinas *Index-Journal*, (Nov. 23, 1933). Unless indicated other-
wise, all quotations concerning this case will be from reports of the
Salinas *Index-Journal* and will hereafter be cited in the text. Although Steinbeck had access to other newspapers, it is fairly certain
that he would have followed the story in his hometown newspaper.
Furthermore, the *Index-Journal*, as will be demonstrated, gave a
peculiar caste to the San Jose lynchings by using related local stories
that may have intrigued Steinbeck.
    Several journalistic works are worth perusing for details of the
case. Many of Royce Brier's accounts in the San Francisco *Chronicle*
are collected in *A Treasury of Great Reporting*, 2d edition, ed.
Louis L. Snyder and Richard B. Morris. A special fiftieth anniversary report in the November 29, 1983, edition of the *San Jose Mercury News*, edited by Harry Farrell, gives valuable interviews with
people present at the lynching or knowledgeable about the events
preceding it. An account by Alvin D. Hyman, "The San Jose Lynchings," appears in *News Stories of 1933: A Collection of Some of the
Best News and Feature Stories of Various Types Which Appeared
in American Newspapers in 1933*, ed. Frank Luther Mott. Brian
McGinty, "Shadows in Saint James Park," *California History* 57
(Winter 1978–79) provides a full account of the events.
    Literary studies of the influence of the lynching on "The Vigi-
lante" include Martha H. Cox, "Steinbeck Used San Jose Hangings

for Short Story with Lynching Theme," *Phoenix* (Apr. 16, 1978), published by San Jose State University; and James Delgado, "The Facts Behind John Steinbeck's 'The Lonesome Vigilante,'" *Steinbeck Quarterly* 16 (Summer–Fall 1983): 70–79.

35. Accounts of the prayer vary. According to one eyewitness, it occurred in the jail at the request of the jailer as he beseeched them to take the right man. Royce Brier first stated that it occurred in the jail cell. The prayer is only one in a series of anomalies in the case. The pairing of the criminals in itself was unusual. Holmes, twenty-nine, who had studied at San Jose State University (then City College), was married and the father of two children. He had separated from his wife and was trying to persuade his current girlfriend to elope with him. Presumably his motive in the kidnapping was to finance the elopement. The Friday, November 17, *Index-Journal* carried a United Press release of an interview with Mrs. Gertrude Estensen, Holmes's girlfriend. She frankly discusses Holmes's desire to elope and his reaction to the kidnapping: "Monday night while mother and I discussed it with him, he said it was an awful thing. I remarked that anyone who would do a thing like that was the lowest kind and he said, 'Yes, that's right.' He talked about it naturally."

Thurmond, twenty-eight, a grade-school dropout, had met Holmes at a gas station. They had discussed the kidnapping for some five weeks and apparently had made one earlier attempt to kidnap Hart by forcing his car into a curb.

The initial ransom demand, issued from a phone in San Francisco, was reported like this in the Friday, November 10, 1933, *Index-Journal:* "We have your son, and want $40,000 for him. Don't get in touch with the police or you will never see your son again." By Monday, November 13, they had lowered their demand to $20,000. The Harts, as often happens in kidnapping cases, received ransom messages from others, one hinting that Brooke was still alive.

36. It is not unusual in such sensational cases for witnesses to appear with fabricated stories. This case was rife with them. For example, the investigation was muddled for a time by a farm woman's report that she had seen five men transferring Hart from a roadster to a sedan (*Index-Journal,* Nov. 22, 1933).

37. Quoted in DeMott, *Steinbeck's Reading,* p. 131.

38. In a special report on the case published Thursday, November 29, 1983, the *San Jose Mercury News* indicates that the plan for lynching had developed over several days. Louis Rossi, a friend of the Harts, reported a central core of ten to twelve leaders "from all walks of life, students from various universities, men from various fraternal organizations."

39. The ground-breaking historical research on the strike movement and Steinbeck's involvement in it has been performed by Jackson J. Benson and Anne Loftis, "John Steinbeck and Farm Labor Unionization: The Backgrounds of *In Dubious Battle*," *American Literature* 52 (May 1980): 194–223.

40. One of the most detailed and objective accounts of conditions of the time is given by Frank J. Taylor, "California's Grapes of Wrath," *Forum* 102 (Nov. 1939): 232–38. The article is reprinted in *The Grapes of Wrath: Text and Criticism*, ed. Peter Lisca, pp. 643–56. See also Carey McWilliams, "California Pastoral," in the same edition, pp. 657–79.

41. Mary McCarthy, "Minority Report," *The Nation* (Mar. 11, 1936): 326–27.

42. Benson, *True Adventures*, p. 324.

43. See Jackson J. Benson, "Through a Political Glass, Darkly: The Example of John Steinbeck," *Studies in American Fiction* 12 (Spring 1984): 45–48.

44. For a moving account of Steinbeck's involvement in the migrant camps see Jackson J. Benson, "Background of *The Grapes of Wrath*," *Journal of Modern Literature* 5 (Apr. 1976): 194–216.

45. Peter Lisca, "'The Raid' and *In Dubious Battle*," in Hayashi, *Study Guide*, pp. 41–45.

46. John Steinbeck, *In Dubious Battle*, p. 5. In the earliest drafts of *In Dubious Battle*, found in the *In Dubious Battle* notebook (held by the Harry Ransom Research Center of the University of Texas, Austin), the account of Jim's background, under his first name of Eddie Wiggin, underwent considerable transformation. Originally, that story focused far more heavily on Eddie's sense of outrage. Alec is described as an angry man, very good in the slaughterhouses, but unable to keep a job because he fought with the bosses. During the hard times, "a kind of vapor of despair seemed to hang in the house." The story focuses upon Alec's terrible rages, then, very suddenly, shifts to Eddie Wiggin in the jail. Here the first attempt broke off.

47. Stephen Crane, *The Red Badge of Courage*, ed. Sculley Bradley et al., p. 121. All quotations are from this edition, and hereafter page numbers will be cited parenthetically.

48. *In Dubious Battle*, p. 249.

49. Ibid., p. 176.

50. *The Grapes of Wrath*, p. 570.

51. That Steinbeck's moods and writing patterns were strongly affected by weather patterns is well established. He himself offers ample testimony. He once speculated to Elizabeth Otis, "It has been colder here than I've ever known it to be. Whole system of weather

seems to be changing. In addition there is an epidemic of pneumonia and influenza out here so we go to town rarely and never to the theater. It is remarkable how cataclysmic human change and natural change work together" (*SLL*, p. 135).

52. In a rather peculiar essay on "Johnny Bear"—peculiar because the author admits that he has little to say about the story—Warren French discusses the notion of the "yellow peril" in Steinbeck's work. Following the argument of his earlier *John Steinbeck*, in which he asserted that the sin of Amy, because of racial prejudices in the town, would destroy the town's sense of order, French argues, "The story thus is part of Steinbeck's long continuing war against complacent 'respectability,' adding to the warning of 'The Harness' and 'The White Quail' against starving people of affection in order to keep up a good front, another 'against putting faith in "good" people any more than "good" causes'" ("'Johnny Bear'—Steinbeck's 'Yellow Peril' Story," in Hayashi, *Study Guide*, p. 58). Thus, French says, "Instead of laboring an unwarranted new interpretation of a story, I would like to develop the passing reference in my earlier analysis to the 'racial prejudices' involved in the response to Johnny Bear's revelations, because if anything about this story puzzles readers today, it is likely to be the town spokesman's overreaction to Johnny Bear's revelation that the respected spinster was not just fornicating, but fornicating with a chinaman" (p. 58).

53. Lisca, *Wide World of John Steinbeck*, p. 96.

54. Owens, *John Steinbeck's Re-Vision of America*, pp. 118–20.

55. Hughes, *Beyond "The Red Pony,"* pp. 80–85.

56. Charlotte Byrd, "The First-Person Narrator in 'Johnny Bear': A Writer's Mind and Conscience," *Steinbeck Quarterly* 21 (Winter–Spring 1988): 12.

CHAPTER 7

1. For all of his concerns about having enough money in early years, Steinbeck had a curious irresponsibility in financial affairs during later years. He could spend money lavishly, give money away on a whim, and also lament that he had no money. In 1954 he wrote to the McIntosh and Otis staff about what he perceived as his shaky financial situation, wondering why he had only $4,500 in the bank out of $70,000 earned income to that point (August 20). He writes, "I went into a tailspin and for a week was so concerned with my brokenness and with the seeming impossibility of ever pulling out that I was incapable of working. In other words, the time taken out for worry about my shaky financial status took the time and more

than the effort of three short stories or one long one" (*SLL*, p. 491).
The editors of *Steinbeck: A Life in Letters* point out, "It should be
understood that he was living in a beautiful house in Paris, maintain-
ing a household, of eight people including family and staff, and driving a new Jaguar" (p. 492).

2. In 1935 Steinbeck wrote Elizabeth Otis, "The publicity on TF
is rather terrible out here and we may have to run ahead of it. Please
ask CF [Covici-Friede] not to give my address to anyone. Curious
that this second-rate book, written for relaxation, should cause this
fuss. People are actually taking it seriously" (*SLL*, p. 111).

3. For Steinbeck's use of sources in composing *East of Eden*, see
Robert DeMott, "'A Great Black Book': *East of Eden* and Dr. Gunn's
Family Medicine," *American Studies* 22 (Fall 1981): 41–57, and his
"Introduction" to *Steinbeck's Reading*, pp. xxxii–xlii.

4. "The Time the Wolves Ate the Vice-Principal," *'47, the Magazine of the Year* 1, no. 1 (Mar. 1947): 26–27.

5. John Steinbeck, *Once There Was a War*, p. 45.

6. Benson, *True Adventures*, p. 512.

7. Steinbeck, *Once There Was a War*, p. 107.

8. John Steinbeck, "The Crapshooter," in *Various Temptations*,
pp. 168–171.

9. Steinbeck, *Once There Was a War*, p. 86.

10. John Steinbeck, "Positano," *Harper's Bazaar* (Aug. 1953),
pp. 41, 68ff.

11. John Steinbeck, "I Go Back to Ireland," *Collier's* (Jan. 31,
1953): 49–50; reprinted as "Green Paradise," *Argosy* 17, no. 5 (May
1956): 41–47.

12. John Steinbeck, "Case of the Hotel Ghost—Or . . . What Are
You Smoking in That Pipe, Mr. S.?" *Louisville Courier-Journal*,
June 30, 1957, reprinted as "Reunion at the Quiet Hotel," London
Evening Standard, Jan. 25, 1958.

13. Benson, *True Adventures*, p. 503.

14. John Steinbeck, *The Forgotten Village*, pp. 52–53. Further
references from the text will be noted parenthetically.

15. The story of Our Lady of Guadalupe is so well known that
Steinbeck undoubtedly heard it often while in Mexico. It is likely
that he would have seen the famous shrine at the old basilica (the
new one was built in 1976) during his visits to Mexico City. But his
attention could also have been drawn to the legend by his reading of
Willa Cather's *Death Comes for the Archbishop*, one of several of
Cather's books that Steinbeck had in his library. He considered
Cather one of the best American authors and may very likely have
read Cather's account of the legend in chapter 4 of the novel.

16. Jody Brant Smith, *The Image of Guadalupe: Myth or Miracle?* pp. 3–4.

17. John Steinbeck, "The Miracle of Tepayac," *Collier's* 122 (Dec. 25, 1948): 22. Further references to this text will be noted parenthetically.

18. Smith, *Image of Guadalupe*, pp. 10–11.

19. Benson, *True Adventures*, p. 616.

20. One notable exception was his November 19, 1948, letter to Bo Beskow:

I still have Gwyn and the children to support. I don't care about her but I want the children well cared for. At first I wanted to kill someone or be killed, even to the extent of walking alone at night in Mexico with a bare machete in my hand but the challenge did not work. I was avoided like the mad dog I guess I was. And that is all over now and a soft benevolence is on me. [*SLL*, p. 342]

21. John Steinbeck, "His Father," *Reader's Digest* 55 (Sept. 1949): 19. Further references will be cited parenthetically.

22. "The Summer Before" was most likely written in May 1954. In a letter of May 22, 1954, Steinbeck wrote, "Last night before I went to sleep I started one of the little stories I want to write just in anticipation of having a room to work in. And after the lights were out I designed two more. I am really champing to get to work" (Benson, *True Adventures*, p. 751). Jackson Benson judges that one of these short stories was "The Summer Before."

23. Steinbeck, "Always Something to Do in Salinas," p. 58.

24. Ibid., p. 59.

25. John Steinbeck, "The Summer Before," *Punch* 128 (May 25, 1955): 647. Further references will be cited parenthetically. One of Steinbeck's descriptions of his pony in "The Summer Before" also appeared in *The Red Pony*. He writes of Jill's holding her breath while he tried to cinch her: "As I tightened the cinch she would take a great breath and swell out her stomach so that when she let the air out, the cinch would be loose the way she liked it. But I could beat her at that game."

26. Steinbeck recalled his sister in a letter to Elaine's mother:

My youngest sister when she was a little girl didn't want to be a girl at all. She felt it the greatest insult that she was a girl. And when you consider that she rode like a cockleburr, was the best pitcher anywhere near her age on the West side of town, and was such a good marble player that the season had to be called off because she had won every marble in town, you can understand why she felt that it was unjust that she should wear little skirts. [*SLL*, p. 581]

27. Dylan Thomas, "Fern Hill," in *The Collected Poems of Dylan Thomas*, p. 180.

28. Robert DeMott considers the possible influence of Poe upon Steinbeck in *Steinbeck's Reading:*

> JS was acquainted with Poe, including "The Murders in the Rue Morgue" (1841) and "The Purloined Letter" (1845), at least by 1920. . . . Some of the grotesque tonal quality of Poe's work figures in JS's serio-comic detective novel, "Murder at Full Moon. . . . " JS considered Poe, like Melville, an example of the American writer who went unappreciated by his native audience: "Even Edgar Allan Poe, who surely wrote more like a European than an American, had to be acclaimed in France before he was acceptable to upper-brow Americans." [p. 168]

29. The most easily accessible source for "The Affair at 7 Rue de M——" and "How Mr. Hogan Robbed a Bank" is *The Portable Steinbeck*, ed. Pascal Covici, Jr. All quotations from these two stories will be from this edition, with page references cited parenthetically.

30. See especially Warren French, "Steinbeck's Winter Tale," *Modern Fiction Studies* 11 (1965): 66–74.

31. "The Short-Short Story of Mankind" has been reprinted several times, mostly in relatively obscure sources. It first appeared under the title "We're Holding Our Own" in *Lilliput* 37 (Nov. 1955): 18–19; as "The Short-Short Story of Mankind" in *Playboy* 5 (Apr. 1958); and under the same title in *Broadside* 1 (June 1966): 14–15, 48. The present text is from *The Playboy College Reader* (New York: Harcourt, Brace Jovanovich, 1971), pp. 443–47. Page references to this text will be cited parenthetically.

32. Louis D. Owens, "Winter in Paris: John Steinbeck's Pippin IV," *Steinbeck Quarterly* 20 (Winter–Spring 1987): 22.

Bibliography

Short Stories of John Steinbeck

Except where noted, the stories are listed in the order of composition, followed by the date of composition entered in parentheses, and the date of first publication. Unpublished stories are identified by the collections holding the original manuscripts.

Early Stories

"Fingers of Cloud: A Satire on College Protervity" (early Winter 1924). *Stanford Spectator* 2, no. 5 (Feb. 1924): 149, 161–64.

"Adventures in Arcademy: A Journey into the Ridiculous" (Spring 1924). *Stanford Spectator* 2, no. 9 (June 1924): 279, 291.

"The Nail" (Spring 1925). Houghton Library, Harvard University.

"Christmas Story" (untitled) (Dec. 1925). Steinbeck Collection, Stanford University.

"The Nymph and Isobel" (Winter–Spring 1926). Houghton Library, Harvard University.

"East Third Street" (Winter–Spring 1926). Houghton Library, Harvard University.

"The Days of Long Marsh" (Winter–Spring 1926). Houghton Library, Harvard University.

"The White Sister of Fourteenth Street" (Winter–Spring 1926). Steinbeck Collection, Stanford University.

"The Gifts of Iban" (by John Stern, pseud.) (1925–26). *The Smokers Companion* 1, no. 1 (Mar. 1927): 18–19, 70–72.

The Pastures of Heaven

The Pastures of Heaven (May–Dec. 1931). New York: Brewer, Warren & Putnam, 1932. Reissued, New York: Robert O. Ballou, 1932. It is difficult to determine the precise order of the stories because Steinbeck wrote in two notebooks and had several false starts on individual stories. "Shark Wicks" was undoubtedly writ-

ten first. In the following list, numerals refer to the final chapter
order in *The Pastures of Heaven*.
3. "Shark Wicks"
4. "Tularecito"
1. "Origins and History of Las Pasturas del Cielo"
   Incomplete draft of "The Battle Farm" ("The Munroes")
   Incomplete draft of "Raymond Banks"
   Incomplete draft of "The Maltbys"
5. "Mrs. Van Deventer and Daughter"
6. "The Maltbys"
7. "The Lopez Sisters"
2. "The Battle Farm" ("The Munroes")
8. "Molly Morgan"
9. "Raymond Banks"
11. "John Whiteside and His House"
10. "Pat Humbert"
"The Maltbys" was republished, with expanded conclusion, as *Nothing So Monstrous*. New York: Pynson Printers at the request of
Ben Abramson, 1936.

The Long Valley and Other Stories of the 1930s

Stories included in *The Long Valley* (New York: Viking Press, 1938)
are marked with an asterisk.
"Saint Katy the Virgin" (composed in verse form, c. 1925; in short
   story form, prior to May 1932). Published as a Christmas book,
   Saint Katy the Virgin. New York: Covici-Friede, 1936.*
"The Gift" (June 1933). *North American Review* 236 (Nov. 1933):
   421–438.*
"The Great Mountains" (Summer 1933). *North American Review*
   236 (Dec. 1933): 492–500.*
"The Murder" (Summer 1933). *North American Review* 237 (Apr.
   1934): 305–12. *Lovat Dickson's Magazine* 3 (Oct. 1934): 442–56.*
"How Edith McGillcuddy Met R. L. Stevenson" (Summer–Fall
   1933). *Harper's Magazine* 183 (Aug. 1941): 252–58.
"The Promise" (Fall 1933–Winter 1934). *Harper's Magazine* 175
   (May 1937): 243–52.*
"The Chrysanthemums" (started late 1933, final draft started Jan.
   31, 1934, completed Feb. 1934). *Harper's Magazine* 175 (Oct.
   1937): 513–19.*
"The Leader of the People" (Winter 1934). *Argosy* 20 (Aug. 1936):
   99–106.*
"The Raid" (May–June 1934). *North American Review* 238 (Oct.
   1934): 299–305.*

"The Harness" (written as "The Fool," May–June 1934). *Atlantic Monthly* 161 (June 1938): 741–49.*

"Flight" (written as "Man Hunt," May–June 1934).*

"Case History" (fragment revised into "The Vigilante," May–June 1934).

"The White Quail" (May–June 1934). *North American Review* 239 (Mar. 1935): 204–11.*

"Addenda to Flight" (June 1934). Incorporated into final version of "Flight."

"Johnny Bear" (June 1934). Published as "The Ears of Johnny Bear." *Esquire* 8 (Sept. 1937): 35, 195–200.*

"The Cow" (a fragment with three starts, June 1934).

"Western Art Colony" (a fragment, June 1934).

"The Vigilante" (Aug. 1934). Published as "The Lonesome Vigilante." *Esquire* 6 (Oct. 1936): 35, 186a–b.*

"The Snake" (Aug. 1934). *Monterey Beacon* (June 22, 1935): 10–11, 14–15. Published as "A Snake of One's Own." *Esquire* 9 (Feb. 1938): 31, 178–80.*

"Breakfast" (Aug. 1934). *Pacific Weekly* 5 (Nov. 9, 1936): 300.*

Later Stories

"The Time the Wolves Ate the Vice-Principal" (July 1944). *Cannery Row*, from which this short story was taken as a rejected intercalary chapter, was completed in late July 1944. *'47, the Magazine of the Year* 1, no. 1 (Mar. 1947): 22–27.

"The Miracle of Tepayac" (Fall 1948). *Collier's* 122 (Dec. 25, 1948): 22–23.

"His Father" (May 9, 1949). *Reader's Digest* 55 (Sept. 1949): 19–21.

"The Affair at 7, Rue de M——" (May 27, 1954). *Harper's Bazaar* 89 (Apr. 1955): 112, 202, 213.

"The Summer Before" (Spring 1955). *Punch* 128 (May 25, 1955): 647–51.

"The Short-Short Story of Mankind" (1955). Published as "We're Holding Our Own." *Lilliput* 37 (Nov. 1955): 18–19; as "The Short-Short Story of Mankind," *Playboy* 5 (Apr. 1958); collected in *The Playboy College Reader*, pp. 443–47. New York: Harcourt, Brace Jovanovich, 1971.

"How Mr. Hogan Robbed a Bank" (1956). *Atlantic Monthly* 197 (Mar. 1956): 58–61.

"Case of the Hotel Ghost—Or . . . What are You Smoking in That Pipe, Mr. S.?" *Louisville Courier-Journal*, June 30, 1957.

Excerpts from Novels or Other Works Reprinted as Short Fiction. The following are listed in alphabetical order:

"The Crapshooter." In *Various Temptations*. New York: Avon Publications, [1955].

"Danny and His Friends." In *A Treasury of Friendship*, compiled and edited by Ralph L. Woods. New York: David McKay, 1957.

"Death of Grampa." In *The Grapes of Wrath at the Flood: The Human Drama As Seen by Modern American Novelists*, edited by Ann Watkins. New York: Harper, 1946.

"The Elf in Algiers." In *Pause to Wonder*, edited by Marjorie Fischer and Rolfe Humphries. Garden City, NJ: Sun Dial Press, 1957.

"Lilli Marlene." In *The Best of The Diners' Club Magazine*, edited by Matty Simmonds and Sam Boal. New York: Regent American Publishers, 1962.

"Sons of Cyrus Trask." *Collier's* 130 (July 12, 1952): 14–15, 217.

"Tractored Off." In *Literature for Our Time: An Anthology for College Freshmen*, edited by Leonard Stanley Brown et al. New York: H. Holt and Company, 1947.

"The Tractors." In *Our Lives: American Labor Stories*, edited by Joseph Gaer. New York: Boni and Gaer, 1948.

"The Turtle." In *Reading I've Liked*, edited by Clifton Fadiman. New York: Simon and Schuster, 1945.

Short Works of Steinbeck Cited

"Always Something To Do in Salinas." *Holiday* 17 (June 1955): 8–9, 152, 153, 156.

"Conversations at Sag Harbor." *Holiday* 29 (Mar. 1961): 60–61, 129, 130, 131, 133.

"Cutting Loose." *Encore: The Sunday Times Book*, edited by Leonard Russell, pp. 151–55. London: Michael Joseph, 1963.

"I Go Back to Ireland." *Collier's* 131 (Jan. 1953): 49–50.

"The Making of a New Yorker." *New York Times Magazine*, part 2 (Feb. 1, 1953): 26–27. Reprinted in *The Empire City: A Treasury of New York*, edited by Alexander Klein, pp. 469–75. New York: Rinehart & Company, 1955.

"My Short Novels." *Wings* 26 (Oct. 1953): 4, 6–8.

"On Learning Writing." *Writer's Yearbook* 34 (1963): 10.

"Positano." *Harper's Bazaar*, Aug. 1953, pp. 41, 68, 70.

"A Primer on the Thirties." *Esquire: Fortieth Anniversary Celebration* 80 (Oct. 1973): 127–31, 364, 366. Reprinted from *Esquire* 53 (June 1960): 85–93.

"Your Only Weapon Is Your Work": A Letter by John Steinbeck to Dennis Murphy, edited by Robert DeMott. San Jose, CA: Steinbeck Research Center, 1985.

Other Works of Steinbeck Quoted From

America and Americans. New York: Viking Press, 1966.
Cup of Gold (1929). New York: Penguin, 1976.
East of Eden. New York: Viking Press, 1952.
The Forgotten Village. New York: Viking Press, 1941.
The Grapes of Wrath (1939), edited by Peter Lisca. New York: Viking Critical Library, 1972.
In Dubious Battle (1936). New York: Penguin, 1979.
Journal of a Novel: The "East of Eden" Letters. New York: Viking Press, 1969.
Letters to Elizabeth: A Selection of Letters from John Steinbeck to Elizabeth Otis, edited by Florian J. Shasky and Susan F. Riggs. San Francisco: Book Club of California, 1978.
The Log from the Sea of Cortez (1952). New York: Penguin, 1976.
The Long Valley (1938). New York: Penguin, 1986.
Once There Was a War (1958). New York: Penguin, 1977.
The Pastures of Heaven (1932). New York: Penguin, 1982.
The Portable Steinbeck, edited by Pascal Covici, Jr. New York: Viking Press, 1971.
The Red Pony. New York: Penguin, 1976.
Steinbeck: A Life in Letters, edited by Elaine Steinbeck and Robert Wallsten. New York: Viking Press, 1975.
Steinbeck and Covici: The Story of a Friendship, edited by Thomas Fensch. Middlebury, VT: Paul S. Eriksson, 1979.
The Winter of Our Discontent. New York: Viking Press, 1961.

Secondary Works

Anderson, Hilton. "Steinbeck's 'Flight.'" *Explicator* 28 (Oct. 1969): item 12.
Antico, John. "A Reading of Steinbeck's 'Flight.'" *Modern Fiction Studies* 11 (Spring 1965): 45–53.
Astro, Richard. *John Steinbeck and Edward F. Ricketts: The Shaping of a Novelist*. Minneapolis: University of Minnesota Press, 1973.
———. "John Steinbeck and the Tragic Miracle of Consciousness." *San Jose Studies* 1 (Nov. 1975): 61–72.

————. "Something That Happened: A Non-Teleological Approach to 'The Leader of the People.'" *Steinbeck Quarterly* 6 (Winter 1973): 19–23. Reprinted in *A Study Guide to Steinbeck's "The Long Valley,"* edited by Tetsumaro Hayashi, pp. 105–11.

Astro, Richard, and Tetsumaro Hayashi. *Steinbeck: The Man and His Work.* Proceedings of the 1970 Steinbeck Conference. Corvallis: Oregon State University Press, 1971.

Autrey, Max L. "Men, Mice, and Moths: Gradation in Steinbeck's 'The Leader of the People.'" *Western American Literature* 10 (Nov. 1975): 195–204.

Barbour, Brian M. "Steinbeck As a Short Story Writer." In *A Study Guide to Steinbeck's "The Long Valley,"* edited by Tetsumaro Hayashi, pp. 113–28.

Barrett, William. *Irrational Man: A Study in Existential Philosophy.* Garden City, NJ: Doubleday Anchor Books, 1962.

Beach, Joseph Warren. "John Steinbeck: Journeyman Artist." In *American Fiction: 1920–1940.* New York: Macmillan, 1941.

Bennett, Robert. *The Wrath of John Steinbeck.* Los Angeles: Albertson Press, 1939.

Benson, Jackson J. "Background of *The Grapes of Wrath.*" *Journal of Modern Literature* 5 (Apr. 1976): 194–216.

————. "John Steinbeck's *Cannery Row:* A Reconsideration." *Western American Literature* 12 (May 1977): 11–40.

————. "Through a Political Glass, Darkly: The Example of John Steinbeck." *Studies in American Fiction* 12 (Spring 1984): 45–58.

————. *The True Adventures of John Steinbeck, Writer.* New York: Viking Press, 1984.

Benson, Jackson J., and Anne Loftis. "John Steinbeck and Farm Labor Unionization: The Backgrounds of *In Dubious Battle.*" *American Literature* 52 (May 1980): 194–223.

Benton, Robert M. "'Breakfast' I and II." In *A Study Guide to Steinbeck's "The Long Valley,"* edited by Tetsumaro Hayashi, pp. 33–39.

————. "A Scientific Point of View in Steinbeck's Fiction." *Steinbeck Quarterly* 7 (Summer–Fall 1974): 67–72.

Beyer, Preston. "The Current Status of John Steinbeck Book Collections." *Steinbeck Quarterly* 17 (Summer–Fall 1984): 87–97.

Bowra, C. M. *The Romantic Imagination.* New York: Oxford University Press-Galaxy Books, 1961.

Byrd, Charlotte. "The First-Person Narrator in 'Johnny Bear': A Writer's Mind and Conscience." *Steinbeck Quarterly* 21 (Winter–Spring 1988): 6–13.

Carpenter, Frederic I. "John Steinbeck: American Dreamer." In

Steinbeck and His Critics: A Record of Twenty-Five Years, edited by E. W. Tedlock, Jr., and C. V. Wicker. Albuquerque: University of New Mexico Press, 1957.

Carr, Duane R. "Steinbeck's Blakean Vision in *The Grapes of Wrath*." *Steinbeck Quarterly* 8 (Summer–Fall 1975): 67–73.

Chapin, Chester F. "Pepe Torres: A Steinbeck 'Natural.'" *College English* 23 (1962): 676.

Court, Franklin E. "A Vigilante's Fantasy." *Steinbeck Quarterly* 5 (Summer–Fall 1972): 98–101. Reprinted in *A Study Guide to Steinbeck's "The Long Valley*," edited by Tetsumaro Hayashi, pp. 53–56.

Cox, Martha Heasley. "In Search of John Steinbeck: His People and His Land." *San Jose Studies* 1 (Nov. 1975): 41–60.

Crane, Stephen. *The Red Badge of Courage*, edited by Sculley Bradley et al. New York: W. W. Norton Critical Edition, 1976.

Davis, Robert Murray. "Steinbeck's 'The Murder.'" *Studies in Short Fiction* 14 (1977): 63–68.

Davison, Richard A. "Hemingway, Steinbeck, and the Art of the Short Story." *Steinbeck Quarterly* 21 (Summer–Fall 1988): 73–84.

Delgado, James. "The Facts Behind John Steinbeck's 'The Lonesome Vigilante.'" *Steinbeck Quarterly* 16 (Summer–Fall 1983): 20–29.

DeMott, Robert. "'A Great Black Book': *East of Eden* and Dr. Gunn's *Family Medicine*." *American Studies* 22 (Fall 1981): 41–57.

———. *Steinbeck's Reading: A Catalogue of Books Owned and Borrowed*. New York: Garland Publishing, 1984.

———. "Toward a Redefinition of *To a God Unknown*." *Windsor Review* 8 (Spring 1973): 34–53.

Ditsky, John M. "A Kind of Play: Dramatic Elements in John Steinbeck's 'The Chrysanthemums.'" *Wascana Review* 21 (Spring 1986): 62–72.

———. "Steinbeck's 'Flight': The Ambiguity of Manhood." *Steinbeck Quarterly* 5 (Summer–Fall 1972): 80–85. Reprinted in *A Study Guide to Steinbeck's "The Long Valley*," edited by Tetsumaro Hayashi, pp. 17–23.

Epstein, Joseph. *Plausible Prejudices: Essays on American Writing*. New York: W. W. Norton & Company, 1985.

Fitzgerald, F. Scott. *Correspondence of F. Scott Fitzgerald*, edited by Matthew J. Bruccoli and Margaret M. Duggan. New York: Random House, 1980.

Fontenrose, Joseph. "'The Harness.'" *Steinbeck Quarterly* 5 (Summer–Fall 1972): 94–98. Reprinted in *A Study Guide to Steinbeck's "The Long Valley*," edited by Tetsumaro Hayashi, pp. 47–52.

————. *John Steinbeck: An Introduction and Interpretation.* New York: Barnes & Noble, 1963.

————. *Steinbeck's Unhappy Valley.* Berkeley: Joseph Fontenrose, 1981.

French, Warren. "'Johnny Bear'—Steinbeck's 'Yellow Peril' Story." *Steinbeck Quarterly* 5 (Summer–Fall 1972): 101–107. Reprinted in *A Study Guide to Steinbeck's "The Long Valley,"* edited by Tetsumaro Hayashi, pp. 57–64.

————. *John Steinbeck.* New York: Twayne Publishers, 1961.

————. "Steinbeck's Winter Tale." *Modern Fiction Studies* 11 (1965): 66–74.

Friede, Donald. *The Mechanical Angel.* New York: Alfred A. Knopf, 1948.

Garcia, Reloy. *Steinbeck and D. H. Lawrence: Fictive Voices and the Ethical Imperative.* Steinbeck Monograph Series, no. 2. Muncie, IN: Ball State University Press, 1972.

————. "Steinbeck's 'The Snake': An Explication." *Steinbeck Quarterly* 5 (Summer–Fall 1972): 85–90. Reprinted in *A Study Guide to Steinbeck's "The Long Valley,"* edited by Tetsumaro Hayashi, pp. 25–31.

Gierasch, Walter. "Steinbeck's *The Red Pony,* II, 'The Great Mountains.'" *Explicator* 4 (1946): item 39.

Girard, Maureen. "Steinbeck's 'Frightful' Story: The Conception and Evolution of 'The Snake.'" *San Jose Studies* 8 (Spring 1982): 33–40.

Gladstein, Mimi R. "'The Leader of the People': A Boy Becomes a Mench." In *Steinbeck's "The Red Pony": Essays in Criticism,* edited by Tetsumaro Hayashi and Thomas J. Moore, pp. 27–37.

Goldsmith, Arnold L. "Thematic Rhythm in *The Red Pony.*" *College English* 26 (Feb. 1965): 391–94.

Gordon, Walter K. "Steinbeck's 'Flight': Journey to or from Maturity?" *Studies in Short Fiction* 3 (1966): 453–55.

Grommen, Alfred. "Who *Is* 'The Leader of the People'?: Helping Students Examine Fiction." *English Journal* 48 (Nov. 1959): 449–56.

Hamby, James A. "Steinbeck's Biblical Vision: 'Breakfast' and the Nobel Prize Acceptance Speech." *Western Review* 10 (Spring 1973): 57–59.

Hawthorne, Nathaniel. *The Complete Novels and Selected Tales,* edited by Norman Holmes Pearson. New York: Modern Library, 1937.

Hayashi, Tetsumaro, ed. *Steinbeck's Women: Essays in Criticism.*

Steinbeck Monograph Series, no. 9. Muncie, IN: Ball State University Press, 1979.

———. *A Study Guide to Steinbeck's "The Long Valley."* Ann Arbor: Pierian Press, 1976.

Hayashi, Tetsumaro, and Thomas J. Moore, eds. *Steinbeck's "The Red Pony": Essays in Criticism.* Steinbeck Monograph Series, no. 13. Muncie, IN: Ball State University Press, 1988.

Hedgpeth, Joel W., ed. *The Outer Shores, Part I: Ed Ricketts and John Steinbeck Explore the Pacific Coast.* Eureka, CA: Mad River Press, 1978.

———. *The Outer Shores, Part II: From the Papers of Edward F. Ricketts.* Eureka, CA: Mad River Press, 1978.

Hemingway, Ernest. *Ernest Hemingway: Selected Letters*, edited by Carlos Baker. New York: Scribner's, 1981.

Houghton, Donald. "'Westering' in 'The Leader of the People.'" *Western American Literature* 4 (Summer 1969): 117–24.

Hughes, Robert S., Jr. *Beyond "The Red Pony": A Reader's Companion to Steinbeck's Complete Short Stories.* Metuchen, NJ: Scarecrow Press, 1987.

———. "The Black Cypress and the Green Tub: Death and Procreation in Steinbeck's 'The Promise.'" In *Steinbeck's "The Red Pony": Essays in Criticism*, edited by Tetsumaro Hayashi and Thomas J. Moore, pp. 9–16.

———. "Steinbeck Stories at the Houghton Library: A Case for Authenticity of Four Unpublished Texts." *Harvard Library Bulletin* 30 (Jan. 1982): 87–95.

———. "Steinbeck's Uncollected Stories." *Steinbeck Quarterly* 18 (Summer–Fall 1985): 79–93.

Hyman, Alvin D. "The San Jose Lynchings." In *News Stories of 1933: A Collection of Some of the Best News and Feature Stories of Various Types Which Appeared in American Newspapers in 1933*, edited by Frank Luther Mott. Boston: Houghton Mifflin, 1934.

John Steinbeck: A Collection of Books and Manuscripts. Santa Barbara, CA: Bradford Morrow Bookseller, 1980.

Jones, Lawrence William. "A Note on Steinbeck's Earliest Stories." *Steinbeck Quarterly* 2 (Fall 1969): 59–60.

———. "An Uncited Post-War Steinbeck Story: 'The Short-Short Story of Mankind.'" *Steinbeck Quarterly* 3 (Spring 1970): 30–31.

Jones, William M. "Steinbeck's 'Flight.'" *Explicator* 18 (Nov. 1959): item 11.

Jung, Carl. *The Collected Works of Carl Jung*, translated by R. F. C. Hull. London: Routledge & Kegan Paul, 1960.

King, Roma A., Jr. *The Focusing Artifice: The Poetry of Robert Browning.* Athens: Ohio University Press, 1968.

Levant, Howard. "John Steinbeck's *The Red Pony:* A Study in Narrative Technique." *Journal of Narrative Technique* 1 (May 1971): 77–85.

————. *The Novels of John Steinbeck: A Critical Study.* Columbia: University of Missouri Press, 1974.

Lewis, Clifford L. "Four Dubious Steinbeck Stories." *Steinbeck Quarterly* 5 (Winter 1972): 17–19.

————. "Jungian Psychology and the Artistic Design of John Steinbeck." *Steinbeck Quarterly* 10 (Summer–Fall 1977): 89–97.

Lisca, Peter. "'The Raid' and *In Dubious Battle.*" *Steinbeck Quarterly* 5 (Summer–Fall 1977): 90–94. Reprinted in *A Study Guide to Steinbeck's "The Long Valley,"* edited by Tetsumaro Hayashi, pp. 41–45.

————. *The Wide World of John Steinbeck.* New Brunswick, NJ: Rutgers University Press, 1958.

Lutwack, Leonard. *Heroic Fiction: The Epic Tradition and American Novels of the Twentieth Century.* Carbondale, IL: Southern Illinois University Press, 1971.

Madeo, Frederick. "'Flight'—An Allegorical Journey." *English Record* 14 (1964): 55–58.

Marcus, Mordecai. "The Lost Dream of Sex and Childbirth in 'The Chrysanthemums.'" *Modern Fiction Studies* 11 (Spring 1965): 54–58.

Marovitz, Sanford E. "The Cryptic Raillery of 'Saint Katy the Virgin.'" *Steinbeck Quarterly* 5 (Summer–Fall 1972): 107–12. Reprinted in *A Study Guide to Steinbeck's "The Long Valley,"* edited by Tetsumaro Hayashi, pp. 73–80.

Martin, Bruce K. "'The Leader of the People' Re-examined." *Studies in Short Fiction* 8 (Summer 1971): 423–32.

May, Charles E. "Myth and Mystery in Steinbeck's 'The Snake': A Jungian View." *Criticism* 15 (Fall 1973): 322–35.

McCarthy, Mary. "Minority Report." *Nation* (Mar. 11, 1936): 326–27.

McMahan, Elizabeth E. "'The Chrysanthemums': A Study of a Woman's Sexuality." *Modern Fiction Studies* 14 (1968): 453–58.

Miller, William V. "Sexual and Spiritual Ambiguity in 'The Chrysanthemums.'" *Steinbeck Quarterly* 5 (Summer–Fall 1972): 68–75. Reprinted in *A Study Guide to Steinbeck's "The Long Valley,"* edited by Tetsumaro Hayashi, pp. 1–10.

Mirrielees, Edith. *Story Writing.* New York: Viking Press, 1962.

Mitchell, Marilyn L. "Steinbeck's Strong Women: Feminine Identity in the Short Stories." *Southwest Review* 61 (Summer 1976): 304–15. Reprinted in *Steinbeck's Women: Essays in Criticism*, edited by Tetsumaro Hayashi, pp. 26–35. Steinbeck Monograph Series, no. 9. Muncie, IN: Ball State University Press, 1979.

Morsberger, Katharine M., and Robert E. Morsberger. "'The Murder'—Realism or Ritual?" In *A Study Guide to Steinbeck's "The Long Valley,"* edited by Tetsumaro Hayashi, pp. 65–71.

Morsberger, Robert E. "In Defense of 'Westering.'" *Western American Literature* 5 (Summer 1970): 143–46.

Mortlock, Melanie. "The Eden Myth as Paradox: An Allegorical Reading of *The Pastures of Heaven*." *Steinbeck Quarterly* 11 (Winter 1978): 6–15.

Norris, Frank. *McTeague*. New York: New American Library, 1964.

Osborne, William R. "The Texts of Steinbeck's 'The Chrysanthemums.'" *Modern Fiction Studies* 12 (Winter 1966–67): 479–84.

Owens, Louis D. *John Steinbeck's Re-Vision of America*. Athens: University of Georgia Press, 1985.

———. "'The Murder': Illusions of Chivalry." *Steinbeck Quarterly* 17 (Winter–Spring 1984): 10–14.

———. "Steinbeck's 'Flight': Into the Jaws of Death." *Steinbeck Quarterly* 10 (Summer–Fall 1977): 103–8.

Peterson, Richard F. "The Grail Legend and Steinbeck's 'The Great Mountains.'" *Steinbeck Quarterly* 6 (Winter 1973): 9–15. Reprinted in *A Study Guide to Steinbeck's "The Long Valley,"* edited by Tetsumaro Hayashi, pp. 89–103.

Piacentino, E. J. "Patterns of Animal Imagery in Steinbeck's 'Flight.'" *Studies in Short Fiction* 17 (Fall 1980): 437–43.

Renner, Stanley. "Mary Teller and Sue Bridehead: Birds of a Feather in 'The White Quail' and *Jude the Obscure*." *Steinbeck Quarterly* 18 (Winter–Spring 1985): 35–45.

———. "Sexual Idealism and Violence in 'The White Quail.'" *Steinbeck Quarterly* 17 (Summer–Fall 1984): 76–87.

Riggs, Susan F. *A Catalogue of the John Steinbeck Collection at Stanford University*. Stanford, CA: Stanford University Libraries, 1980.

———. "Steinbeck at Stanford." *Stanford Magazine* 4 (Fall–Winter 1976): 14–21.

Robbe-Grillet, Alain. *For a New Novel: Essays on Fiction*. New York: Grove Press, 1965.

Ruggiers, Paul. *The Art of the Canterbury Tales*. Madison: University of Wisconsin Press, 1965.

St. Pierre, Brian. *John Steinbeck: The California Years*. San Francisco: Chronicle Books, 1983.

Seixas, Antonia. "John Steinbeck and the Non-Teleological Bus." In *Steinbeck and His Critics: A Record of Twenty-Five Years*, edited by E. W. Tedlock and C. V. Wicker. Albuquerque: University of New Mexico Press, 1957.

Sheffield, Carlton. *John Steinbeck: The Good Companion*. Portola Valley, CA: American Lives Endowment, 1983.

Shestov, Lev. *Athens and Jerusalem*, translated by Bernard Martin. New York: Simon & Schuster, 1968.

Shuman, R. Baird. "Initiation Rites in Steinbeck's *The Red Pony*." *The English Journal* 59, no. 9 (Dec. 1970): 1252–55.

Simmonds, Roy S. "The First Publication of Steinbeck's 'The Leader of the People.'" *Steinbeck Quarterly* 7 (Winter 1975): 13–18.

———. "John Steinbeck, Robert Louis Stevenson, and Edith Mc-Gillcuddy." *San Jose Studies* 1 (Nov. 1975): 29–39.

———. "The Original Manuscripts of 'The Chrysanthemums.'" *Steinbeck Quarterly* 7 (Summer–Fall 1974): 102–11.

———. "The Place and Importance of 'The Great Mountains' in the Red Pony Cycle." *Steinbeck's "The Red Pony": Essays in Criticism*, edited by Tetsumaro Hayashi and Thomas J. Moore, pp. 17–26.

———. "Steinbeck's 'The Murder': A Critical and Bibliographical Study." *Steinbeck Quarterly* 9 (Spring 1976): 45–53.

Simpson, Arthur L. "'The White Quail': A Portrait of an Artist." *Steinbeck Quarterly* 5 (Summer–Fall 1972): 76–80. Reprinted in *A Study Guide to Steinbeck's "The Long Valley,"* edited by Tetsumaro Hayashi, pp. 11–16.

Smith, Jody Brant. *The Image of Guadalupe: Myth or Miracle?* Garden City, NJ: Doubleday & Company, 1983.

Snyder, Louis L., and Richard B. Morris, eds. *A Treasury of Great Reporting*. 2d ed. New York: Simon & Schuster, 1952.

Stone, Donal. "Steinbeck, Jung, and *The Winter of Our Discontent*." *Steinbeck Quarterly* 11 (Summer–Fall 1978): 87–96.

Street, Webster. "Remembering John Steinbeck." *San Jose Studies* 1 (Nov. 1975): 109–27.

Sweet, Charles A., Jr. "Ms. Elisa Allen and Steinbeck's 'The Chrysanthemums.'" *Modern Fiction Studies* 20 (June 1974): 210–14.

Tammaro, Thomas M. "Erik Erikson Meets John Steinbeck: Psychosocial Development in 'The Gift.'" *Steinbeck's "The Red Pony": Essays in Criticism*, edited by Tetsumaro Hayashi and Thomas J. Moore, pp. 1–9.

Tedlock, E. W., and C. V. Wicker. *Steinbeck and His Critics: A Record of Twenty-Five Years*. Albuquerque: University of New Mexico Press, 1957.

Thomas, Dylan. *The Collected Poems of Dylan Thomas*. New York: New Directions, 1957.

Timmerman, John H. *John Steinbeck's Fiction: The Aesthetics of the Road Taken*. Norman, OK, and London: University of Oklahoma Press, 1986.

————. "John Steinbeck's Use of the Bible: A Descriptive Bibliography of the Critical Tradition." *Steinbeck Quarterly* 21 (Winter–Spring 1988): 24–39.

Vogel, Dan. "Steinbeck's 'Flight': The Myth of Manhood." *College English* 23 (1961): 225–26.

Ware, Elaine. "Struggle for Survival: Parallel Theme and Techniques in Steinbeck's 'Flight' and Norris's *McTeague*." *Steinbeck Quarterly* 21 (Summer–Fall 1988): 96–103.

West, Philip J. "Steinbeck's 'The Leader of the People': A Crisis in Style." *Western American Literature* 5 (Summer 1970): 137–41.

Woodward, Robert H. "John Steinbeck, Edith McGillcuddy, and *Tortilla Flat*." *San Jose Studies* 3 (Nov. 1977): 70–73.

————. "The Promise of Steinbeck's 'The Promise.'" *Steinbeck Quarterly* 6 (Winter 1973): 15–19. Reprinted in *A Study Guide to Steinbeck's "The Long Valley,"* edited by Tetsumaro Hayashi, pp. 97–103.

————. *The Steinbeck Research Center at San Jose State University: A Descriptive Catalogue*. San Jose Studies no. 11 (Winter 1985).

Index